Food Activism

Food Activism: Agency, Democracy and Economy

Edited by
Carole Counihan and Valeria Siniscalchi

B L O O M S B U R Y

LONDON • NEW DELHI • NEW YORK • SYDNEY

Bloomsbury Academic

An imprint of Bloomsbury Publishing Plc

50 Bedford Square
London
WC1B 3DP
UK

1385 Broadway
New York
NY 10018
USA

www.bloomsbury.com

Bloomsbury is a registered trade mark of Bloomsbury Publishing Plc

First published 2014
Reprinted 2014

British Library Cataloguing-in-Publication Data
A catalogue record for this book is available from the British Library.

ISBN: HB: 978-0-85785-832-0
PB: 978-0-85785-833-7
ePDF: 978-1-47252-020-3
ePub: 978-0-85785-834-4

Library of Congress Cataloging-in-Publication Data
Food activism : agency, democracy and economy / edited by Carole Counihan and
Valeria Siniscalchi.
pages cm
ISBN 978-0-85785-833-7 (pbk.) – ISBN 978-0-85785-832-0 (hardback) –
ISBN 978-0-85785-834-4 (epub) 1. Food supply–Social aspects. 2. Food
supply. 3. Food industry and trade. 4. Agriculture–Economic
aspects. 5. Agriculture–Social aspects. 6. Political participation.
I. Counihan, Carole, 1948- II. Siniscalchi, Valeria.
HD9000.5.F5477 2014
363.8'5–dc23
2013035093

Typeset by Apex CoVantage, LLC
Printed and bound in Great Britain

Contents

Preface and Acknowledgments

We started collaborating on a project on food activism in 2009, when our mutual friend Cinzia Scaffidi of Slow Food put us in touch with each other. We thank Cinzia for launching a friendship and a collaboration that has blossomed over the years into this book and many good times. We organized panels at the 2010 and 2011 annual meetings of the American Anthropological Association on the topic of food activism, and we are grateful to the participants in those sessions for broadening our perspectives and extending our thinking: Yve LeGrand, Cristina Grasseni, Sue Johnston, Richard Wilk, Claire Lamine, Nancy Rosenberger, Ellen Messer, David Beriss, Inez Adams, Joan Mencher, Penny Van Esterik, Amanda Green, and Marc Edelman. We thank the contributors to this volume for their fine work, remarkable punctuality, and patience with our relentless editing. We thank Millersville University, Boston University Metropolitan College, and the École des Hautes Études en Sciences Sociales for their support. Our gratitude goes to Boston University Gastronomy MLA coordinator Rachel Black for her friendship and help in providing us with the assistance of graduate student Emily Contois, whom we thank for her indispensable, meticulous, and cheerful editorial assistance throughout the book's preparation. We thank Louise Butler and Sophie Hodgson of Bloomsbury for their support of this project and the two anonymous reviewers for their excellent feedback. We thank Valeria's husband, photographer Franco Zecchin, for the cover photo that symbolizes the wide range of food activism, and Carole's husband, anthropologist Jim Taggart, for his steadfast encouragement; we are grateful to both for their insightful feedback as the project was taking shape. We also thank the friends who helped us to summarize food activism in a single photograph under the Marseille sun.

Notes on Contributors

Carole Counihan is professor emerita of anthropology at Millersville University and has been a visiting professor at Boston University, the École des Hautes Études en Sciences Sociales (Marseille), the University of Cagliari, and the University of Gastronomic Sciences (Italy). She authored *The Anthropology of Food and Body* (1999), *Around the Tuscan Table* (2004), and *A Tortilla Is Like Life* (2009). She co-edited *Food and Culture* (1997, 2008, 2013) and *Taking Food Public* (2012), and is editor of *Food and Foodways* journal.

Greg de St. Maurice is a PhD candidate in cultural anthropology at the University of Pittsburgh. He has an MSc in social anthropology from Oxford University and MAs in international relations from American University and Ritsumeikan University. He received a Fulbright grant to conduct dissertation fieldwork in Kyoto, Japan, in 2012–2013. His primary research interests include place-making, food and agriculture, and globalization.

Elizabeth Fitting is an anthropologist in the Sociology and Social Anthropology Department of Dalhousie University, Canada. Her ethnography *The Struggle for Maize: Campesinos, Workers, and Transgenic Corn in the Mexican Countryside* (2011) was recently translated into Japanese. Her work on the livelihoods of Mexican maize producers and anti-GMO campaigns has been published in *Agriculture and Human Values, Focaal,* Psyche Williams-Forson and Carole Counihan's *Taking Food Public,* and Gerardo Otero's *Food for the Few.*

Marie-France Garcia-Parpet is senior researcher at the Institut National de la Recherche Agronomique (INRA) in Paris and member of the Centre de Sociologie Européenne (CNRS-EHESS). She has studied the social construction of markets in France and Brazil and the globalization of wine markets. She is currently working on the organic certification market. Her publications include *Le marché de l'excellence: Les grands crus à l'épreuve de la mondialisation* (2009).

Hanna Garth is a PhD candidate in anthropology at the University of California, Los Angeles, who is studying the ways in which the changing food-rationing system in Cuba affects household and community dynamics and in turn individual subject positions. She has conducted research in the Philippines, Chile, Peru, and

Houston, Texas, and is the editor of the volume *Food and Identity in the Caribbean* (Berg, 2013).

Joan E. Gross (PhD, University of Texas, 1985) is professor of anthropology at Oregon State University, where she helped start the Food in Culture and Social Justice program. She is the author of "Capitalism and Its Discontents: Back-to-the-Lander and Freegan Foodways in Rural Oregon" and "Constructing a Community Food Economy," both published in *Food and Foodways.* She is currently working on food activism in Oregon and Ecuador.

Teresa M. Mares is assistant professor of anthropology at the University of Vermont and is affiliated with the Transdisciplinary Research Initiative in Food Systems. She received her PhD (2010) in sociocultural anthropology from the University of Washington. Her research focuses on Latino/a immigrant foodways and food access in the United States. She has recently published articles in *Food and Foodways, Latino Studies, Agriculture and Human Values,* and *Environment and Society.*

Birgit Müller is senior researcher at LAIOS-Centre national de la recherche scientifique in Paris and has studied post-socialist factories and environmental movements in Europe and Latin America. She is carring out a project on "Food, Property and Power: Agricultural Technologies as Global Policies and Local Practices" in the Food and Agriculture Organization of the United Nations, Canada, and Nicaragua. Her books include *Disenchantment with Market Economics: East Germans and Western Capitalism* (2007) and *The Loss of Harmony: The Politics of Policy Making in Multilateral Organizations* (2013).

Nefissa Naguib is research professor at Chr. Michelsen Institute and Associate Professor of social anthropology at the University of Bergen, Norway. She has conducted research in Egypt since 1990. Among her latest publications are *Movements of People in Time and Space*; *Water, Women and Memory: Recasting Lives in Palestine*; and *Interpreting Welfare and Relief in the Middle East.* She also co-produced the documentary *Women, War and Welfare in Jerusalem.*

Theodoros Rakopoulos received his PhD from the Anthropology Department of Goldsmiths, University of London. He is currently a postdoctoral fellow at the Human Economy Programme, University of Pretoria. His research interests include cooperativism, solidarity economies, Sicily, and the Greek crisis. He has published in *Re-public.*

Daniel Reichman teaches anthropology at the University of Rochester. His book *The Broken Village: Coffee, Migration, and Globalization in Honduras* was published in 2011. He is currently studying the impact of traceability protocols on coffee production in the Americas.

Valeria Siniscalchi is associate professor at the École des Hautes Études en Sciences Sociales (Centre Norbert Elias), where she teaches economic anthropology. She has conducted research in Italy and the French Alps on the politics of nature, work, industrial districts, and food movements, especially Slow Food, the topic of a forthcoming book. Her publications include *Antropologia culturale: Un'introduzione* (2001, 2012) and *Frammenti di economie: Ricerche di antropologia economica in Italia* (2002).

Delphine Thivet is pursuing a PhD in sociology at the École des Hautes Études en Sciences Sociales with a project on the transnationalization of peasant movements. She has published "Des paysans contre la faim. La souveraineté alimentaire, naissance d'une cause paysanne transnationale," in *Terrains & Travaux* (2012), and "A Nation without Hunger? Current Threats to Food Security in Contemporary India," in Åshild Kolås and Jason Miklian (eds.), *Invisible India: Hidden Risks within an Emerging Superpower* (2013).

Wim Van Daele is currently finalizing his joint PhD in interdisciplinary studies at the Center Leo Apostel and in comparative cultural sciences at Ghent University in Belgium. His work explores the heterogeneous connections between food and various spheres of life in a Sri Lankan context. He has published articles in *Contributions to Indian Sociology, International Development Policy, Food and Foodways,* and several other journals.

Part I

Introduction

Ethnography of Food Activism

Valeria Siniscalchi and Carole Counihan

Introduction

The idea for this book was born during fieldwork. We met doing research on the same subject—the Slow Food movement—but along two different pathways, one focusing "from above" on the movement's headquarters, the other focusing "from below" on the local grassroots chapter leaders. When two anthropologists meet on the same research site and discover each other, they can have diverse reactions, one being the realization: "my" field is no longer only mine! But we took a different tack and decided to join our paths and perspectives rather than building walls between them.

We began our cooperation by organizing a double session on food activism, a topic that encompassed our fieldwork and aimed to extend to other related projects as well, at the 2010 Annual Meeting of the American Anthropological Association in New Orleans. From this panel, and from a second double session we organized the following year at the association's Annual Meeting in Montreal, was formed the initial nucleus of this volume. Our idea was to compare diverse forms of activism centered on food initiated by both consumers and producers. We decided to draw flexible borders that allowed us to consider together individual and collective mobilizations with a variety of forms, actors, and strategies in diverse parts of the world.

By *food activism* we mean efforts by people to change the food system across the globe by modifying the way they produce, distribute, and/or consume food. Although our goal in this book is to be inclusive rather than exclusive and to present and analyze a broad range of activism, we decided not to include antihunger movements because these are so vast as to warrant their own book.

The geographic range of these chapters—including sites in Cuba, Mexico, Colombia, Sri Lanka, Egypt, Japan, Italy, France, Canada, and the United States—shows that food activism is a worldwide movement taking place in both the Global North and the Global South. An important element that emerges from reading across the cases is that the actions and ideologies of food activism are connected through transnational flows, like those linking peasants in India and Brazil through La Via Campesina's struggles for food sovereignty, and those linking consumers in the

United States to coffee producers in Honduras through fair trade and transparency regimes. Taken together, the chapters allow us to analyze food activism as a set of multisited practices and reveal how concepts and strategies are used and appropriated from one group or place to another. For example, we can see how the anti-GMO movement in Colombia borrows yet differs from its Mexican counterpart, and how urban Sri Lankan food activists transform ritual meanings surrounding food that are typical of the countryside into forms that make sense to international funding agencies. The chapters reveal the changes that occur over time in the forms of mobilization and their aims, for example, how the spontaneous coming together of a small group of Oregonians seeking to revitalize local food production and consumption evolved into a permanent organization with paid employees, a funding structure, and a formal mission statement.

Anthropology and Ethnography of Food Activism

Increasing numbers of studies in anthropology and the social sciences look explicitly at diverse forms of food activism, including studies of ethical consumption, commodity chains, local food, community-supported agriculture, and the anti-GMO movement (Borras, Edelman, and Kay 2008; Carrier and Luetchford 2012; Dubuisson-Quellier 2009; Fitting 2011; Lamine 2008; Pratt 2007; Siniscalchi 2013; Williams-Forson and Counihan 2011). As Richard Wilk says, "Food has long been a focus for political and social movements in many parts of the world; food is a potent symbol of what ails society, a way of making abstract issues like class or exploitation into a material, visceral reality" (2006: 21–22). Many recent studies of food activism focus on the North American context; for example, Clare Hinrichs and Thomas Lyson's (2009) edited book gives extensive coverage of U.S. alternative food practices, from CSAs to farmers' markets to chicken labeling. Sandor Katz (2006) provides an overview of seed saving, labor struggles in the food industry, vegetarianism, farmers' markets, home fermentation, and other challenges to food-system consolidation and degradation in the United States. Mark Winne (2011) also focuses on efforts to change the North American food system with case studies of meat production, school food, and food sovereignty, while Alison Alkon and Julian Agyeman's (2011) collection explicitly highlights how low-income people and communities of color strive for sustainability and environmental justice in the North American food system, which is plagued with race and class inequalities.

Some studies take a more global approach to food activism, such as Eric Holt-Giménez's (2006, 2009, 2011) writings on peasant struggles for food justice and Rachel Schurman and William Munro's (2010) collection about social movements against biotechnology and agribusiness. Wynne Wright and Gerad Middendorf's (2008) anthology uses the concepts of agency and structure to anchor several articles about challenges and changes in food production around the world, such as fair trade banana production in the Dominican Republic, red meat production in New Zealand and South Africa, a community food-sharing program in Toronto, and farming in Puerto Rico. Our book aims to contribute to this body of work by investigating how globalization instigates and structures food activism and how activists experience globalization, by providing a holistic look at diverse kinds and scales of food activism in a range of global contexts, and by mustering an explicit ethnographic perspective and comparative approach.

Just as the idea of this book was born in the field, it aims to validate the centrality of fieldwork, and one of its distinctive elements is the adoption of an ethnographic approach to food activism. Ethnography highlights diverse insider perspectives on ongoing lived processes. Each case study—from those focused on highly localized mobilizations to those examining transnational movements—is grounded in a deep understanding of activists' visions and practices in specific cultural settings. The researchers approach food activism using a variety of methods. They look at food activism in its social and cultural context—linked to economic, political, and ideological forces and taking place at diverse scales and in different forms.

The authors position themselves at different vantage points, some at the heart of a movement and others on the periphery. They choose varying foci, including activists' discourses, values, practices, forms of resistance, political and economic dynamics, challenges, and successes. Authors share a common search for an "empirical alignment" between observed phenomena and qualitative analysis (Olivier de Sardan 2008: 7–8). At the same time, like all ethnographers, they navigate a fine line between being participants and observers, between being involved insiders and detached outsiders, a tension that is perhaps particularly acute in the study of activism. Alexander Koensler and Amalia Rossi write, "The study of social movements, in fact, often involves tension between the disengaged posture of scientific observation and the ideological beliefs of the researcher. This can call into question the theoretical foundations, results, and boundaries of ethnographic work, and causes numerous dilemmas in the ethnographic relationships with activists" (2012: 15; our translation). Like all ethnographers, the authors here are always also involved persons whose perspectives are never completely neutral. Moreover, as Judith Okely affirms, during fieldwork the anthropologist is forced to take a position and "must either be involved or perish" (2012: 14).

Just as activists hold a variety of political ideologies, from revolutionary to conservative, so ethnographers have different analytical positions (cf. Edelman 2001: 301–303), and the authors in our volume are no exception, even while varying in their critical posture and efforts to balance competing views. As Wilk reminds us, "The range of groups involved in food activism covers the entire spectrum from left to right and can create unlikely alliances between conservative religious groups and Marxists. Each of these activist and policy communities is itself culturally constituted and amenable to study using all the tools of economic anthropology" (2006: 22). In this volume, for example, Nefissa Naguib faces a difficult challenge in providing an insider's look at the Muslim Brotherhood's use of food in its religious activism, a view that differs radically from other accounts that emphasize the Brotherhood's hard-line fundamentalism. From certain points of view this insider's perspective may be considered insufficiently critical; at the same time, it is important to remember, as Jean-Pierre Olivier de Sardan writes, that "our charge.... is to render familiar and comprehensible the subjects of our research, whether they are culturally close or distant" (2008: 21; our translation), even though this mission may at times undermine a more critical stance.

What Is Food Activism, and What Is Not?

Food activism takes aim at the capitalist system of production, distribution, consumption, and commercialization. We include in food activism people's discourses and actions to make the food system or parts of it more democratic, sustainable, healthy, ethical, culturally appropriate, and better in quality. It is an umbrella that permits us to include spontaneous actions like Cubans refusing government food or Sardinian women making choices to valorize local food consumption, organized groups like the local community coalition Ten Rivers Food Web in Oregon or the citywide urban garden program in Seattle, and transnational social movements like Slow Food, La Via Campesina, or fair trade.

The comparative study of food activism investigates its form, ideologies, and levels of political commitment. Sometimes immediate concrete struggles against neoliberalism appear as food activism through their forms of action and expressions of dissent, such as those of Canadian wheat farmers seeking to maintain the single-desk sales of wheat. At other times food activism is manifest in ethical commitments that extend beyond the food sphere, as in the antimafia goals of the Sicilian agricultural cooperatives, or the environmental and cultural heritage ideals of Mexican activists manifest in efforts to outlaw genetically modified corn. Aimee Shreck proposes a useful typology of activism that includes (1) acts of resistance composed of people's explicit nonparticipation in hegemonic systems and their challenges to it, (2) redistributive acts aimed at more equitable distribution of resources that are steps toward future change, and (3) radical social action seeking "positive structural transformation of the system resulting in something qualitatively different" and more equitable for all (2008: 127–128). Specific food activist initiatives may fall on a continuum between these forms of militancy as well as between spontaneous and institutionalized, individual and collective.

This book showcases all kinds of actors holding a range of social and political affiliations and positions—from explicit, militant, politically aware activists to people who resist for less articulate, less political, and more personal reasons. People acting to change the food system or speaking out against it in whole or in part include consumers, academics, farmers, chefs, environmentalists, "professional" activists, political activists, religious activists, and business owners. Some initiatives engage several diverse actors; for example, the Kyoto local food movement links farmers, chefs, and consumers, whereas other actions engage mainly single constituencies, such as the Canadian wheat farmers. Still others struggle to include diverse constituencies, like the white Seattle activists grappling to deal with the food needs of Latino immigrants. In the Sicilian antimafia food cooperatives, the leaders and some of the farmers declared themselves to be political activists, whereas other farmers participated in the cooperatives simply to have a good job. This raises the issue of how any activist initiative balances individual motivations with the impact of collective action: the apolitical farmworkers contributed to the success of the cooperatives through their labor even though they did not hold the same ideals as the more politicized leaders.

The critical approaches of activists are not always explicit or cohesive. For example, disgruntled Cuban consumers commit quiet, spontaneous, and unorganized acts of resistance to the Cuban state by spreading rumors about adulterated government food. They express opposition that goes beyond food and links individual choice to political opposition. Slow Food members around the world share a goal of "good, clean, and fair" food but differ in their commitment and strategies, with some emphasizing changed consumption and others valorizing local economies or promoting biodiversity by protecting local foods. Some case studies fall at the very edges of activist practice, like the tactics of the young Muslim Brothers who distribute free food to the populace for religious and political conversion, or the coffee-labeling and transparency regimes established by private corporations as marketing strategies. Our choice of an expansive perimeter permits us to include cases located at the boundaries of food activism, through which we can reflect critically on the limits and meaning of the term.

Finally, food activism is a fruitful term for examining together the diverse forms of dissent and resistance practiced by political activists, farmers, restaurateurs, producers, and consumers. Their common goal is to have control over or take charge of production, distribution, or food choice, but their discourses and practices may range from aiming for an overreaching political impact to simply seeking closer ties between producers and consumers on the local stage.

Spaces and Places of Activism

The question of scales of political action is another thematic axis of this volume. Some mobilizations are based in groups with a collective image and common identity, like the Sri Lankan members of the Movement of National Land and Agricultural Reform or the Slow Food activists. In other cases, food activism involves more gradual and less visible efforts, like those of French biodynamic grape growers, who make changes in production methods and seek a place within French wine hierarchies, or the Oregonian members of the Ten Rivers Food Web, who promote farmers' markets and support local agriculture.

The case studies fall on a continuum from those that are more locally based to those that are more globally focused. Some that operate mainly on the local stage are, for example, the urban garden directors and their clients in Seattle; the women of Cagliari, Italy, who aim to revitalize their local food system; and the chefs and consumers in Kyoto, Japan, who valorize local heirloom vegetables. Concentrating on the local stage gives attention to specific enactments and definitions of agency and democracy. Furthermore, their valorization of local food creates the "local" itself, and this gives particular impetus to food movements by grounding them in imagined local "communities" (cf. Appadurai 1998; Gupta and Ferguson 1999; Low and Lawrence-Zùniga 2003).

Several of the case studies move beyond the local stage to examine actions more fully embedded in national or transnational sociopolitical contexts. Sicilian food-production cooperatives are illuminated by the history of the mafia, political opposition to it, and the critical economic ties between southern Italian producers and northern Italian consumers. The activism of Canadian wheat producers challenges national political legislation on the selling of wheat that affects Canadian farmers' ability to compete in global markets. Anti-GMO activism in Mexico and Colombia takes different forms due to the different cultural meanings of corn but is linked through common interests into a transnational network of activists. Taken together, the chapters show how activism takes place on narrow or broad stages in diverse settings with local, national, and international connections and highlight the migration of ideas and modes of action across geographic, social, and cultural contexts.

Agency and Power

Agency in food activism refers to how people act on, connect to, and transform economic or social relations while expressing either support or dissent. We believe with Sherry Ortner that social actors "are always involved in, and can never act outside of, the multiplicity of social relations in which they are enmeshed....relations of power, inequality and competition" (2006: 130–131). For example, the agency of Cuban consumers is limited by the coercive power of the state, and so they practice a quiet underground resistance to the food system. In contrast, Italian women in Sardinia are able to speak out freely in public against the food system, but their agency is constrained by gender-role expectations. Slow Food leaders' ability to promote local economies by developing high-quality artisanal products called *Presidia* bumps up against competition with other high-quality products valorized by other labeling systems.

The different forms of agency observed in the chapters in this volume confront different degrees of power. Josée Johnston (2008: 96) gives a definition of agency based in a Foucauldian concept of power as situated everywhere—in its institutional consolidations and in its everyday reinforcements through human actions. In this view, if power is pluralistic, fragmented, and everywhere, so agency must also be pluralistic, ubiquitous, and enacted through small everyday acts that demonstrate "the capacity to affect outcomes." Agency can only be understood, Amy Guptill (2008: 205) argues, by examining the "relationships among the desire for change, strategies for change, and ultimate success"; in other words, agency involves motivation, action, and results—all conditioned by individual and institutional power relations. This ties into Ortner's emphasis on "intentionality," which "differentiates agency from routine practices" (2006: 136). Moreover, Ortner points out that although agency appears to reside in individuals, it "is always in fact interactively negotiated" (2006: 151–152) as individuals confront other people and social institutions, just as Sardinian women in their food activism must cope with implicit cultural standards of appropriate female behavior as well as male-dominated political and economic structures.

Through their agency food activists express and navigate diverse forms of power. We can consider the power of charismatic leaders as well as the power of organized or spontaneous groups who give individuals strength in numbers (cf. Wolf 2001). But we also need to consider the power of the market, of industry, of the state, and of commercial lobbies that constrain or structure agency. Activists construct relationships, forms of opposition, or negotiations with and through these power structures and power holders by employing diverse strategies. Some actors are legitimate players, and others move on the margins of classic political arenas or in entirely new spaces they carve out. As June Nash (2005: 3) points out, just as global institutions must be flexible, so also must be the social movements that challenge them. Some movements display this capacity for adaptation in their actions, alliances, political strategies, and organizational structures.

Although these groups are often formed around resistance or promote an egalitarian militancy, they are not necessarily free of hierarchy, and as movements gain permanence and structure they inevitably have to deal with internal power dynamics. Movements undergo transformation over time through institutionalization, internal tensions, expansion, and narrowing or reforming of their goals or membership. Consideration of processual dimensions is indispensable to understanding food activism. Some of the cases presented—like the Ten Rivers Food Web in Oregon or the Movement of National Land and Agricultural Reform in Sri Lanka—reveal tensions stemming from bureaucratization and organizational change and their impact on members' conflicts over reproducing the organization itself versus enacting change in the world. Other cases permit analysis of the evolution of the cause and the ways dissent is channeled, integrated, or isolated.

Democracy and Economy

How the movements define, imagine, practice, and promote democracy is a key issue, and they manifest a range of forms, from radical conceptions of collective equality to libertarian notions of individual freedom. Democracy is expressed, for example, through consumer choice, regulation of food production, control of food distribution, and goals for universal access to resources. Some movements, like Slow Food, highlight a conception of food democracy defined as universal access to tasty, healthy, sustainable, and fairly produced food, whereas others, like

La Via Campesina, emphasize food sovereignty and its focus on local control of food production and distribution. Some movements emphasize gender, race, and class equality, while others ignore these social distinctions in favor of a concept of democracy based on market choice. Clearly democracy is a strategic concept wielded according to the particular goals and contexts of specific activist efforts.

Food activist initiatives give varying emphases to democratic and economic goals, which are sometimes aligned and sometimes at odds. Some movements may want to change the world, and others may simply want to promote better food. Some focus on local food and direct links between producers and consumers to reduce food miles, to promote knowledge about food, and to sustain local economies rather than multinational food companies (cf. Dubuisson-Quellier 2009). Underlying all the practices is a critical approach to systems of food production, distribution, or consumption, which can be expressed as a focus on greater social and economic justice.

Democracy is an explicit goal of some but not all food activist efforts, being overshadowed in some cases by other aims, such as a cleaner environment, better economic returns, or a "human economy" (Hart, Laville, and Cattani 2010). Different forms of food activism engage with the economy in diverse ways. According to Stephen Gudeman (2012: 96) "economy contains two realms: that of community and that of market or impersonal trade...These two faces of economy are complexly intertwined, and the border between them is often indistinct." The community dimension involves the social relations of production, distribution, and consumption, whereas the market dimension emphasizes exchange relations and the impersonal logic of the profit motive. Food activists often try to exploit the community dimension to affect the market dimension, for example, by creating farmers' markets or fair trade regimes to link producers and consumers in personal relationships that accrue economic benefits to both.

Organic, local, biodynamic, vegetarian, anti-GMO, fair trade, and food democracy are concepts that run through food activism. They hold diverse meanings in different contexts. The chapters in this book use ethnographic approaches to delve deeply into how diverse actors across the globe wield these concepts in their struggles around food. They open up a world of action and analysis that we hope will inspire future studies to fill gaps and promote further understanding of the significant growing global practices of food activism.

References

Alkon, A. H., and Agyeman, J. (eds.) (2011), *Cultivating Food Justice: Race, Class, and Sustainability*, Cambridge, MA: MIT Press.

Appadurai, A. (1998), *Modernity at Large: Cultural Dimensions of Globalization*, Minneapolis: University of Minnesota Press.

Borras, S., Edelman, M., and Kay, C. (eds.) (2008), *Transnational Agrarian Movements Confronting Globalization*, Hoboken, NJ: Wiley-Blackwell.

Carrier, J. G., and Luetchford, P. (eds.) (2012), *Ethical Consumption: Social Value and Economic Practice*, Oxford: Berghahn.

Dubuisson-Quellier, S. (2009), *La consommation engagée*, Paris: Sciences Po, les Presses.

Edelman, M. (2001), "Social Movements: Changing Paradigms and Forms of Politics," *Annual Review of Anthropology*, 30: 285–317.

Fitting, E. (2011), *The Struggle for Maize: Campesinos, Workers, and Transgenic Corn in the Mexican Countryside*, Durham, NC: Duke University Press.

Gudeman, S. (2012), "Community and Economy: Economy's Base," in J. Carrier (ed.), *A Handbook of Economic Anthropology* (2nd edn.), Cheltenham, UK: Edward Elgar, 95–108.

Gupta, A., and Ferguson, J. (eds.) (1999), *Culture, Power, Place: Explorations in Critical Anthropology*, Durham, NC: Duke University Press.

Guptill, A. (2008), "Infertile Ground: The Struggle for a New Puerto Rican Food System," in W. Wright and G. Middendorf (eds.), *The Fight over Food: Producers, Consumers and Activists Challenge the Food System*, State College: Pennsylvania State University Press, 203–224.

Hart, K., Laville, J. L., and Cattani, A. D. (eds.) (2010), *The Human Economy*, Cambridge: Polity.

Hinrichs, C. C., and Lyson, T. A. (eds.) (2009), *Remaking the North American Food System: Strategies for Sustainability*, Lincoln: University of Nebraska Press.

Holt-Giménez, E. (2006), *Campesino a Campesino: Voices from Latin America's Farmer to Farmer Movement for Sustainable Agriculture*, Oakland, CA: Food First.

Holt-Giménez, E. (2009), "From Food Crisis to Food Sovereignty: The Challenge of Social Movements," *Monthly Review*, 61/3: 142–156.

Holt-Giménez, E. (ed.) (2011), *Food Movements Unite! Strategies to Transform Our Food Systems*, Oakland, CA: Food First.

Johnston, J. (2008), "Counterhegemony or Bourgeois Piggery? Food Politics and the Case of FoodShare," in W. Wright and G. Middendorf (eds.), *The Fight over Food: Producers, Consumers and Activists Challenge the Food System*, State College: Pennsylvania State University Press, 93–119.

Katz, S. E. (2006), *The Revolution Will Not Be Microwaved: Inside America's Underground Food Movements*, White River Junction, VT: Chelsea Green.

Koensler, A., and Rossi, A. (2012), "Introduzione: Comprendere il dissenso," in A. Koensler and A. Rossi (eds.), *Comprendere il dissenso: Etnografia e antropologia dei movimenti sociali*, Perugia, Italy: Morlacchi Editore, 13–32.

Lamine, C. (2008), *Les AMAP: Un nouveau pacte entre producteurs et consommateurs?* Gap, France: Yves Michel.

Low, S. M., and Lawrence-Zùniga, D. (eds.) (2003), *The Anthropology of Space and Place: Locating Culture*, Oxford: Blackwell.

Nash, J. (2005), "Introduction: Social Movements and Global Process," in J. Nash (ed.), *Social Movements: An Anthropological Reader*, Oxford: Blackwell, 1–26.

Okely, J. (2012), *Anthropological Practice: Fieldwork and Ethnographic Method*, Oxford: Berg.

Olivier de Sardan, J. P. (2008), *La rigueur du qualitatif: Les contraintes empiriques de l'interprétation socio-anthropologique*, Louvain-la-Neuve, Belgium: Academia-Bruylant.

Ortner, S. B. (2006), *Anthropology and Social Theory: Culture, Power and the Acting Subject*, Durham, NC: Duke University Press.

Pratt, J. (2007), "Food Values: The Local and Authentic," *Critique of Anthropology*, 27/3: 285–300.

Schurman, R., and Munro, W. A. (2010), *Fighting for the Future of Food: Activists versus Agribusiness in the Struggle over Biotechnology*, Minneapolis: University of Minnesota Press.

Shreck, A. (2008), "Resistance, Redistribution, and Power in the Fair Trade Banana Initiative," in W. Wright and G. Middendorf (eds.), *The Fight over Food: Producers, Consumers and Activists Challenge the Food System*, State College: Pennsylvania State University Press, 121–144.

Siniscalchi, V. (2013), "Slow versus Fast: Économie et écologie dans le mouvement Slow Food," *Terrain* 60: 132–147.

Wilk, R. (2006), "From Wild Weeds to Artisanal Cheese," in R. Wilk (ed.), *Fast Food/Slow Food: The Cultural Economy of the Global Food System*, Lanham, MD: Altamira, 13–28.

Williams-Forson, P., and Counihan, C. (eds.) (2011), *Taking Food Public: Redefining Foodways in a Changing World*, New York: Routledge.

Winne, M. (2011), *Food Rebels, Guerrilla Gardeners, and Smart-Cookin' Mamas: Fighting Back in an Age of Industrial Agriculture*, Boston: Beacon.

Wolf, E. R. (2001), *Pathways of Power: Building an Anthropology of the Modern World*, Berkeley: University of California Press.

Wright, W., and Middendorf, G. (eds.) (2008), *The Fight over Food: Producers, Consumers and Activists Challenge the Food System*, State College: Pennsylvania State University Press.

Part II

Local Engagements

–2–

Food Activism in Western Oregon

Joan E. Gross

Introduction

I am both a participant in and an observer of the local food movement (LFM) in Western Oregon. I came into this field both from a desire to connect with good local food and from an applied research project I conducted on rural food insecurity (Gross and Rosenberger 2009). When I moved to Oregon in 1989, I was attracted by the long growing season, the sheep in the fields, and the proximity to the ocean. I quickly discovered that there was no outlet for local seafood in town, and the only lamb in the stores came from New Zealand. The price of apples in the store bore no relation to the piles of apples that were rotting in our neighbors' yards. I began thinking about these various disconnects in the food system when I discovered that Oregon had the highest hunger rate in the nation.[1] While interviewing food-insecure rural residents in 2004, I witnessed the physical results of living on cheap and emergency food. People who were missing legs from diabetes talked about the abundance of breads and pastries donated to the emergency food system and the scarcity and expense of fresh vegetables and fruit. I read about how these same rural areas, which had become food deserts, once exported a variety of food. I came to realize that the local food system needed to be changed and that I could help do it.

This chapter addresses the activism of the Ten Rivers Food Web (TRFW), whose mission is to build resilient food systems which provide healthy food for all. My connection to this organization began four years before it became a focus of my research. I was a founding board member, a low-income network chair, vice president, and president. Since we had no staff for the first five years, board members did all the work of the organization: staffing tables at community gatherings, holding fundraisers and educational events, and writing grants. I began spending so much time on the organization that I felt compelled to include it in my research agenda. In what follows, I pay particular attention to forms of human agency in the local food movement and the challenges of scaling up an organization from an ad hoc nucleus of motivated people to an organization with staff members. In the second part of this chapter, I look more carefully at who the food activists involved in this social change are, what brought them into the local food movement, and what sustains their interest in it.

Acknowledging and Growing a Diverse Food Economy

As outlined in the productionist paradigm (Lang and Heasman 2004), American farmers sell their crops on the commodity market or to food conglomerates and the food eventually shows up in chain grocery stores and restaurants. This state of affairs has received a lot of press as the industrial food system has come under attack for degrading both the environment and health. But this is not the whole story. J. K. Gibson-Graham points out that what is usually regarded as "the economy" is restricted to wage labor, commodity market exchange, and capitalist enterprise, but capitalism is "just one particular set of economic relations situated in a vast sea of economic activity" (2006: 70). They illustrate this with the image of an iceberg where wage labor and production for a market in a capitalist firm jut out on top, but underneath the surface lies a diverse noncapitalist economy that includes cooperatives, self-provisioning, volunteering, and barter. Capitalocentric hegemony impedes us from properly acknowledging the many ways in which people provide for themselves and their communities. This is most apparent when we consider food. In Figure 2.1, I offer a food system–centered iteration of Gibson-Graham's (2006: 70) icon of the iceberg.

In Figure 2.1, the top of the iceberg is dominated by global markets and transnational corporations reducing food to its monetary value. Below the surface of the water, you see an expanded view of foodways, many of which consciously work against the global capitalist food system and others of which sit comfortably within the dominant system.[2] This image highlights the massive participation in noncapitalist and small-scale food activities that bring people closer to the sources of their food through growing, foraging, or cooking, and closer to other people. One might say that they resocialize economic ties around food.

This background is relevant to the following discussion of the LFM in the mid–Willamette Valley of Oregon. Activists combat the global industrial food system by supporting the local production of sustainably produced food and venues where it can be procured locally. Goals of LFMs are multiple: to reduce the environmental impact of large-scale agriculture based on chemical inputs and monocultures, as well as the long-distance shipment of food; to increase access to fresh fruits and vegetables for people of all income levels; to support the economic viability of small farmers over the corporate control of the food system; and to create ties between producers and consumers. Food activists, then, work below the tip of the iceberg to reduce local dependency on global markets and to increase knowledge about the origin of one's food.

There are many ways that LFMs go about accomplishing these goals. They are necessarily influenced by the social, ecological, and economic environments in which they are located. The LFM studied here is situated in a place of small towns and cities surrounded by agricultural land and small farms that produce a large diversity of crops. It is easy to find houses with sizable yards, the climate is mild, there

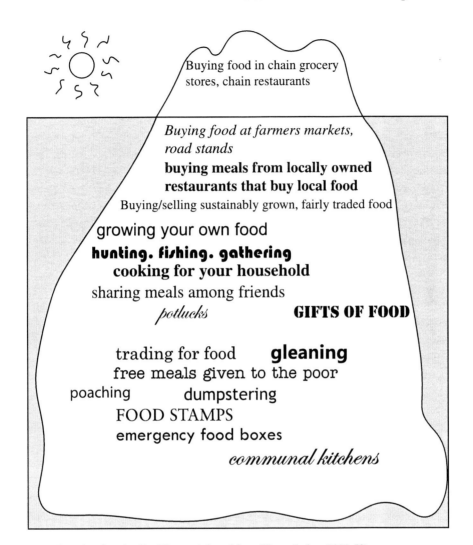

Buying food in chain grocery stores, chain restaurants

Buying food at farmers markets, road stands

buying meals from locally owned restaurants that buy local food

Buying/selling sustainably grown, fairly traded food

growing your own food

hunting. fishing. gathering

cooking for your household

sharing meals among friends

potlucks   **GIFTS OF FOOD**

trading for food   **gleaning**

free meals given to the poor

poaching   dumpstering

FOOD STAMPS

emergency food boxes

communal kitchens

Figure 2.1   Our Complex Food System (adapted from Gibson-Graham 2006: 70).

is no water shortage, and the soil is good for the most part. The major employer is a land grant university, and opportunities to learn about food growing and processing are available through the university's extension program. These properties have oriented the LFM toward smallholder food producers. Oregon's well-known environmental activism and its less-known food insecurity have also helped shape the LFM, which has privileged direct action on local projects rather than indirect policy work. Currently the focus is on equipping rural farmers' markets to be able to accept payment through the Supplemental Nutrition Assistance Program (SNAP) and the funding to be able to increase the value of their SNAP award when used at the farmers' market.[3]

The Birth and Development of a Community Food Organization

Fifty community members attended an informal discussion on hunger in Oregon on January 11, 2004. David Graeber (2009) would call this an "affinity group"—the elementary particle of voluntary association. Manuel DeLanda (2006) uses the term *meshwork* and defines it as a flexible, nonhierarchical, decentralized, self-organizing group. We were a coalition of people with different interests—health, the environment, farming, poverty, and the economy. We came to see how all these were related through food, and we all had a desire to reorient our local food system. From that first time, a group of us continued to meet regularly. We had an employee of the U.S. Department of Agriculture, an early organic farmer, food bank and grocery cooperative workers, church representatives, environmental activists, and anthropologists. We toyed with naming ourselves a "food policy council," but we wanted to work concretely on projects, rather than indirectly on policies, so instead we chose the term *food web* because we were attracted by the imagery of linking all the different facets of food production and consumption together. When we talked about geographic focus, I introduced the notion of foodshed (Kloppenburg, Hendrickson, and Stevenson 1996); with Oregon's strong structure of local watershed councils, this idea resonated with the group. But foodsheds have a stronger social component than watersheds, and we eventually decided to map our geographic focus onto political entities that encompassed a significant amount and variety of food. We agreed to cover three contiguous counties in the mid–Willamette Valley, containing seafood on the coast, diverse vegetables and fruits in the valley, and grains and pasture in the foothills of the Cascade Range. One of our members commented that there were ten rivers running through this region, so we became the Ten Rivers Food Web. In 2005 we targeted five areas that members wanted to work on: a community processing facility, food literacy, farm-to-institution alliances, local farm coordination, and low-income projects. Group members concentrated on one of the five areas and took on projects and contributed labor and sometimes money to their specific projects.[4]

This type of structure is not valued by funders. They are interested in supporting organizations that have a singularity of purpose, articulated in clear vision and mission statements and demonstrated through projects with outcomes and subsequent evaluations. Rather than focusing on building an organization that would be well positioned to acquire external funding, members used the umbrella of the organization to pursue their own interests. However, people eventually did want external funding to ramp up the projects they were involved with, and this forced the affinity group to restructure itself into a nonprofit organization so that we could apply for grants, and donors could get tax deductions. Suddenly, we needed officers, an accountant, and a lawyer. Group members became board members. Eventually, we constructed agendas to move us through business at our meetings. The imposition of structured rules of discourse forced people to recognize that we were no longer an affinity group brought together by a general sense of interest and camaraderie but a structured organization with an explicit purpose.

Developing a strategic plan led to the alienation of several longtime board members as the various interests represented on the board were squeezed into a narrower focus necessary for funding agencies. Many of us experienced cognitive dissonance in resisting corporate control of the global industrial food system and then restructuring our organization on a business model in order to access funds. To fight against the advertisement of junk food and then work on "branding" our organization to advertise our own goals seemed a bit disingenuous. Often meetings were contentious.

Having received a small grant or two made us eligible to apply for large grants, but this entailed focusing even more on our organizational capacity. We attended countless hours of facilitated meetings over a period of six months in the process of creating a new strategic plan. The 2011 plan outlined four project areas (community food organizing, food literacy, access to local food for all, food-producer support) and five organizational areas (staffing, facilities and systems, board development, marketing and communications, fund development). We were told that the mission and vision statements we created should roll off our tongues, but many of us were left stuttering. New board members were brought on who wasted no time in asking about the organization's mission and vision. My inclination was to tell them about the history of our coming together and about showing films at the public library, about organizing in neighborhoods to do garden food swaps, about opening an emergency food pantry on the college campus, about facilitating discussions between restaurant owners and farmers, about bringing grass-seed farmers together to talk about growing beans and grains. But most of these activities were associated with a particular board member, rather than with TRFW as an organization.

Building organizational structure paid off in funding for staff and projects. Our budget had grown from zero to four digits in four years and then from four to six digits in another two years. While we claimed to be serving three counties, all of us lived in the central county and had no time or money to do outreach in the other two. Funding allowed us to hire community food organizers for the two surrounding rural counties and an executive director who could work full-time on projects. Nevertheless, external funding came with strings attached, and those strings created structures that impeded the human agency that began the movement. Rosalinda Guillén (2011: 308) writes of this often uncomfortable process of transitioning from a meshwork into a recognized hierarchical organization: "And then whatever it was we started from the beginning dissolves into something totally different that all of a sudden needs to be 'funded,' needs to be 'organized' and needs to be 'directed.'"

As organizations become driven by donors and projects (as funders and strategic plans require), they limit their capacity to be responsive to local needs and to be creative (Batta et al. 2011: 97). One local food activist in our group put it this way:

> It seems like when you're a smaller operation dealing with small amounts of money, there's nothing hanging over you. When you've gotten big grants and there's a bunch of money, there's definitely more fire to be doing things because there are expectations that go with that money. And I don't know if that changes goals and aims of the organization and what direction they want to go because they have to be pleasing people and an idea that they had six months ago, they have to stick with because that was on paper.

To summarize, in the first stage of development a group of people found that coming together in a loose organization gave them the social support and a bit of financial assistance to pursue linked interests. In the second stage, a new cast of characters joined an established organization and felt constrained by organizational documents to proceed in a prescribed direction. In both stages, however, individual food activists work against the global industrial food system, and it is to them that we now turn our gaze.

Food Activists

In the course of my involvement with TRFW, I have conducted semistructured interviews with twenty-nine local food activists.[5] Twenty-one women and eight men with birth years from 1940 to 1988 are in the sample. All but one would be identified as white.[6] The majority had modest incomes and fell into the 15 percent income tax bracket ($8,500–$34,500). Fifteen of them are on the board or staff of TRFW. The others volunteer or work for partner organizations, including local direct-market farms. My sample includes four farmers who own or rent their land, five people who work on farms, and ten people who receive a salary from a nonprofit organization that includes food access or localization in its mission. Three of them first served as volunteers in AmeriCorps, a national program that places people with nonprofit organizations, and two are current AmeriCorps volunteers. Only three participants were born and raised in Western Oregon, though most of the older participants have spent over thirty years in the area. Within the group are people who helped found the state's organic certification organization and who established the local natural food co-op newsletter, as well as the president of the state farmers' market association. Other study participants run community gardens, farmers' markets, and CSAs. All of them are affiliated with more than one local food organization. Most of them attend countless meetings of organizations that are striving to expand local food production and markets and to connect low-income residents with healthy local food.

Despite the high level of activism in my sample, I found that some people were uncomfortable labeling themselves as activists or even as part of a movement. I heard, "I'm not really a movement person," "I was never a joiner," and "I'm more of a solitary activist than a group activist." Many considered it fundamental to edu-cate the self in order to be a resource person for others and to inspire people to make the food system more localized, sustainable, and justice oriented. This brings up the question of scale. Is one an activist if the site of the action is one's own body? What about one's household or one's circle of friends? Mobilizing for change rather than unconsciously accepting a given structure shows human agency, but should we con-sider activists a woman who takes the time to prepare fresh, local food for her family and a person who decides that he will no longer eat factory-produced meat? Both of these people are repudiating the existing order and taking power for themselves. Marion Nestle's (2000) suggestion that we must "vote with our forks" exemplifies how the personal is political and economic. I have found that the transformation of their own eating habits often served as a gateway for individuals to get involved in food activist organizations. This leads me to conclude that any challenge to the food system is a form of activism, even at the level of individual choice and even if people don't consider themselves activists.

Food is integral to our daily lives, and practices around food are at least partially unconscious, conforming to the way that the people closest to us eat. Changing one's food habitus, or the unconscious tendencies one acquires in the practice of everyday life, involves raising the act of eating to a level of consciousness, and new practices may be positioned against family foodways. One participant cited her father's death from diabetes and poor eating habits as the reason she altered her own. Several infor-mants, on the other hand, cited the importance of eating meals together as an aspect of their family foodways that they try to continue, although they have shifted away from the central importance of meat. Thirteen of the twenty-nine participants spoke of periods of vegetarianism. Most of them now eat local meat. Emma explained it in this way:

> I was a vegetarian for a few years, but I often felt that the reasons I was vegetarian were different from why other people were and my reasons shifted over time....A lot of people were attracted for humanitarian reasons, to a lesser extent eating low on the food chain. I guess that I feel that it is okay to eat higher on the food chain, better to eat a local chicken from down the street than tofu that caused a rainforest to be cut down in Brazil.

Emma emphasizes the importance of constructing a local food economy over a vegetarianism connected to global agribusiness but disconnected from local roots.

Contact with a particular social movement or a book they read are common ways that people reported raising their consciousness. Participants also described the real-ization that there was something wrong with their own and their culture's foodways when traveling abroad. Finding oneself in a different food culture introduces the possibility of breaking one's own food habitus. I call this "food culture shock."[7] Several people gave enthusiastic descriptions of what was good about foreign foodways that contrasted with mainstream American foodways.[8] Jaya articulated this particularly well:

> In Cinque Terre I was just mesmerized and I think, coming back to it, that's probably what inspired me to get involved in the local food movement. More specifically just the relationship or the role of food in that community seemed so embedded in place and in this deep history and it just shaped their landscape but it didn't seem like this man against nature sort of thing. It seemed much more a relationship between the place and the people and I am really attracted to that because it spoke to the identity of the people and the identity of the place and that's when it's really interesting to me.

Tammy expressed a similar sentiment about her experiences in two different continents:

> Mexico and Australia absolutely affected my attitude! Experiencing how others prepare, value, share, and culture food is a tremendously beneficial thing for anyone. In my own way, I'm always interested in the relationships people have with food. In southern Mexico for instance, people in many communities are poor beyond the imagination of most US citizens. However, their diets and their food culture are fantastically rich. They have the ability to coax food plants out of scant fertile soil, they know how to find and use native foods, they utilize foods efficiently and value "waste," and they understand the magic of simplicity. They have a fundamentally respectful relationship with their food.

Jaya and Tammy, both in their thirties, were first devoted environmentalists and later came into the food movement. Other participants just marveled at the time that was spent cooking and eating long, drawn-out meals in other countries and how enjoyable it was. After a study-abroad experience in Belgium, Dave said, "It was my first experience of a different food culture where I really did feel like I had a window into making food a more important part of my life. I was amazed at how small the refrigerator was."

Dave's last comment relates to the freshness of food, another common theme that was linked to the habit of shopping at markets instead of large grocery stores. Karrie remembered the following:

> I saw in German farmers' markets a style of shopping that was very practical rather than trendy like U.S. farmers' markets can be. People really came to shop with their baskets and bags in hand and filled them up with the week's provisions. The markets were crowded with buyers rather than people out for a romantic stroll listening to music and walking their dogs.

Ten people mentioned the freshness and good taste of the food in other cultures. Zoey said that food was more abundant in the United States than in Russia, but "it had a lot less flavor." Asa was impressed by knowledge about food in France: "people know what vegetables are and they're more discerning." Even when food was scarce, these Americans were impressed by the hospitality people in other cultures showed in giving their best food to their guests, even when they barely had enough.

One participant commented, "The isolation and self sufficiency [of Costa Rica and New Zealand] we found inspiring and invigorating and, again, the simpler life-style reinforced the idea that that's something we wanted to work towards, or work for." In their travels, participants also discovered food activists bent on changing their food systems: better nutrition and sustainable living in Mexico; food-producer co-ops, animal rights, and genetically modified organism (GMO) labeling in England; land-use laws in Germany; and food sovereignty in Thailand.

To sum up, living temporarily in a foreign food system shocked these activists into thinking about how food habits could be different. One older participant talked about reverse food culture shock when she returned to the United States after living for two years in the eastern Mediterranean, where she shopped daily in open markets but also was in contact with refugees who had very little to eat. She told about having a temporary breakdown in a grocery store where it seemed as if the food stretched on forever and she couldn't find anything to make for her family among all the pack-aged goods.

Connection with growing food was another important gateway into the local food movement. This included growing up on a farm; interning on a farm as a young adult; getting to know a farmer at a farmers' market; growing organic vegetables in a community garden plot, in one's backyard, or as a Peace Corps volunteer; and buy-ing a farm after retirement. Participants listed eight different organizations dealing with farming and gardening that they belonged to. Five of the ten informants born before 1957 said that they were part of the "back-to-the-land" movement and that that had definitely affected their attitude toward food. The back-to-the-land move-ment was part of an alternative social movement and had a strong focus on grow-ing one's own food and attempting to be self-sufficient (Belasco 2007). Two of the people born after 1975 also cited self-sufficiency but situated it within the context of environmental degradation and peak oil, stating that they feared being dependent on food from distant sources.

Buying, cooking, and eating food were also cited as gateways into food activism. Two people mentioned being introduced through natural food stores and farmers' markets. Four participants said that their intense interest in cooking brought them into the local food movement. Kayla, a young food organizer, explained the connec-tions in this way:

> It actually was cooking [that brought me into the movement]. When I went to college after the first year I wanted to drop out and go to culinary school but after apprenticing with a chef that summer, he was like "you should stay in school, get your undergrad and then after that at least you'll have that to fall back on". Then I was like "Well I'm in school, what can I do that's related to food that might make sense?" I was always

interested in environmental and social justice and how food tied those things together as well as just the enjoyment of cooking, it just made a lot of sense to me. Like "Oh yeah food issues influence all these other things that I was interested and passionate about."

Kayla finished her degree and focused her career goals on working for change in the food system.

Participants listed related organizations and movements they were involved in. Eleven environmental organizations were listed, as well as general movements around global sustainability, sustainable living, and opposition to car use. Social justice was the next most common theme, with specific mention of affordable housing, rural development, immigration reform, and, especially, food access. Four people credited their faith communities (both Christian and Buddhist) for leading them into work for food justice. Participants also engaged in other forms of counterculture, such as antiwar, home birth, and de-schooling movements.

The way in which people first connected with the LFM tended to affect their program priorities. I remember one TRFW meeting in particular when people of an environmentalist bent stated that our focus should be on food production because if enough food was produced locally, people would automatically have access. Those on the social justice side had to remind them that supply is not the same as distribution; as a result, plans to support a local emergency food pantry were sustained. Steven saw the split between producers and low-income consumers as one of the more difficult ones to negotiate as a community food organizer in a rural county:

I also work with building partnerships around local foods movements and trying to convince different stakeholders about the importance of different issues. So we have some people who are really into the hunger movement and trying to connect them with the local foods people who tend to be the growers and making both sides understand each other better. There's not animosity but there's differences in opinions. On the hunger side, food is too expensive and needs to be cheaper and on the local food side you have farmers and fisherman that are trying to get a fair wage for their product and therefore have to sell it at a high price. And trying to bridge that gap and make both sides understand each other better so that we can all move together as a community around food systems work is hard.

The people who didn't self-identify as food activists explained their role as "leading by example." In this, they mirrored the self-described activists, who also saw part of their role as modeling the change they wanted to see in the world. Both TRFW and the food action team of the city's Sustainability Coalition have included in their vision statements a time in the future when a certain percentage of the food eaten in the region/city will be locally sourced.[9] Despite the impossibility of determining such a figure exactly, some sampling indicates that it grew from 2 percent in 2008 to 7 percent in 2011 (Payne 2011). When I asked my informants to estimate what percentage of the food they consume is local, the figures ranged from 40 to 95 percent. Peter, who is sixty-seven years old, explained:

> If we don't grow it ourselves, mostly we get it at the Co-op and I only buy Oregon wines and I only buy local beers. I'll bet 90% of what we eat is local.... We mostly buy local cheese. You can't get shredded wheat and other breakfast cereal and those are so convenient so we go to the store for those. Sugar, we buy. Can't get local sugar. We don't use as much. I'm just thinking about things that come in the door—breakfast cereal and sugar. You know I've almost cut out citrus and I'm glad I did because now when I get an orange or a grapefruit, I'm astonished at how much more I enjoy it.

Cathy, who is just three years younger than Peter, was equally adamant about eating locally:

> We have lived on 12 1/2 acres in rural Benton County since 1979 and have gardens every year. We now have year-round gardens, thanks to my husband's willingness to work out in the cold. In fact, we have a fresh salad from our garden every night, even in the coldest parts of winter. The salads also boast reconstituted tomatoes we dried the previous summer and/or other vegetables I canned or pickled (eggplants, green beans, etc.) and garbanzos or other beans we grew or were grown locally.

Eating locally is important to the younger generation of food activists as well. Julie, thirty-three years old, reported:

> Probably 80% of my food is barter and it's probably all from the farmers' market. We live off of veggies, local bread and meat from the market. And the rest of the stuff is bought at the co-op like our pasta. So I'd say like the other 20% that we don't barter for we buy at the co-op and maybe 5 to 10% of that is local. I don't think the pasta is. All the dairy is local, the veggies, the fruit, because we just eat what's in season. And then I do a lot of my own drying. I'll get stuff at the market when its abundant and then dry and can. So that's what we eat when it's off season. I try not to buy things when they're not in season and local. I've gotten out of the mindset of craving asparagus when it's not growing. I just don't do that anymore.

Asa, age twenty-nine, has no land of his own but made sure that he could have chickens and a garden at his rental. Upon moving to the area, he quickly established contacts with local growers and fruitful landscapes:

> A lot of our food comes from the farm I work at, because this place is very generous and if you work here you can take home vegetables which is great. We also have chickens, have a pretty good garden growing and usually our protein comes through some opportunistic thing. Somebody has just caught a fish or somebody has some lambs to sell. We try to buy things in larger quantities, but through local sources. Some of the food comes through trades, some of the food is wild gathered, in terms of the very plentiful

blackberries here and mushrooms and things like that, as well as "you pick" other fruit and then trades through the market as well.

Peter and Julie both alluded to changing their own food habits in order to eat locally grown food; for example, Peter does not buy citrus since citrus does not grow where he lives, but his appreciation of it has grown more intense. Julie has given up eating fresh food out of season that she would have to buy at the store. This way she can trade her own produce at the farmers' market and fill her kitchen and save the money for necessary farm equipment. All of these participants mentioned that they don't think about what to cook independently of what they have. Rather than focusing on deprivation, the food activists I interviewed were proud of their environmentally sound eating and their degree of self-sufficiency. Perhaps more important, most activists expressed enjoyment of the food, considering it as a pleasure as well as nourishment. Both Cathy and Asa are very accomplished cooks and spend a good deal of time perfecting recipes with local ingredients.

It must be said that few activists in other realms can enjoy the fruits of their labor at every meal. Even though the ulterior motives of food activists are to shrink income gaps, support local economies, stop destroying the natural environment, and make good food more accessible, the enjoyment of food is not an insignificant element in the lives of activists. I made a point of asking people to describe a meal that they thoroughly enjoyed, and I was struck by how often people described meals that they had eaten in the past few days that included home cooking and local produce. The meals varied from the fast cooking of fresh vegetables from the garden to elaborate preparations that stretched over days. Steven gave an example of the latter:

> I made a ham for Easter, it was one of our hams and I brined it and cured it for a week and then smoked it for 8 hours and then I'm trying to think, we probably just had like a salad and some kale or collards, ideally rutabagas. I love rutabagas. So you have that kind of a meal where it takes a lot. It wasn't like I thought of it that day and then put it together. It was something that was planned for months.

The production of a meal is a source of entertainment for many of the food activists, in both its preparation and its consumption. It is also a performance in which one demonstrates one's food-procuring and preparation skills. On the whole, food activists reported eating very well without spending much money for food. They do this by inserting themselves into food production and by using nonmonetary systems of exchange. For both farmers and farmworkers, the farmers' market is a key site where people trade what they have a lot of for what they want in order to diversify their diet. In addition to the delight of receiving lots of high-quality food without spending money, people increase their social ties with other food producers. Asa commented:

> At the market where we worked everyone at the end was always trading and giving. It was really cool because you'd come home at the end with goat cheeses and bread and

pastries and all kinds of neat stuff. You eat really well that way and affordably. Good food is expensive but when you're dealing with individuals who are producing the food instead of corporations who are producing the food, there's a lot more room for negotiation and exchange. So you can get high end stuff for not very much money.

Another group that local food activists belonged to was the local alternative currency organization.[10] In addition to trading, local food activists can eat high-end food without an outlay of cash by foraging. Mushrooms were the most consistently mentioned foraged food, especially chanterelles, which are the easiest for amateurs to recognize. Participants also gathered fiddlehead ferns and mussels.

When I asked activists what they appreciated most about food in this area, answers included the "long growing season," "good water supply," and abundance and variety of food. Knowing the farmers and how close by the food is grown was mentioned several times. In general, everyone was appreciative of the "food culture" and of supporting local food in all its richness. This was often contrasted with what they found when they returned to visit family in other parts of the country.

Conclusion

Chad Lavin (2012) and Julie Guthman (2011) criticize LFMs for abandoning the rhetoric of citizenship and state action for that of consumerism by elevating the consumption of local food to the level of political action. Lavin points out a deep suspicion of conventional politics that seems to pervade the movement and the understanding of the market as the solution to political problems. He asks whether consumerist politics is a ruse that distracts citizens from meaningful political engagement or whether it speaks to a lack of opportunities for political action. The organization and individuals examined in this chapter highlight consumption in the work to reorient the food system, but consumption is not synonymous with "the market." Foraging, growing, and trading for food and treating food preparation and eating as primary forms of pleasure and entertainment are all practices of the LFM that sidestep the market. Changing policy is only one way to combat the multinational corporations that control the global food system. Working below the surface to diversify the ways people obtain and think about food is another way to attack corporate control, which eventually has a political effect. TRFW chose direct action over policy work, and the activists that align with this organization illustrate the desired model in their own daily practices. The LFM is certainly representative of new social movements that try to change civil society by transforming values, lifestyles, and symbols in contrast to earlier, more overtly political social movements (Melucci 1996). It may also be an example of what Alberto Melucci calls "regressive Utopianism" (1996: 104) since it seeks to recreate a food system using many elements of older agrarian systems. However, being actively involved in social change protects the participants from the false notion that society is coterminous with one's own solidarity group, a feature Melucci has found in other forms of regressive Utopianism.

The food activists who participated in this study weaned themselves away from highly processed, cheap industrial foods to which they had grown accustomed and increased their consumption of locally produced food, some of which they grew themselves. This shift in foodways reconnects local food activists to their ecosystem and to each other, serving to alleviate what has been referred to as "nature deficit" as well as the social isolation that characterizes late capitalism (Louv 2011; Putnam 2000). In transforming their own foodways, they joined with others in parallel social movements and formed communities of practice in which their foodways came to resemble each other's, rather than those of the families they came from.

I suggest that the food system is a privileged entry point when one is trying to reconceive the economy in an alternative manner. When capitalism is understood as a unified structure, it cannot be chipped away at or gradually replaced but must be transformed entirely in one fell swoop. This makes the task so mammoth as to be hopeless (Gibson-Graham 1993). If, instead, we acknowledge the differences between types of market transactions and the myriad noncapitalist economic forms that permeate our food system, incremental changes in the food system can make tangible differences in the lives of individuals, families, and communities.

Notes

1. Oregon has consistently ranked among the states with the highest rates of hunger (later revised to "very low food security") since the U.S. Department of Agriculture began collecting statistics in 1995.
2. I included the federally mandated Supplemental Nutrition Assistance Program (SNAP) program (food stamps) and other emergency food programs because they are not entirely part of the market-driven system found at the tip of the iceberg. I am well aware of the history of the food stamp program as a way to use surplus crops but wanted to emphasize the entitlement nature of the program.
3. Since TRFW assisted the Corvallis and Albany farmers' markets to begin accepting SNAP EBT cards in 2007, $162,190 of government assistance has gone directly to local farmers, and the amount increases every year.
4. TRFW has collaborated with over twenty organizations, illustrating Neva Hassanein's (2012) point that food democracy must be based on a coalition of groups focusing on different problems in order to transform the food system.
5. Pseudonyms have been used.
6. According to the 2010 census the population of the three counties is approximately 90 percent white, with Latinos, Asians, and Native Americans/Alaskan Natives making up the rest. For the importance of whiteness and gender in the alternative food movement, see Slocum 2007.

7. Food culture shock goes beyond what Julie Guthman (2011) calls *Europhilia.*

8. Negative comments from poorer areas of the world included food insecurity, food safety, monotonous diets, the cutting down of old growth to farm, and the killing of endangered species to eat.

9. TRFW's goal was 30 percent by 2012, but the most recent vision statement removed the date while keeping the percentage. The Sustainability Coalition's is 60 percent by 2020, but they are considering reducing it to 40 percent.

10. This system, derived from the Ithaca HOUR, is based on time spent in human labor, and products are revalued accordingly. An hour of washing windows is worth the same as an hour of translating Russian, for example.

References

Batta, F., Brescia, S., Gubbels, P., Guri, B., Jean-Baptiste, C., and Sherwood, S. (2011), "Transforming NGO Roles to Help Make Food Sovereignty a Reality," in E. Holt-Giménez (ed.), *Food Movements Unite!* Oakland, CA: Food First.

Belasco, W. (2007), *Appetite for Change: How the Counterculture Took on the Food Industry,* Ithaca, NY: Cornell University Press.

DeLanda, M. (2006), *A New Philosophy of Society: Assemblage Theory and Social Complexity,* New York: Continuum.

Gibson-Graham, J. K. (1993), "Waiting for the Revolution, or How to Smash Capitalism while Working at Home in Your Spare Time," *Rethinking Marxism,* 6/2: 10–24.

Gibson-Graham, J. K. (2006), *A Postcapitalist Politics,* Minneapolis: University of Minnesota Press.

Graeber, D. (2009), *Direct Action: An Ethnography,* Oakland, CA: AK Press.

Gross, J., and Rosenberger, N. (2009), "The Double Binds of Getting Food among the Poor in Rural Oregon," *Food, Culture, and Society,* 12/4: 47–70.

Guillén, R. (2011), "Transforming Our Food System by Transforming Our Movement," in E. Holt-Giménez (ed.), *Food Movements Unite!* Oakland, CA: Food First.

Guthman, J. (2011), *Weighing In: Obesity, Food Justice, and the Limits of Capitalism,* Berkeley: University of California Press.

Hassanein, N. (2012), "Practicing Food Democracy: A Pragmatic Politics of Transformation," in C. Counihan and P. Williams-Forson (eds.), *Taking Food Public: Redefining Foodways in a Changing World,* New York: Routledge.

Kloppenburg, J., Hendrickson, J., and Stevenson, G. W. (1996), "Coming in to the Food Shed," *Agriculture and Human Values,* 13/3: 33–42.

Lang, T., and Heasman, M. (2004), *Food Wars: The Global Battle for Mouths, Minds, and Markets,* Sterling, VA: Earthscan.

Lavin, C. (2012), "The Year of Eating Politically," in C. Counihan and P. Williams-Forson (eds.), *Taking Food Public: Redefining Foodways in a Changing World,* New York: Routledge.

Louv, R. (2011), *The Nature Principle: Human Restoration and the End of Nature-Deficit Disorder,* Chapel Hill, NC: Algonquin.

Melucci, A. (1996), *Challenging Codes: Collective Action in the Information Age,* Cambridge: Cambridge University Press.

Nestle, M. (2000), "Ethical Dilemmas in Choosing a Healthful Diet: Vote with Your Fork!" *Proceedings of the Nutrition Society,* 59: 619–629.

Payne, S. (2011), "Local Eats Week: A Celebration of All Ingredients Locally Grown," *Corvallis Gazette Times,* October 20, http://www.gazettetimes.com/entertainment/dining/local-eats-week-a-celebration-of-all-ingredients-locally-grown/article_56c08292-fb55-11e0–913e-001cc4c002e0.html, accessed March 18, 2013.

Putnam, R. (2000), *Bowling Alone: The Collapse and Revival of American Community,* New York: Simon and Schuster.

Slocum, R. (2007), "Whiteness, Space and Alternative Food Practice," *Geoforum,* 38/3: 520–533.

3

Engaging Latino Immigrants in Seattle Food Activism through Urban Agriculture

Teresa M. Mares

Introduction: This Country Is Full of Farmers!

Just days before the tenth anniversary of the World Trade Organization protests that shut down Seattle's streets in late 1999, Eric Holt-Giménez, executive director of Food First,[1] addressed a captivated audience at the University of Washington. Holt-Giménez had been invited by organizers from the Community Alliance for Global Justice, and his talk opened a series of events organized to commemorate the protests and discuss the lessons learned over the preceding ten years. While completing my graduate studies in cultural anthropology, I had become deeply involved with the alliance's Food Justice Project and was thrilled to see the large crowd that turned out for the event. A decade after the "Battle of Seattle," Holt-Giménez spoke eloquently about the global food crisis, the devastating impacts of policies like the North American Free Trade Agreement (NAFTA) for farmers in the Global South, and the inspiring ways that grassroots groups around the world were challenging corporate-controlled food systems through organizing for food sovereignty.

Having finished a series of interviews with Latino/a day laborers earlier that week, one vignette that Holt-Giménez shared was especially poignant for me that night. He stated:

> You know, there's a sick joke amongst older farmers here because the average age of a farmer in the United States is approaching sixty right now ... in ten years the average age of the American farmer is going to be *dead*. Nonetheless, this country is full of farmers! They are standing on the street corners looking for work. They come from Mexico, Honduras, Nicaragua, Guatemala, Colombia, Panama. They've been displaced! They mow our lawns, they pump our gas, they cook our food in the fancy restaurants, those are farmers. We're surrounded by farmers. They're out of work.

In these brief lines, Holt-Giménez synthesized a complex contradiction that persists in our agricultural and service sectors—connecting the movement of people from Mexico to the United States in search of work with the devastation of rural livelihoods in Latin America. Seattle is just one of many U.S. cities where this movement is touching down into local communities, with Latino/a farmers experiencing radical changes in their foodways and overall well-being as they build new lives in the United States (Mares 2012, 2013). Holt-Giménez's analysis came at an especially opportune time for me, as I grappled with the challenge of connecting what I was learning through my ethnographic study with on-the-ground actions for food justice.

Three months after this event, newly appointed Seattle mayor Mike McGinn and the city council announced that 2010 would be the "Year of Urban Agriculture." This announcement dovetailed with a highly publicized visit from Will Allen, chief executive officer of Growing Power,[2] who has earned international recognition for his innovative efforts in rebuilding urban food systems. He came to Seattle to network with food justice activists and offer his guidance to several community projects. Along with many of my fellow urban agriculture enthusiasts, I was deeply inspired by Allen's call for a "good food revolution" and his commitment to making local and healthy foods accessible to communities of color and the poor. Nevertheless, the strategic timing of the city's declaration to coincide with his visit gave me reason to pause and reflect. After several years of research, I had become all too aware of how urban agricultural projects did not always translate into concrete steps toward food justice, especially for the Latino/a community. Would 2010, the "Year of Urban Agriculture," really be any different?

This chapter traces the trajectory of food activism in Seattle to connect the discourses of food sovereignty and food justice with an analysis of the city's urban agricultural landscape. Despite Seattle's exciting developments in building more localized food systems, I argue that Latino/a immigrants, especially those who are undocumented, remain marginalized from these efforts. I focus specifically on urban agriculture to analyze both the barriers that marginalize the food and agricultural knowledge of Latino/a immigrants living in the city and also the broader consequences of this marginalization. My analysis draws on my own shifting positionality in the field cultivated through deep and sustained ethnographic fieldwork on urban agriculture and food access for Latino/a immigrants in the Seattle area. Working with the land became synonymous with doing ethnography, and the tangible reminders of my fieldwork—dirt beneath my fingernails, a farmer's tan, and oddly shaped vegetables—regularly found their way into my home and into my research. The less tangible reminders—new friendships, growing commitments, and a need to make my findings accessible and useful—shaped my project in an even deeper and more sustained manner.

I begin this chapter by outlining the main historical trends in urban agriculture over the past 100 years to demonstrate how these trends are linked to political changes and social movements at both the national and grassroots level. I then connect these historical trends to more recent discussions concerning food justice and food sovereignty that advocate for urban agriculture as a promising alternative. After describing the urban agricultural landscape of Seattle, I turn to an analysis of the barriers that prevent broader and more meaningful Latino/a participation in urban agriculture. I draw on interviews with organizational staff and my own experiences working in and observing the local food system, and I suggest some potential solutions. I conclude by outlining how the movements for sustainable food systems in Seattle could be strengthened through a more concerted effort to engage the knowledge and experiences of Latino/a residents.

A Brief History of Growing Food in Cities and the Movements That Inspire It

Urban agriculture in the United States extends back to the end of the nineteenth century and is linked to similar histories in the United Kingdom, where the Allotment Act of 1887 was passed as a strategy to pacify farmers whose common lands had been enclosed by large landowners. Largely responding to national crises such as the Great Depression and World Wars I and II, allotment gardening was also utilized as a means to feed and control the poor in U.S. cities (Warner 1987). Not unlike the current politics over the sites of community gardens, allotment gardens during this period were located on vacant lots, where the security of tenure depended on the owner's financial interests and the development value of the land. Alternately known as war gardens, liberty gardens, victory gardens, and relief gardens, these spaces were intimately tied to larger processes of human migration, militarization, and economic transformation. World War I marked a major wave of allotment gardening and brought with it an explicit connection to American patriotism and the obligations of citizenship. Those who contributed to the war effort as food producers, who were "formerly thought of as poor people in want of food and instruction, ... became full-fledged patriotic citizens" (Warner 1987: 17). The National War Garden Commission worked at the federal level to promote patriotism through gardening, and following the end of World War I, war gardens were triumphantly renamed victory gardens, a rebranding that continued through World War II. At one point in 1944, "victory gardens produced 44 percent of the fresh vegetables eaten in the United States" (Hynes 1996: xii).

Some historians claim that community gardens declined in both number and political significance following World War II, a change linked to "the transition to large-scale agriculture and the expansion of the food distribution system" (Saldivar-Tanaka and Krasny 2004: 399). In another piece, Devon Peña and I (2010) challenge this telling of history, arguing that it overlooks an alternative history of "home kitchen gardens" among working-class and immigrant families. Nevertheless, scholars agree that urban agriculture took on new political and social forms in the late 1960s and 1970s. Rather than responding to national food shortages, this wave of urban gardening was motivated by the emergence of the civil rights movement, the environmental movement, and community reactions to increasing urban decline (Saldivar-Tanaka and Krasny 2004; Schmelzkopf 1995; Warner 1987). These movements produced a new set of politics within urban gardens, and these physical spaces became symbolic of broader struggles against social, economic, and racial injustices. This generation of urban gardeners, many of whom called themselves "guerrilla gardeners," worked at the grassroots level, often in opposition to local policies and land-use plans.

Researchers have demonstrated the multiple benefits of urban agriculture, in terms of fostering community development, alleviating food insecurity, and renewing connections between people and place (Armstrong 2000; Blair, Giesecke, and Sherman 1991; K. Brown and Jameton 2000; Glover 2003, 2004; Hynes 1996; Landman 1993; Peña 2005; Pinderhughes 2003; Saldivar-Tanaka and Krasny 2004). More recently, there has been a lively debate about the viability of urban agriculture in ensuring food security for U.S. city dwellers. In July 2012 Maurice Hladik penned an opinion piece citing a previous article about the viability of urban agriculture, claiming that "the author got carried away and used this as yet another example of how the urban farming movement has a meaningful impact on the nation's overall food supply. As if four heads of lettuce were really going to have an impact on feeding the world!" What is particularly problematic in Hladik's argument—in addition to his dramatic underestimation of the production value of urban farming—is his valuation of urban agricultural projects in narrow quantitative terms of dollars and pounds, rather than more holistic measures. Advocates for local food and urban agriculture often point to the ways that more localized supply chains can better support the availability of foods that are "culturally appropriate," more nutritious, and less polluting. These measures are not addressed by Hladik and are all worthy of further consideration and scientific inquiry.

In the face of climate change, dwindling fossil fuels, and sustained economic crises, urban dwellers around the globe are seeking more sustainable and socially just ways to feed the world. The renewed attention to the potentials of urban agriculture has become intimately linked with social movements that challenge the global industrialized food system and find promise in more localized alternatives (Allen and Wilson 2008; Holt-Giménez 2009; Patel 2008; Schiavoni 2009). Urban agricultural projects in cities across the United States continue to draw inspiration from the social movements of the 1960s and 1970s (especially the environmental and civil rights movements) but are now also inspired by contemporary movements for "good food," following the work of leaders like Will Allen. Multiple discourses (including local food, community food security, food justice, and food sovereignty) comprise what is more broadly conceived as the "food movement" but differ in terms of their motivations, strategies, and critiques (Mares and Alkon 2011). Significantly, this food movement is not limited to the United States, and innovations in urban agriculture have transformed cities in Brazil (WinklerPrins and de Sousa 2005), Cuba (Altieri et al. 1999; Buchmann 2009), Tanzania (Owens 2010), and Uganda (Maxwell 1995). Indeed, many researchers have argued that urban agriculture is a central piece of building sustainable, resilient cities around the world (Despommier 2010; Mougeot 2006; Nordahl 2009).

Despite these innovative transformations, scholars have questioned whether and how the strategies endorsed by community food advocates perpetuate the reach of neoliberal logic in addition to race- and class-based inequalities (Alkon 2008; Allen 2004; Allen and Guthman 2006; S. Brown and Getz 2008; Guthman 2008; Pudup 2008). The need for a deeper, transnational analysis of the food system and more radical visions of transformation is met in part by the discourses of food justice and food sovereignty. The discourse of food justice is inspired by the movements for local food and community food security but argues that access to healthy and culturally appropriate food and the land on which it is produced is marked by structural racism and classism. The discourse of food sovereignty, inspired by the international peasant movement La Via Campesina, argues that food and trade policies must be defined by and for the benefit of food producers, not by the large agrifood corporations that benefit most from neoliberal market arrangements. These two discourses (and the movements they inspire) transcend geophysical boundaries to challenge the political and market-based structures that are responsible for food injustices. When studying urban agricultural projects, these discourses also help to center critiques on the problematic ways that food systems—both local and global—are marked by class- and race-based inequalities that shape how food and the resources required to produce it are both unevenly distributed.

Drawing on Arjun Appadurai and Arturo Escobar's concept of the "translocal," Gerda Wekerle (2004) argues that the food justice movement is best understood as translocal. This translocality transforms relationships between community members, civil society institutions, and the state, but it also opens up new opportunities to form institutional alliances and coalitions across geographic boundaries. An acknowledgment of translocal relationships is especially relevant when seeking to understand the shifting foodways of Latino/a immigrants who have been displaced and forced to migrate in search of work. From a planning perspective, Wekerle argues, "food justice movements, as place-based movements engaged in local organizing and community development, represent an engaged citizenry that should be of interest to urban planners focused on various forms of citizen planning" (2004: 378). Noteworthy in her analysis are the assumptions embedded within the term *citizen*. Although she raises questions about the role of the state in translocal and transnational movements, Wekerle does not specifically engage with the multiple meanings of citizenship or the reality that political citizenship is often foreclosed to those who might be part of an otherwise "engaged citizenry."

Charles Levkoe (2006) also sees promise in the food justice movement's potential to facilitate more democratic food systems through transforming "consumers" into "citizens" by modeling a "healthy democracy" at the grassroots level. He states, "Through food justice movements, a vision of food democracy has been adopted which directly challenges anti-democratic forces of control, exploitation, and oppression. Food democracy refers to the idea of public decision-making and increased access and collective benefit from the food system as a whole" (2006: 91). Levkoe claims that the benefits of developing civic virtues and critical perspectives through food justice organizing expand beyond the food system to build an overall stronger community. However, like Wekerle, Levkoe also does not complicate the notion of citizenship, merely representing citizenry as a level of engagement to which mere consumers should aspire.

On the other hand, the international farmers' movement La Via Campesina has developed the concept of food sovereignty, elevated the struggles and rights of third world peasant farmers (especially women), challenged the impacts of neoliberal trade and agricultural policies, and emphasized the importance of working in solidarity across international borders (see Thivet, this volume). Food sovereignty demands consideration of fundamental inequalities in land distribution, resource management, and corporate control. Holt-Giménez argues that "food sovereignty is a much deeper concept than food security because it proposes not just guaranteed access to food, but democratic control over the food system—from production to processing, to distribution, marketing, and consumption" (2009: 146).

Although the food sovereignty movement has largely developed through the mobilization of rural peasant farmers, agrifood scholars and activists see great potential in furthering the movement in urban contexts. Raj Patel, a development sociologist who is himself an active participant in food movements, argues that the vision of food sovereignty is

> important not only because it has been authored by those most directly hurt by the way contemporary agriculture is set up, but also because it offers a profound agenda for change for everyone…as it…aims to redress the abuse of the powerless by the powerful, wherever in the food system that abuse may happen. (2008: 302)

Also active in global and national food movements, Christina Schiavoni (2009) agrees with Patel and finds potential in connecting the framework of food sovereignty to the food justice activism within urban centers across the country.

Ethnography with Muddy Hands: Cultivating Methodology from the Ground Up

Between 2005 and 2009 I conducted fieldwork in the Seattle area on the multiple ways that Latino/a immigrants interacted with the local food system, focusing specifically on food access and provisioning. The broader research questions guiding this study were (1) What networks, strategies, and resources do Latino/a immigrant households utilize to define and act on their food needs? (2) How do state and civil society institutions respond to the food needs of Latino/a immigrants through their policies, practices, and discourses? (3) What do these strategies, practices, and policies and their underlying motivations tell us about the symbolic importance of food and the meanings that people attach to their own sustenance and the broader food system? (4) How do the articulations between people and their food systems complicate the dynamics of agency and social structure?

In addition to archival research, my fieldwork involved participant observation at Marra Farm, a four-and-a-half-acre site in south Seattle; at five Spanish-language gardening classes I helped to coordinate during 2007 and 2008; and at a hot-meals site in 2009 that primarily serves Latino day laborers. My study also included two sets of semistructured interviews. In the first set, I spoke with representatives from thirteen Seattle-area agencies working on food issues, including direct service providers, organizations working in urban agriculture, and institutions doing political advocacy work related to food systems. My main objective was to gather information about what the individual staff members understood about the food needs of the Latino/a immigrant community, and whether and how these organizations sought to address these needs. In the second set, I interviewed forty-six first-generation immigrants who had moved to the United States from various regions of Latin America. The sample included an equal number of men and women, all over the age of eighteen. Thirty-five were from Mexico, three from Peru, two from Honduras, two from El Salvador, and one each from Guatemala, Cuba, Nicaragua, and Ecuador. I asked these participants about their experiences growing food, both in their home countries and in the United States; their perspectives on health and eating; and their experiences with different agencies in the Seattle food system. Both sets of interviews were recorded, transcribed, and coded for common themes and outlying perspectives. In this chapter, I use pseudonyms when referring to individual interviewees but have maintained the actual names of the community organizations for which they worked.

My years conducting fieldwork coincided with a particularly transformative period in Seattle's food activism, and over the course of my study, I was struck by how rapidly the local food system was changing. Built on exceptionally fertile soils and blessed with abundant rainfall, Seattle has become a model for national efforts in building food movements. The city has experienced a growing number of neighborhood farmers' markets (currently fourteen), the 2008 passage of the Local Foods Action Initiative, the formation of the Puget Sound Regional Food Policy Council, and the cultivation of seventy-five community gardens coordinated by Seattle's P-Patch Program. Current urban agriculture projects take various forms, including community gardens, community-supported agriculture (CSA) programs, farmers' markets, and school gardens. In these urban agriculture projects, governmental institutions and grassroots activism meet, with official support from the municipal P-Patch program and the Puget Sound Regional Food Policy Council contrasting with the active bulldozing of the guerrilla gardens that have sprouted along city bike trails.

The most prominent player in Seattle's urban agricultural landscape is the P-Patch Program, which began in the early 1970s. As of 2012 the program coordinated seventy-five gardens (with twelve more in development) where over 4,400 gardeners cultivated more than 2,200 plots ranging in size from 100 to 400 square feet. More than 1,000 people are on the wait list for a plot at any one time, and the average time to obtain a plot varies between three months and four years, depending on the site. These gardens are located in public housing communities, on privately owned land, and on a number of city lots (P-Patch Program 2012). As of 2007, 55 percent of gardeners were low income, 20 percent were people of color, 48 percent lived in apartments, and 77 percent had no access to gardening space where they lived. Increasing the level of participation for communities of color and other underserved groups is a goal of the program.

The fourteen farmers' markets in Seattle are coordinated by multiple nonprofit and community-based organizations. Several of these markets operate year-round, and all of them regularly offer prepared foods and entertainment. The two more prominent organizations, the Neighborhood Farmers Market Alliance and the Fremont Market, honor benefits from various food assistance programs, including the Supplemental Nutrition Assistance Program (SNAP), Senior Farmer's Market Nutrition Program (FMNP), and the Women, Infants, and Children (WIC) Nutrition Program.[3]

Barriers in Expanding Latino/a Involvement in Urban Agriculture in Seattle

While I was excited by the changes I witnessed in Seattle's food system and took great delight in choosing from the heirloom varieties of tomatoes and apples that appeared each weekend at my neighborhood farmers' market, I could not shake my observations that access to these spaces was clearly limited for the working class and communities of color. The narratives that Latino/a research participants shared with me about their food practices only reinforced these observations (Mares 2013). While there is no doubt that the various institutions in the city are producing many changes in the local food system, it is also clear that this change is happening unevenly and is marginalizing Latino/a immigrants, particularly those without U.S. citizenship.

Out of the forty-six interview participants from Latin America, only four were growing food in the city, with an additional three growing herbs. Only eight mentioned shopping at the farmers' markets, even while many shared memories of doing their daily shopping at open-air markets in Latin America. None of the Latino/a participants mentioned CSA programs. However, interviews also revealed that the majority had grown food in their home countries, and the memories of the gardens and farms they cultivated often brought smiles to their faces and prompted stories of time spent with their families and the sharing of recipes. Of the forty-six, thirty-seven had grown food before migrating to the United States, including those who had moved from both rural and urban areas from northern Mexico to the highlands of Peru, and most had positive memories about the gardens and the farms they had cultivated before migrating.

The low participation in urban agriculture in the United States, despite a high level of agrifood knowledge and experience in their home countries, signals multiple barriers preventing people from engaging in urban agricultural projects and the social movements that push them forward. The barriers that Latino/a immigrants face reflect the limitations of nonprofit and governmental agencies working in urban agriculture and include the following: challenges working within historically white institutions; inadequate resources (including funding and staff) and an institutional inability to allocate the use of resources for the benefit of Spanish-speaking families; institutional difficulties in defining and doing effective outreach with Latino/a residents; a disconnect between institutions and community members about the needs and preferences of the Latino community, including information about how to access community spaces; and the differential access to services and land among refugee and immigrant groups due to citizenship status.

It became clear through my fieldwork that the institutions working in urban agriculture are full of staff members who see the potential in working more with Latino/a immigrants who have deep knowledge about growing food. Ruth, who worked with Seattle Tilth, had this to say:

> I mean, I guess you could say, it seems kind of obvious, and I don't want to jinx us, but there is the challenge of being a historically white organization. I think that's our challenge in general. It's a historically white organization. But our world is changing at a very rapid pace, and a lot of things that are historically white are changing.... Well, like, any white, historically white place, it's a monoculture! And we teach about that, but we're not even following our own curriculum to diversity! Because that's what we teach, that any biological system is a stronger one if it's more diverse, so honestly, I think the organization will fail if it's not able to diversify!... Because, in practical terms what it might mean is a lot of new growing techniques, new crops, new solutions to problems, new approaches to food production in an increasingly urbanized area. I mean, we are all kind of inventing a whole new thing together, really.

Ruth understands that the infusion of new knowledge and new solutions from diverse populations could contribute to the transformation of Seattle's food system into something more relevant and meaningful for marginalized communities. Nevertheless, her ability to carry out these commitments is constrained by the histories and structures that govern the institution for which she works.

Another theme that came through the organizational interviews was trying to do the best work possible with inadequate institutional resources. Paula, who worked for P-Patch, talked about the continuous challenge of never having enough funding and staff, a challenge that had become especially pressing with the general economic downturn. However, just as important, she also acknowledged a more fundamental (and potentially more solvable) problem of allocating the resources that the organization already possessed. I asked Paula about the current level of Latino/a participation, and after wryly joking that she could count all of the Latino/a gardeners on one hand, she told me that it had actually decreased in recent years. I asked her if she knew the reason for this decline, and she responded:

> Yes! It basically comes down to our outreach, our outreach ability. I think that at the base level, probably once we were able to get more people in the gardens there might be other things that would need to change to meet people's needs better. But, right now, just even getting people to participate in the program is about outreach, I don't think the outreach itself would be that difficult. I mean, based on other times when we had people that were able to do that.

Although P-Patch had identified the Latino community as "underserved" by their program, Paula did not feel that this had translated into specific actions.

Other participants admitted that they had questions about the most appropriate form of outreach or program delivery within the Latino/a community. During my interview with Melissa, a woman with whom I worked extensively at Marra Farm throughout the duration of my fieldwork, we talked about the challenges that Lettuce Link (a program working at Marra Farm) faced in trying to work with Spanish-speaking individuals. She reflected on their bilingual gardening classes, held in collaboration with Seattle Tilth, and admitted, "I don't think that classes are perhaps the right format. And is that unique for Spanish-speaking immigrants? I don't know."

Another institutional barrier was the lack of information about the needs and desires of Latino/a immigrants with respect to food and its production, a problem noted by Leslie, who was central to the passage of the Local Foods Action Initiative through her position within the city council. Although Leslie's office identified the promotion of urban agriculture as one priority within the Local Foods Action Initiative, she acknowledged that they needed more information about community needs, telling me:

> For example, people will say, "well, low-income people don't have time to garden" and we'll come back and say, "well, what we are hearing from the Somali community, for example, or from the southeast Asian refugee community, for example" *we haven't* heard as much from the Hispanic community, or Latino communities, but in fact, this [gardening opportunity] is *really* what they want.

In my interviews with Latino/a community members, I learned that becoming engaged in community gardens was indeed something that people desired. However, the primary reason people did not become involved was that they had little access to information about how to sign up for a plot, what the fees were, or whether they had access to the program without providing citizenship documents. One solution would be a more sustained and informed effort to disseminate this information in a bilingual format.

The differences in the information available to diverse immigrant and refugee communities living in Seattle is connected, at least in part, to the fact that many refugees are able to access services not available to Latino/a immigrants who have arrived through unofficial channels. Paula described this as an additional challenge that her organization faced in doing outreach within the Latino community:

> I think the whole issue around documentation is really big, it's sort of why and how people are here is a really big difference, at least with P-Patch and the other immigrant communities we are working with. Most of them are here with some level of support from a public agency. Either they're refugees that are involved in resettlement programs…they're enrolled, they may be connected with churches that have sponsors for them, or a lot of the communities are in public housing so they have all of the resources that come with being in a public housing community and they have addresses that we can record and there are often community workers, community outreach workers that we can partner with. And with the Latino community, the immigrant community, I think people are living their lives here and making their own way and there certainly are associations and ways that if we were doing a planned outreach, we could connect with people through but it's not the same level of official support.

In fact, several of the public housing communities that Paula referred to have large gardening areas that residents are able to access in addition to ongoing educational programs designed to increase involvement in food cultivation or build awareness of the crops that grow well in Seattle's climate. However, the Seattle Housing Authority, the largest provider of public housing in the city, requires that all residents provide proof of U.S. citizenship or "eligible immigration status." This forecloses the possibility of undocumented workers and their families accessing these housing options and the gardening opportunities that go along with them.

These interrelated barriers demonstrate not only the structural and systemic challenges that are responsible for low rates of Latino/a participation in Seattle's urban agriculture projects but also the collective will on the part of institutional staff to make their programs and services more effective and inclusive. As important, they point to a need to envision more creative opportunities for Latino/a immigrants to engage in growing their own food, which many of my interviewees indeed desired and had the experience and knowledge required to do. In order for this vision to become actualized it is essential that a stronger connection is forged between the Latino/a community and the institutions central to pushing the food movement forward.

Significantly, these kinds of barriers are not only endemic to Latino/a participation in Seattle's urban agriculture efforts but have been observed with respect to the participation of diverse communities of color in the alternative food movement more generally. Activists and scholars guided by the framework of food justice have drawn attention both to the barriers and to the grassroots efforts to overcome them that have been led by and for communities of color around the United States (Alkon and Agyeman 2011; Gottlieb and Joshi 2010). In other areas of the country, there are noteworthy examples of Latino/a-led efforts in urban agriculture, among them the Nuestras Raices program in Holyoke, Massachusetts, and the South Central Farm in Los Angeles, California (whose original site was bulldozed in 2006; Lawson 2007). What makes these two examples especially significant is their attention to culturally appropriate forms of organizing and governance that stemmed from the Latino/a founders and their visions for change.

While the Latino/a individuals whom I interviewed did not offer any specific solutions to the barriers outlined above, their narratives about gardening and farming at home and my broader ethnographic findings both illuminate some potential directions forward (Mares 2012). Moreover, it is important that institutions working on food issues build stronger connections with Latino/a-led community-based organizations (including those not working specifically on food issues) to consider the most culturally appropriate forms of urban agriculture for Latino/a residents, which may very well resemble kitchen gardens located near the home rather than allotment-style gardening. Engaging in this work has tremendous potential to improve the overall food security of Latino/a residents in Seattle while further democratizing Seattle's food activism.

Conclusion: Urban Agriculture as a Matter of National Importance

Nearly one hundred years after the first war gardens were built, urban agriculture once again became an official matter of national importance with the rebuilding of the White House garden in 2009. Shortly after President Barack Obama took office, First Lady Michelle Obama and a team of local schoolchildren dug up a section of the first family's lawn, the first time it had been used for growing food since Eleanor Roosevelt grew her own victory garden during World War II. The building of this garden seemed to signal at least the possibility of a more progressive food and agriculture policy in the Obama administration. Although the realization of this possibility remains uncertain at the beginning of Obama's second term, the significance of the White House garden goes beyond the vegetables it produces for the first family. This garden, as a clear national symbol, grants both legitimacy and visibility to the practices, possibilities, and values that are linked to a shift toward more sustainable food systems in urban areas. However, through its very location at the epicenter of the nation, this garden also represents a significant mainstreaming of attitudes toward alternative food systems in the United States. The city of Seattle is no exception to this mainstreaming trend, and as I have shown in this chapter, there are real consequences for individuals and families who are consistently excluded from the mainstream alternative food movements because of their race/ethnicity and citizenship status.

Over the five years that I was involved in food-related fieldwork and activism in Seattle, I witnessed the movements around food change in response to both on-the-ground mobilization and changes at the regional and national level. When I first started this project in 2005, *food justice* was rarely used to describe what was happening all around us. However, these conversations have changed over the past several years, and *food justice* is now a term that Seattle's food activists use with great frequency. This transition is a hopeful one as it allows food activists to center their critiques on the ways race- and class-based inequalities have shaped access to food and the means to produce it. It seems as though the time is, quite literally, ripe for substantive efforts to engage all Seattle residents in declaring a "good food revolution" and building a food system that serves everyone's needs.

What is key in promoting an inclusive and representative food movement in Seattle, or in any city for that matter, is a critical awareness of how local food activism is necessarily conditioned by relations of power. As I have balanced my academic and activist commitments (not always with the greatest of ease), I have navigated these relations of power and have attempted to illuminate the diversity of perspectives present in my field site both in my academic writing and in public reports I have shared with community members and research participants (Mares 2011). This chapter is just one small effort to share my research findings in a way that draws attention to the types of local knowledge that community-based ethnographic research is uniquely capable of providing.

However, I maintain that the movement forward should be informed not only by a local discourse and movement for food justice but also by a vision of local democracy guided by the global movement for food sovereignty. As a movement and set of principles, food sovereignty prioritizes the knowledge and experience of farmers and is especially important when considering the needs of farmers who have been displaced from their original lands. Indeed, their lack of food security while living in the United States is bound to a denial of sovereignty in their homelands. To return to Holt-Giménez's point raised at the beginning of this chapter, displaced farmers from the Global South often hold tremendous knowledge about local food systems, and integrating this knowledge has the potential to democratize contemporary efforts in food activism. Given the complexity of the challenges we face in building food systems that are both just and sustainable, it is imperative that the vision guiding us forward is likewise capable of addressing this complexity and that we, as scholar-activists, recognize expertise and knowledge wherever it may be found.

Notes

1. Food First/Institute for Food and Development Policy is a think tank based in Oakland, California, that engages in research, policy analysis, education, and advocacy on issues connected to hunger, poverty, and the environment.

2. Growing Power is a nonprofit organization that provides training, outreach, and technical assistance on issues connected to urban agriculture and land trusts. With operations based in Milwaukee and Chicago, Growing Power is active nationally through their Regional Outreach Training Centers.
3. According to the "Sound Food Report," in 2005 the Neighborhood Farmers Market Alliance markets housed 129 vendors, grossed $3,958,742 in vendor sales, and had $62,292 in WIC checks and $31,006 in senior FMNP checks redeemed (Garrett et al. 2006: 98). This report also notes that none of the markets in Seattle except for the Pike Place Market has a permanent site and that the locations of two of the most popular markets, those in Columbia City and the University District, are the most threatened.

References

Alkon, A. (2008), "Black, White, and Green: A Study of Urban Farmers' Markets," PhD diss., University of California, Davis.

Alkon, A., and Agyeman, J. (eds.) (2011), *Food Justice: Race, Class, and Sustainability,* Cambridge, MA: MIT Press.

Allen, P. (2004), *Together at the Table: Sustainability and Sustenance in the American Agrifood System,* University Park: Pennsylvania State University Press.

Allen, P., and Guthman, J. (2006), "From 'Old School' to 'Farm to School': Neoliberalization from the Ground Up," *Agriculture and Human Values,* 23/4: 401–415.

Allen, P., and Wilson, A. B. (2008), "Agrifood Inequalities: Globalization and Localization," *Development,* 51/4: 534–540.

Altieri, M. A., Companioni, N., Cañizares, K., Murphy, C., Rosset, P., Bourque, M., and Nicholls, C. (1999), "The Greening of the 'Barrios': Urban Agriculture for Food Security in Cuba," *Agriculture and Human Values,* 16/2: 131–140.

Armstrong, D. (2000), "A Survey of Community Gardens in Upstate New York: Implications for Health Promotion and Community Development," *Health and Place,* 6/4: 319–327.

Blair, D., Giesecke, C., and Sherman, S. (1991), "A Dietary, Social, and Economic Evaluation of the Philadelphia Urban Gardening Project," *Journal of Nutrition Education,* 23: 161–167.

Brown, K., and Jameton, A. (2000), "Public Health Implications of Urban Agriculture," *Journal of Public Health Policy,* 21/1: 20–39.

Brown, S., and Getz, C. (2008), "Privatizing Farm Worker Justice: Regulating Labor through Voluntary Certification and Labeling," *Geoforum,* 39/3: 1184–1196.

Buchmann, C. (2009), "Cuban Home Gardens and Their Role in Social-Ecological Resilience," *Human Ecology,* 37/6: 705–721.

Despommier, D. (2010), *The Vertical Farm: Feeding the World in the 21st Century,* New York: Thomas Dunne.

Garrett, S., Naas, J., Waterson, C., Henze, T., Keithly, S., and Radke-Sproull, S. (2006), Sound Food Report: Enhancing Seattle's Food System, A report to the city of Seattle, June 20, 2006.

Glover, T. (2003), "The Story of the Queen Anne Memorial Garden: Resisting a Dominant Cultural Narrative," *Journal of Leisure Research*, 35/2: 190–212.

Glover, T. (2004), "Social Capital in the Lived Experiences of Community Gardeners," *Leisure Sciences*, 26: 143–162.

Gottlieb, R., and Joshi, A. (2010), *Food Justice*, Cambridge, MA: MIT Press.

Guthman, J. (2008), "Neoliberalism and the Making of Food Politics in California," *Geoforum*, 39/3: 1171–1183.

Hladik, M. (2012), "Commentary: Urban Farming Is an Urban Myth," AgProfessional (July 27, 2012), http://www.agprofessional.com/news/Urban-farming-is-an-urban-myth--163861346.html, accessed March 17, 2013.

Holt-Giménez, E. (2009), "From Food Crisis to Food Sovereignty: The Challenge of Social Movements," *Monthly Review*, 61/3: 142–156.

Hynes, P. J. (1996), *A Patch of Eden: America's Inner-City Gardeners*, White River Junction, VT: Chelsea Green.

Landman, R. H. (1993), *Creating Community in the City: Cooperatives and Community Gardens in Washington DC*, Westport, CT: Bergin & Garvey.

Lawson, L. (2007), "The South Central Farm: The Dilemma of Practicing the Public," *Cultural Geographies*, 14/4: 611–616.

Levkoe, C. Z. (2006), "Learning Democracy through Food Justice Movements," *Agriculture and Human Values*, 23: 89–98.

Mares, T. (2011), "Community Report: We Are Made of Our Food: Latino/a Immigration and the Practices and Politics of Eating," Community Alliance for Global Justice (July 2011), http://www.seattleglobaljustice.org/wp-content/uploads/MaresCommunityReport2011.pdf, accessed January 25, 2013.

Mares, T. (2012), "Tracing Immigrant Identity through the Plate and the Palate," *Latino Studies*, 10/3: 334–354.

Mares, T. (2013), "'Here We Have the Food Bank': Latino/a Immigration and the Contradictions of Emergency Food," *Food and Foodways*, 21/1: 1–21.

Mares, T., and Alkon, A. H. (2011), "Mapping the Food Movement: Addressing Inequality and Neoliberalism," *Environment and Society: Advances in Research*, 2: 68–86.

Mares, T., and Peña, D. (2010), "Urban Agriculture in the Making of Insurgent Spaces in Los Angeles and Seattle," in J. Hou (ed.), *Insurgent Public Space: Guerrilla Urbanism and the Remaking of Contemporary Cities*, New York: Routledge, 241–254.

Maxwell, D. (1995), "Alternative Food Security Strategy: A Household Analysis of Urban Agriculture in Kampala," *World Development*, 23/10: 1669–1681.

Mougeot, L. (2006), *Growing Better Cities: Urban Agriculture for Sustainable Development*, Ottawa: IDRC Books.

Nordahl, D. (2009), *Public Produce: The New Urban Agriculture,* Washington, DC: Island Press.

Owens, G. R. (2010), "Post-Colonial Migration: Virtual Culture, Urban Farming and New Peri-urban Growth in Dar Es Salaam, Tanzania, 1975–2000," *Africa: Journal of the International African Institute,* 80/2: 249–274.

Patel, R. (2008), *Stuffed and Starved,* New York: Melville House.

Peña, D. (2005), *Mexican Americans and the Environment: Tierra y Vida,* Tucson: University of Arizona Press.

Pinderhughes, R. (2003), "Poverty and the Environment: The Urban Agriculture Connection," in J. K. Boyce and B. G. Shelley (eds.), *Natural Assets: Democratizing Environmental Ownership,* Washington, DC: Island Press, 299–312.

P-Patch Program. (2012), "P-Patch Community Garden Program 2012 Fact Sheet," http://www.seattle.gov/neighborhoods/ppatch/documents/2012P-PatchSheet.pdf, accessed July 10, 2012.

Pudup, M. B. (2008), "It Takes a Garden: Cultivating Citizen-Subjects in Organized Garden Projects," *Geoforum,* 39/3: 1228–1240.

Saldivar-Tanaka, L., and Krasny, M. E. (2004), "Culturing Community Development, Neighborhood Open Space, and Civic Agriculture: The Case of Latino Community Gardens in New York City," *Agriculture and Human Values,* 21: 399–412.

Schiavoni, C. (2009), "The Global Struggle for Food Sovereignty: From Nyéléni to New York," *Journal of Peasant Studies,* 36/3: 682–689.

Schmelzkopf, K. (1995), "Urban Community Gardens as Contested Space," *Geographical Review,* 85/3: 364–381.

Warner, S. B., Jr. (1987), *To Dwell Is to Garden,* Boston: Northeastern University Press.

Wekerle, G. R. (2004), "Food Justice Movements: Policy, Planning, and Networks," *Journal of Planning Education and Research,* 23/4: 378–386.

WinklerPrins, A., and de Sousa, P. S. (2005), "Surviving the City: Urban Home Gardens and the Economy of Affection in the Brazilian Amazon," *Journal of Latin American Geography,* 4/1: 107–126.

4

Resistance and Household Food Consumption in Santiago de Cuba

Hanna Garth

Introduction

On a hot summer afternoon in Santiago de Cuba, Yaicel, the granddaughter of a local farmer, reflected on Cuba's domestic agriculture system:

> What they do here, the majority of the farmers, the State gives them [supplies] like seeds so that they grow crops and raise animals, the State gives them a percentage and the rest goes to the population....But everything comes from the State, the farmers grow, they get to keep very little and the rest goes to the State. (interview, Santiago de Cuba, 2008)

A growing number of food activists and food researchers are using La Via Campesina's notion of "food sovereignty" as the standard for better food systems that advocate for the interests of farmers, the poor, and a variety of environmental and social movements. This idea of food sovereignty, defined as "people's right to healthy and culturally appropriate food produced through ecologically sound and sustainable methods, and their right to define their own food and agriculture systems" (Via Campesina 1996), is fundamentally based on democratic control of the food system by the citizenry and agricultural workers. In socialist Cuba decisions about food imports, agriculture, and development are made centrally by the national government without voter input. There is no corporate or other business influence on the Cuban agriculture system; it is entirely decided by the state. Part of the rationale behind state control over the food system is precisely the need to maintain equitable distribution of food and to prevent people from exploiting scarcities and profiting by producing and selling directly to the public.

After outlining the contemporary Cuban food system, this chapter details how consumers experience it. The data presented here reveal nostalgia for previous periods of abundant cheap imported foods as well as consumers' struggle to deal with their dissatisfaction with the current food system. I focus on three ways consumers in Santiago de Cuba resist unfavorable aspects of the food system and consequently practice a form of food activism: (1) complaints and discursive resistance, (2) the exercise of purchasing power and the refusal to consume, and (3) rumors about food.

Background on the Cuban Food System

The Cuban farming system is a unique form of socialist agriculture. After the revolution in 1959 over half of the previously privately owned farmland in Cuba was redistributed, and farms over 988 acres were placed under state control as part of agrarian reform (Alvarez 2004). The land was nationalized, and several large sugar plantations were converted into national cooperatives. Whereas under Soviet land reform the large estates were redistributed to peasants and small farmers, in Cuba the state declared the land to be collectively owned by hundreds of thousands of small farmers who could cultivate the land as tenants or sharecroppers (Gomez 1983). The farmers did not have the right to lease or sell the property, and they were required to turn over the crop yields to reach certain quotas determined by the state depending on national need. The famers could sell to the state any crop yields above the quotas. This was one of the central ways in which farmers earned income. The 1963 agrarian reform act effectively made the Cuban state the owner and manager of most of Cuba's farmland (Alvarez and Messina 1996). Beginning in the 1980s, "integral brigades" consisting of blue- and white-collar workers from all over the country were required to spend a certain amount of days each season collecting the harvests (Gey 1990). They were paid their usual state salary for their agricultural work. This system continues today.

The Cuban socialist food and agriculture systems were established with heavy and ongoing investments via subsidies, preferential trade agreements, and in-kind donations from the Soviet Union and the Council for Mutual Economic Assistance. In 1990, as a result of the collapse of the Soviet Union, Cuba plummeted into a period of economic hardship that the state called the "Special Period in Time of Peace." Due to the drastic decrease in imports of agricultural inputs from the Soviet Bloc, during this period Cuba's agricultural production and export economy were devastated.

After the collapse of the Soviet Union, and thirty years after the previous agrarian reform, in October 1993 the Cuban state established a new cooperative farming system consisting of Unidad Basico de Produccion Cooperativa (basic units of co-operative production, UBPCs). The UBPC system leases state land to farmers for an indefinite period. The UBPCs have production quotas of what they must sell to Aco-pio, Cuba's state-run agricultural procurement system, and little autonomy in their primary crop "in order to maintain a balance of production throughout the country" (Alvarez and Messina 1996: 178). With the establishment of this system Cuban agricultural production slowly increased and remains fairly diverse, with the majority dedicated to sugarcane, cereals, vegetables, fruits, and tubers (U.S. Department of Agriculture [USDA] 2008). The UBPCs produce foods for export as well as domestic consumption. Cuba's top export crops today are tobacco (cigars), sugar, seafood, and rum (made from sugarcane).

Despite the relative success of UBPCs for domestic production compared to earlier agricultural approaches in socialist Cuba, in the first decade of the 2000s Cuba's global food imports increased to approximately $1.5 billion annually and totaled 84 percent of Cuban food consumption in 2008 (USDA 2008). Basic staples such as wheat, corn, powdered milk, flour, and soybean oil make up 75 percent of imports (MercoPress South Atlantic News Agency 2011).

In October 2000 U.S. president Bill Clinton signed the Trade Sanctions Reform and Export Enhancement Act; this allowed U.S. firms to export food and agricultural products to Cuba, and since 2002 the United States has become Cuba's largest supplier of food and agricultural products. All of Cuba's imports are handled by the government agency Alimport (Empresa Cubana Importada de Alimentos). In the case of purchases from the United States, Alimport coordinates payment through a third-party country and manages the distribution of these imports within Cuba. All sales to Cuba must be made in cash; no credit is ever issued. Cuba has consistently ranked among the top ten export markets for U.S. soybean oil, dried peas, lentils, dried beans, rice, powdered milk, and poultry. Cuba also has been a major market for U.S. corn, wheat, and soybeans (USDA 2008). By 2003 Cuba was ranked thirty-fifth among countries importing food and agricultural products from the United States, and since 2000 Cuba has spent over $2.2 billion on agricultural imports from the United States (Alvarez 2004).

Cuba imports food and agricultural products from several other nations across the globe. Vietnam is Cuba's second-largest food supplier after the United States. Cuba purchases about 8 percent of Vietnam's total rice exports (USDA 2008). In 2006 Cuba signed a $1.8 billion bilateral trade agreement with China to cover a wide variety of products including food, refrigerators and other domestic appliances, and technologies for developing Cuba's nickel and oil industries (USDA 2008: 32). Canada provides much of Cuba's dried peas (*chicharros*), wheat and a mixture of grains (*meslin*), frozen beef, and powdered milk (Agriculture and Agrifood Canada 2012).

The Cuban food system has become increasingly dependent on the global food system—for 80 percent of its citizens' nourishment—and particularly on exports from the United States. Although Cuba can decide which products are imported from where, it has little control over the production or processing of those food products. Cuba's dependence on food imports and lack of control over the production of those imports is not new; Cuba's food system has relied on imports since colonial times. Even before these most recent import trends Cuba's food system relied very heavily on Soviet material aid, which included subsidized food imports.

How Cuban Consumers Use the Food System

This state system of shifting food-importation practices has a profound impact on the everyday lives of people living in Cuba. During the period of Soviet material aid from the 1960s to the 1980s Cubans grew accustomed to products imported from the Soviet Bloc, such as canned meats and desserts and packaged pastries and candies. Soviet aid helped domestic agriculture to flourish, and prices for domestically produced foods remained low. During the "Special Period" in the 1990s, agricultural and food imports that had formed the basis for Cuba's food system since the 1960s decreased abruptly, and the food system changed radically; many food products became scarce, and those that were available were difficult for average Cubans to access due to their increased prices. Additionally, school cafeterias, day-care centers, and government job sites provided fewer and lower-quality foods than they had before. In order to deal with the food shortages, the state attempted to introduce new foods into the Cuban diet, for instance, by substituting soy and other vegetable proteins for meat and dairy and encouraging people to eat more vegetables, tubers, and legumes. Many Cubans were displeased with these changes; the Santiagueros of diverse race, class, and neighborhood groups who participated in my study voiced concerns and frustrations with the manner in which the Cuban state was changing the food system (cf. Garth 2009).

Domestic Food-Distribution System

Cuba's unique food-rationing system was officially established on March 12, 1962. Every Cuban is eligible for a ration card of basic food items, commonly referred to as *la libreta*. Prices are very heavily subsidized, but households must still pay a small amount for the rationed food. The original ration booklet optimistically included ham, cheese, pepperoni, sausage, beef, pork, lamb, goat, fish, seafood, fruits, and vegetables; however, many of these items were never actually available. During the course of my research in Santiago, the items available in the ration slowly fluctuated with national scarcities and surpluses. The rations are distributed at *bodegas, placitas/puestos,* and *carnicerias,* and people often have to go to several different locations to collect all of their rations.[1]

Household members must also travel to various markets across the city to supplement the ration. State-subsidized peso markets are known to have the lowest prices, but they also tend to have the least and lowest-quality foods. They usually sell less perishable foods such as garlic, onions, and various kinds of tubers. Nonetheless, because the prices are so low many consumers seek out these markets first. Consumers also frequent nonsubsidized peso markets once they have acquired what they can more cheaply. Although these markets often have irregular and inconsistent supplies, they are frequently the only places to buy certain types of food items (such as lettuce, tomatoes, and other highly perishable fruits and vegetables). Finally, the hard-currency markets are often the only option for many of the products Cubans consider necessary, including additional cooking oil, imported spices, bouillon cubes, and certain dry goods. Cuba's hard currency, the Convertible Cuban Peso (CUC, called *Divisa* or *Chavitos*), came into circulation in 2004.[2] At the time of my research the CUC was equivalent to $1.08. However, Cubans are not paid in CUC but in the Cuban national peso. There are 25 national pesos per CUC. Pesos may be exchanged for CUC at banks and state-run money-exchange centers.

In addition to all of these official sources, many households acquire food through the black market of goods and services that operates outside of the official formal state power. In Cuba black market activity includes situations where the production, possession, consumption, purchase, or sale of the product is illegal. The availability of foods on the black market constantly fluctuates, as do prices, but in situations of extreme scarcity this is often the only channel though which to procure things. Additionally, goods will often be cheaper on the black market than in CUC or peso markets. Most consumers constantly monitor all of these markets in order to ensure that they are getting the best prices (cf. Garth 2009).

This description illuminates the complexities and difficulties of navigating food acquisition in Santiago. Cubans' experiences of the food system before the "Special Period," and their subsequent experiences of food scarcity and difficult access during the "Special Period," influence present-day expectations for the food system. Historically the Cuban diet was based heavily on meat and starch, and Cubans resist the new food system because it limits access to these historically important foods. Although Cuba is not a democracy and Cubans do not have food sovereignty, there are still possibilities for resistance within the current system.

I will elaborate on three areas of small, everyday resistance that I characterize as forms of food activism in Santiago de Cuba. I define *food activism* as individual or collective forms of agency used to resist an inadequate food system that does not provide users with sufficient access to affordable, culturally appropriate, and adequate-quality foods. It may take several different forms, including protests and other large-scale forms of collective resistance, as well as small-scale actions such as refusal to purchase or consume certain foods and discursive resistance through complaints and discussions of the problems with the current food system. I define *agency* as the capacity to act in a way that impacts the practices of everyday life based on conscious and unconscious desires that are historically and socially mediated. Resistance is a form of agency.

Resistance and Household Food Consumption in Santiago de Cuba Today

This chapter is part of a larger project that aims to examine how household members use the current food system and, in turn, how the tactics employed to acquire food strain, shift, and strengthen social relationships, thus affecting household and community social dynamics. I conducted sixteen months of fieldwork between 2008 and 2011 in Cuba's second-largest city, Santiago de Cuba, located on the southeastern side of the island. I collected data via systematic observation of household food acquisition and consumption behaviors, time allocations for these practices, and semistructured interviews among twenty-two households with over 100 household members ranging in age from seventeen to ninety-nine years. Households included in the study had at least two household members, with at least one of working age (eighteen to sixty years old). In Cuba a household is a residential unit that consists of kin, fictive kin, and close friends who share in economic and social activities. Due to the sociohistorical particularities of the Cuban food system, in this chapter I focus on food activism via consumption practices rather than production. My research provides critical insight into everyday Cuban household life that has not previously been systematically studied anthropologically (cf. Garth 2009, 2013).

Complaining and Discursive Resistance

Complaining about the quality and quantity of food available in Santiago de Cuba was a daily pastime for most of my research participants, especially about the worst period of food scarcity in their lifetime, the Special Period of the 1990s. Most Santiagueros have traumatic and significant memories of those years, which they frequently juxtapose with complaints about the current food system. For instance, memories of poor-quality bread during the Special Period are often recalled in comparison to the bread available today. Throughout my fieldwork in Santiago it seemed like on any given day someone complained to me about bread—specifically, the rationed bread rolls, distributed to everyone daily. These extremely inexpensive rolls are the least favored type of bread among my research participants, yet nearly everyone consumes them because the next cheapest bread costs more than ten times the price of this roll. Shortages or pilfering of ingredients for the rolls caused variations in flavor, texture, shape, and color that generated an uproar of complaints. Here Elvira remembers how awful the food situation was at the height of the Special Period during the 1990s:

> When the situation started, started to get bad, the food [was] horrible, terrible, and so many lines!…and a roll of bread?! To eat that bread was terrible!!! (interview, Santiago de Cuba, spring 2011)

In efforts to save money the Cuban state has substituted many dairy and meat products with soy versions, another source of ongoing complaints. For most of my research participants, the most reprehensible soy product by far is the "soy ground meat" (*picadillo de soya*). Carolina explained:

> Soy is very aggressive for the Cuban body, for the stomach, it's very hot and since the climate here is so hot our bodies are not adjusted to such hot foods. Not all bodies are

the same no? Some people, like from northern climates can eat soy, but not Cubans. (interview, Santiago de Cuba, summer 2008)

Carolina's classification of soy as a food that is too hot for Cuban bodies, a reference to humoral pathology, is a common complaint for Santiagueros (cf. Garth 2013b).[3] Soymilk and yogurt are also sources of many food complaints for other reasons, though these products seem to be more accepted than soy-based meat substitutes, likely because dairy is not as central as meat to the Cuban diet. Nevertheless, many of my research participants noted that their children reject the free soymilk and soy yogurt they receive in the ration because they don't like the taste or it upsets their stomachs. Here again the underlying issue is that Cubans were accustomed to bovine-based dairy products and are not satisfied with the state-based decision to switch to soy-based "dairy."

Complaints about the availability and accessibility of food items are also prevalent. Whereas before the Special Period, Santiagueros were accustomed to accessing a wide variety of fruits, vegetables, grains, and meats at low prices in the state peso markets, now fewer and fewer items are available in these lower-cost markets and are available for purchase only in Cuba's second currency, the CUC. Santiagueros complain to one another about the difference in quality between items available in the national peso versus the CUC, as Maria Julia did:

> But let me tell you, in the [peso] stores where you could get gelatin, that supposedly is for children, that gelatin does not have the same flavor as the one that they sell in the [CUC] store, *in CUC.* (interview, Santiago de Cuba, 2011)

Reflecting on the contraction of the rationing system and the need to purchase more unsubsidized foods in order to survive in Cuba, Orlando, a 64-year-old Santiaguero who is independently employed and relatively well-off, notes the ways in which these changes affect Santiagueros:

> There are many people who have had a lot of difficulty; the revolution began to—to change things for everyone. The situation is difficult, they give us [the ration]…but it's not enough. Do you know how much we have to spend to buy [things like oil] in addition to what they give us? So that we can survive. (interview, Santiago de Cuba, summer 2008)

Santiagueros express dissatisfaction with their food system in many ways; their complaints are part of a broader understanding of what comprises a decent cuisine and are part of a quiet resistance through which they hold the Cuban state to a higher standard. Through these complaints they discursively resist the current status of state provisioning and implicitly demand access to higher-quality, affordable foods. Complaining about food quality and accessibility is widespread among close friends and family, but it is also commonly overheard in public places, for instance, while waiting in line for rations or at stores. This certainly impacts Cubans' impressions of food quality. Although complaining is widespread, it does not appear to have much of an impact on improving food quality; rather, it serves to create solidarity among the populace and provide an outlet for consumers to vent frustrations.

Food Rumors and Hidden Transcripts

Rumors and hidden transcripts, veiled forms of speech used to quietly critique power (Scott 1985), are forms of narrative expression that my research participants used to discuss and debate their changing social world. During my fieldwork in 2010 and 2011 two food-related rumors were in wide circulation among Santiagueros of differing races, classes, genders, and neighborhoods. Both of these rumors were said to have video footage that could prove their truthfulness; however, I never actually saw the videos even after relentlessly insisting on seeing them. The first rumor, however, was accompanied by a PowerPoint presentation with pictures detailing the acts in question, which I was able to see. One of my research participants began telling me that she did not trust state meat and that she believed that the state would often use different, lower-quality meats than they advertised. I must have seemed unconvinced, because she insisted that we stop the interview and load this PowerPoint onto her computer so that she could prove to me what was really happening: state restaurants (in some versions of the rumor it was a state Chinese food restaurant) were serving rat meat and presenting it as rabbit. The PowerPoint presentation included pictures of the process of preparing this dish, displaying photos of live rats, beheaded rats with fur, skinned rats, and finally the roasted rat on a plate with a lettuce garnish, which was supposedly sold as rabbit. While this PowerPoint presentation could easily have been a hoax, what is important is that people continued to circulate the rumor and revealed their distrust of and dissatisfaction with the food system.

The second rumor also involved rats. In this case, while undertaking surprise inspections of the state bakeries, the new provincial socialist party leader discovered rat feces, cockroaches, and other vermin inside the flour and other ingredients for making the rationed bread. I was told that there was video footage verifying this rumor but was never able to access the footage. Nonetheless, the rumor itself indicated distrust of and dissatisfaction with the state food system. However, in this case, the presence of the provincial party leader suggests that the state was not the culprit. The provincial leaders rectified the situation by inspecting all of the provincial bakeries, disposing of contaminated ingredients, and vowing to maintain clean and healthy facilities in the future. Here the blame was on the employees of the state bakeries rather than on local-level functionaries or higher-level state leadership.

In any case, these rumors are a form of hidden transcripts that research participants used to express frustration and dissatisfaction with their food system. In contemporary Cuba, overt expressions of dissonance can have negative consequences, such as sanctions and the loss of certain rights, and many of my research participants feared public forms of resistance. Hidden transcripts allowed them to express their dissatisfaction in a safer form of veiled speech in public contexts. Many spoke in veiled language even with their closest friends and family because they feared that someone might be eavesdropping or spying on their conversations even in their own homes.

Hidden transcripts have a long history in Caribbean communication, possibly beginning with the musical and folkloric traditions of slave society, such as *refranes*, or sayings that were used as a "means of resisting oppression from a more or less safe position" (Barcia 2008: 119). This history of veiled communication may have given rise to the forms of indirect and valenced speech that are common in Cuba today that may express nonalignment with or resistance to Cuban state master narratives. These present abstract ideas that are espoused as collective national sentiments, but they may be particularly inauthentic cultural or political lenses for interpreting experiences (Barker 1991; Duranti 2006). Under a system where overt protest is not possible, cryptic speech and communication via rumor are crucial forms of discursive resistance to the master narrative (see also Gal 1995; Humphrey 1994; Scott 1985). As Nancy Scheper-Hughes (1998) illuminates, rumors can be a way of "warning others," of sounding an alarm. As Cubans experience the decline in the quality and quantity of foods available to them, they use rumors as a form of protest.

Purchasing Power and the Refusal to Consume

Rumors, hidden transcripts, complaining, and contestation of the introduction of new ingredients into Cuban cuisine are clear displays of resistance that are sometimes coupled with practical resistance through action. In this section I focus on three examples of the refusal to purchase (and consume) certain foods and the use of alternative purchasing strategies as forms of resistive action that are, however, open only to those with financial security. The urban poor cannot afford to be selective about what they eat but must eat the cheap available foods whether they like them or not.

One example of resistance through purchasing power is the rejection of state-subsidized beer. To celebrate Carnival in Santiago, during the month of July, the state provides very heavily subsidized "dispensed" beer in huge metal drums, which costs a fraction of the price of other alcoholic beverages, yet few choose to drink it. Many of my research participants across all ages and socioeconomic groups complained that the state beer tasted bad, was too flat, and caused illness. Rather than consume it, they preferred to either drink less or borrow money to buy the more expensive and better-tasting beer. This "better" beer, also produced by the state, is presumed to be made with better-quality ingredients, comes in labeled bottles and cans, and costs about three times as much as the cheaper "state" beer.

Not eating workplace cafeteria lunches is another rather common refusal of heavily subsidized state foods among my research participants. Margarita, a thirty-year-old white Santiaguera, explained to me that if she did not have the extra money to buy lunch at work, she would rather not eat for the duration of the workday than eat the cafeteria food. She described the rice and beans as mushy, watered down, and flavorless. She claimed that the lunches never included meat because the cafeteria workers always pilfered the meat for themselves or reserved it for the managers. The meals came with boiled *viandas* (tubers or plantains), but they were often undercooked or overcooked and flavorless. For Margarita, no amount of desperation could bring her to eat these meals that she described as "disgraceful."

The refusal to consume free hospital foods (or, more specifically, refusal to allow hospitalized loved ones to consume this food) was also strikingly common. In the midst of my research with a middle-class mixed-race family, the youngest household member, Mayelin, age nineteen, was hospitalized in her fifth month of pregnancy when she became consistently hypertensive. At the time doctors told her that she would remain hospitalized until she gave birth. Although the hospital provided her with free low-sodium meals three times a day, her family and in-laws refused to allow her to eat any of the hospital food. They insisted on bringing her three meals, an afternoon snack, and boiled drinking water every day. Both families shared the responsibility of making special low-sodium meals and making the daily trek with food to the high-risk maternity ward. One evening, as Mayelin was opening steaming plastic containers with rice, split pea soup, pork chops, and boiled yucca, the hospital food cart came by to distribute the exact same meal that we had prepared. I thought this was ironic, considering that I had seen the strain that preparing and delivering these meals put on the family. As I was about to comment on this, Mayelin's mother-in-law, Elvira, turned toward us in disgust and exclaimed that she wanted to leave the room because the hospital food looked and smelled horrible. She did not actually leave the room but proceeded to comment on how disgusting and disrespectful the hospital food was, loud enough so that all of the other patients in the partition-less room could hear her as they ate their hospital-food dinner. When visiting hours were over and we left, Elvira continued to complain with disgust about the hospital food. Although I did not have a reaction of disgust, the hospital food appeared to be dry and did not smell as if it was well seasoned. Elvira implied that now that I had seen and smelled the food, I should surely understand why they insisted on bringing Mayelin every meal, even if it was for four more months.

These three cases illustrate how Santiagueros use purchasing power to enact quiet resistance when they feel that the minimum standards of quality have not been met. Low-priced items provided by the state ensure minimum nutrition or, in the case of state beer, a way to relax and enjoy summer celebrations. However, because they do not meet minimum local standards, many consumers refuse to consume them.

These cases might support the common theory that people appreciate goods and services more if they have to pay for them; however, they do pay a nominal fee for the state dispensed beer and workplace cafeteria lunches. Furthermore, in Cuba there are countless goods and services that are provided at virtually no cost by the state, such as education and medical treatment, and it is rare to find anyone who refuses them. In the case of the food refusals outlined above, there is an underlying tone of disgust. People seem to actually take offense at the idea of eating these foods, which are not all that different from the foods that people readily consume in their everyday lives. Indeed, the ingredients are imported through the same channels and sourced from the same government warehouses. These foods, however, were not prepared as a labor of love by a family member but rather by the hands of a government employee.

Making Sense of Everyday Resistance in Contemporary Santiago de Cuba

People use narrative expression, including complaints, to make sense of experiences (Frank 1995; Garro 2000, 2003; Mattingly 1998).[4] Cubans' constant discussion of past events, especially the Special Period, indicate their centrality in these interlocutors' lives. Their focus on present and past food problems in Cuba serves as a way to imagine possibilities for and anxieties about the future.

In a setting where mass organization for protest is strictly prohibited, people in Santiago de Cuba use hidden transcripts as a discursive form of protest within households and among friends. Complaints about the quality of bread, meat, and other foods communicate a literal meaning that the quality of the actual food item is substandard and also imply that the state, the sole provider of these foods, is to blame for the poor quality. In some cases, complaints about low-quality food are actually not a literal reference to the item being discussed but an implicit critique of the Cuban state safely cloaked in irony. Cautious, discreet, nonattributable dissent and small-scale isolated actions among friends have been central to coping with the struggles of daily life in Cuba during the Special Period and into the present. This type of resistance is not unique to food activism. Discursive resistance and hidden transcripts are mobilized in response to many of the elements of the Cuban socialist state with which citizens are dissatisfied, including problems with housing, education, transportation, and human rights.

Consumers also enact agency through their purchasing power and refusal to consume disgusting state-provided foods. This form of resistance, though not directly voiced, is noticed by the state and the intermediaries that provide these foods. The ability to use consumption practices as tools of resistance is often an option only for those with more privilege whose choices are not only about the items' quality and cost but also about the social acceptability and social capital (or lack thereof) connected to the consumption of certain items, like the state-provisioned beer during Carnival. Despite the lack of explicit citizen participation in structuring the Cuban food system, through these small forms of political action Santiagueros are able to quietly voice their problems with their food system.

Conclusions

In Cuba the struggle for food-related social justice is based on locally conceived standards for a justified and decent cuisine, which are grounded in longings for the previous food system that existed before the Special Period of the 1990s. During that time, Soviet material aid afforded Cubans access to a variety of imported foods and the agricultural supports necessary to maintain Cuba's domestic food production. Food prices were low, and a variety of foods were widely available to the public. Now that Cuba no longer relies on Soviet material aid, agricultural production and food-import costs are higher. The quality and quantity of food accessible to the average consumer have been drastically reduced.

In Santiago de Cuba resistance is expressed mainly through individual, household, or very small-scale community consumption practices and actions. Consumption is the main realm of agency for food activists in Santiago de Cuba. Through hidden transcripts, other forms of discursive resistance, and refusal to consume certain items, consumers in Santiago de Cuba promote a form of food activism that attempts to maintain previously met standards for food. These forms of resistance are part of food activism and allow individuals to engage in covert political actions that are very different from more explicit political action, such as food riots. However, in a context where such political action is prohibited, these forms of resistance are essential to furthering a better-quality and more just food system.

Acknowledgements

I would like to acknowledge my friends in Santiago who have made this project possible by sharing their stories with me. In particular, I thank the Casa del Caribe for supporting my work, along with my doctoral committee members: Carole Browner, Linda Garro, Jason Throop, Akhil Gupta, and Robin Derby. Thanks to Sarah Grant for comments on an earlier draft. I would also like to thank the volume editors Carole Counihan and Valeria Siniscalchi. This project was generously funded by several organizations, including the Social Science Research Council, the National Science Foundation, the University of California Cuba Initiative, the University of California, Los Angeles (UCLA) Latin American Institute, the University of California Diversity Initiative for Graduate Study in the Social Sciences program, the UCLA Department of Anthropology, the UCLA Center for Study of Women, and the UCLA Eugene and Cota Robles Fellowship. All errors are my own.

Notes

1. In March 2011 the monthly ration per person included 5 pounds of white rice, 10 ounces of beans, 3 pounds refined sugar, 1 pound raw sugar, 1 kilogram of salt,

4 ounces of coffee, and 250 milliliters of oil, as well as a roll of bread per day. Meat products include 6 ounces of chicken, 11 ounces of fish, 10 eggs, and 8 ounces of ground meat mixed with soy. All of these items cost about 25 national pesos a month, or about one dollar. People with certain chronic conditions, such as high cholesterol, diabetes, cancer, and renal problems, are able to purchase additional or different food items.

2. In 1993 the government began to allow Cubans to use foreign currency legally; previously, the possession of hard currency was a punishable crime. Cuba operated on a dual U.S. dollar–Cuban peso economy until 2004, when dollars ceased to be accepted and the CUC was introduced.

3. The logic of humoral pathology has been traced back to ancient Greece and is commonly found throughout Latin America. Humoral pathology is based on the idea that the human body consists of four humors—blood, phlegm, black bile, and yellow bile—each of which has characteristics of wetness, dryness, hotness, and coldness. Foods and drinks are also thought to have these characteristics.

4. Across many different types of discursive expression, actors consciously and subconsciously hold memories of the past as they act within and think through present situations (Heidegger 1962; Husserl 1982 [1913]; Ochs 2004; Ochs and Capps 2000; Ricoeur 1981).

References

Agriculture and Agrifood Canada (2012), "Agri-Food: Past, Present and Future Report: Cuba," http://www.ats-sea.agr.gc.ca/lat/4678-eng.htm, accessed May 31, 2012.

Alvarez, J. (2004), *Cuba's Agricultural Sector,* Gainesville: University Press of Florida.

Alvarez, J., and Messina, W. A., Jr. (1996), "Cuba's New Agricultural Cooperatives and Markets: Antecedents, Organization, Early Performance and Prospects," in *Cuba in Transition,* 6, Washington, DC: Association for the Study of the Cuban Economy.

Barcia, M. (2008), *Seeds of Insurrection,* Baton Rouge: Louisiana State University Press.

Barker, P. (1991), *Regeneration,* New York: Plume.

Duranti, A. (2006), "Narrating the Political Self in a Campaign for the U.S. Congress," *Language in Society,* 35/4: 467–497.

Frank, A. (1995), *The Wounded Storyteller: Body, Illness, and Ethics,* Chicago: University of Chicago Press.

Gal, S. (1995), "Language and the 'Arts of Resistance': Review Essay," *Cultural Anthropology,* 10: 407–424.

Garro, L. (2000), "Cultural Knowledge as Resource in Illness Narratives," in C. Mattingly and L. Garro (eds.), *Narrative and the Cultural Construction of Illness and Healing,* Berkeley: University of California Press, 70–87.

Garro, L. (2003), "Narrating Troubling Experience," *Transcultural Psychiatry*, 40/1: 5–43.

Garth, H. (2009), "'Things Became Scarce': Food Availability and Accessibility in Santiago de Cuba Then and Now," *NAPA Bulletin*, 32: 178–182.

Garth, H. (2013a), "Cooking Cubanidad," in H. Garth (ed.), *Food and Identity in the Caribbean*, London: Berg.

Garth, H. (2013b), "Disconnecting the Mind and Essentialized Fare: Identity, Consumption, and Mental Distress in Santiago de Cuba," in N. J. Burke (ed.), *In Sickness and Health: Encountering Wellness in Cuba and the U.S.*, Berkeley: University of California Press.

Gey, P. (1990), "Cuba: A Unique Variant of Soviet-Type Agriculture," in K. Wadekin (ed.), *Communist Agriculture: Farming in the Far East and Cuba*, New York: Routledge, 90–106.

Gomez, O. (1983), *De la finca individual a la cooperativa agropecuaria*, Havana: Editora Política.

Heidegger, M. (1962), *Being and Time*, trans. J. Macquarrie and E. Robinson, London: SCM Press.

Humphrey, C. (1994), "Remembering an 'Enemy': The Bogd Khann in Twentieth-Century Mongolia," in R. S. Watson (ed.), *Memory, History, and Opposition under State Socialism*, Santa Fe: School of American Research Press, 21–44.

Husserl, E. (1982 [1913]), *Ideas Pertaining to a Pure Phenomenology and to a Phenomenological Philosophy*, trans. F. Kersten, The Hague: Nijhoff.

Mattingly, C. (1998), *Healing Dramas and Clinical Plots: The Narrative Structure of Experience*, Cambridge: Cambridge University Press.

MercoPress South Atlantic News Agency (2011), "Cuba Admits Food Imports Bill Is Up 25% and 'Miracles Are Running Out,'" April 16, http://en.mercopress.com/2011/04/16/cuba-admits-food-imports-bill-is-up-25-and-miracles-are-running-out, accessed May 31, 2012.

Ochs, E. (2004), "Narrative Lessons," in A. Duranti (ed.), *A Companion to Linguistic Anthropology*, Malden, MA: Blackwell.

Ochs, E., and Capps, L. (2000), *Living Narrative: Creating Lives in Everyday Storytelling*, Cambridge, MA: Harvard University Press.

Ricoeur, P. (1981), "Narrative Time," in W.J.T. Mitchell (ed.), *On Narrative*, Chicago: University of Chicago Press.

Scheper-Hughes, N. (1998), "Truth and Rumor on the Organ Trail," *Natural History Magazine* (October): 48–57.

Scott, J. C. (1985), *Weapons of the Weak: Everyday Forms of Peasant Resistance*, New Haven, CT: Yale University Press.

U.S. Department of Agriculture (USDA) (2008), "Cuba's Food and Agriculture," http://www.fas.usda.gov/itp/cuba/cubasituation0308.pdf, accessed May 31, 2012.

Via Campesina (1996), "The Right to Produce and Access to Land (Statement on Food Sovereignty)," http://www.voiceoftheturtle.org/library/1996%20Declaration%20of%20Food%20Sovereignty.pdf, accessed April 17, 2012.

5

Women, Gender, and Agency in Italian Food Activism

Carole Counihan

Introduction

This chapter presents four women's experiences of food activism in Italy to analyze the different challenges and opportunities they encounter. The chapter considers their experiences against the backdrop of gender relations in Italian society, where women have a long history of holding primary responsibility for cooking and other domestic work and have been disadvantaged in the workplace (Counihan 2004). The four women take action in the public sphere to improve the quality of food, promote local food and food producers, and educate others about good food. They act through a variety of channels in different ways, but all of them find meaning in their work. I examine their actions and agency in their food activism.

My definition of agency builds on Antonio Gramsci's query, "In posing the question what is a human being, we mean what can human beings become, whether, that is, humans can dominate their own destiny, can 'make themselves,' can create a life" (1955: 27; my translation). Agency is this ability to create or shape one's own life; more explicitly, it can be defined as doing meaningful work that has social value (Sacks 1974). In this chapter I define agency in the context of women's food activism as the ability to propagate one's values, forge meaningful social connections, and effect real material changes in the world in freely chosen and personally significant ways. I use data gathered in Cagliari, Sardinia, in 2011 from ethnographic interviews with the women and observations of their activism to explore their agency.

In Italy food carries historical, cultural, sensory, and expressive richness for both men and women, although they have very different responsibilities surrounding it.[1] Traditionally women have done most of the shopping, cooking, and cleaning up; these activities represent their general responsibilities for social reproduction, including nurturing, child care, and other forms of "unpaid family labor" (Saraceno 2011), such as ironing, washing clothes, and cleaning the house. Concomitant with this private-sphere burden and probably in part because of it, women are more likely to hold "precarious" positions in the public sphere that are part-time, temporary, without full benefits, and less likely to lead to lifelong careers (Fantone 2007). It is beyond the scope of this chapter to analyze in detail these labor force dynamics and their impact on gender roles, but they form a context where food activism offers women a rich sphere for self-activation since it involves the food work they know so well but enables them to extend it out into the public, where they play important if often unremunerated roles.

Food Activism and Gender

In this chapter, I use the term *food activism* to refer to efforts to promote social and economic justice through food practices. This is my term and was not used by the people I interviewed, who found the words *activism* (*attivismo*) and *food activism* (*attivismo alimentare*) to be inaccurate or too militant. They were more comfortable with the term *alternative foodways* (*alimentazione alternativa*), which I told them was the topic of my study when I asked to interview them. They were, however, more likely to describe their practices in specific rather than general terms, for example, talking about Slow Food, didactic farms, or local food. I find *food activism* useful as an umbrella term to refer to diverse alternatives to the agro-industrial food system, including farmers' markets, purchasing groups, vegetarianism/veganism, organic/free-range/biodynamic production, farm-to-school programs, school and community gardens, and other initiatives that aim to promote food democracy—the ability for all to attain high-quality, affordable, sustainable, and culturally appropriate food (Lang 1999).

Few studies on food activism address gender directly, but what data there are suggest that women are at the forefront of grassroots efforts to change the food system in many different cultural contexts including the United States, Canada, and Latin America (Allen and Sachs 2007; Barndt 1999; Field 1999; Hayes-Conroy and Hayes-Conroy 2010; Moffett and Morgan 1999; Schroeder 2006; Villagomez 1999).[2] Women become food activists because they are the main food preparers all over the world, they are more often poor and vulnerable to hunger, and they prioritize children's interests; they have been main players in child-feeding programs, food-purchasing groups, and community kitchens and gardens (Field 1999: 201–203). Women have organized to improve their poor working conditions and low wages as fast-food workers, supermarket cashiers, field hands, and produce packers (Barndt 1999). They lead in community-supported agriculture, farmers' markets, and training programs for food workers (Allen and Sachs 2007). Food is a channel through which marginalized women have been able to achieve "personal and political empowerment" (Moffett and Morgan 1999: 225).

But in spite of this strong female presence, Patricia Allen and Carolyn Sachs (2007: 13–14) claim that "there is a curious absence of feminism per se in women's efforts to create change in the agrifood system." In other words, female food activists often do not link the ills of the food system to gender inequality and thus do not make gender change central to food-system change. Nonetheless, in Italy food activism offers women the opportunity to act publicly and politically—opening up the question about its potential to bring about changes in Italian society and gender relations beyond the food system.

Studying Food Activism in Cagliari

Generalizing about Italian foodways is tricky because there is much diversity of cuisine and culture by region as well as by class, national origin, marital status, occupation, and age, but there are also commonalities that make a case study valuable. I studied food activism in Cagliari, the capital and largest city on the island of Sardinia, for several reasons. The island has always had an important agropastoral economy, which faces competition from increasingly globalized foodways manifest in expanding distribution networks and a high density of supermarkets.[3] As the regional and provincial capital, Cagliari is the center of Sardinian politics, culture, history, and commerce. There are 156,000 residents in the city and 563,000 in the surrounding metropolitan area, comprising a third of the island's total population of 1,675,000 (Istituto Nazionale di Statistica [ISTAT] 2011). Its major port makes it an important economic and communications center and attracts a steady stream of tourists and immigrants. Today Cagliari's alternative food practitioners—those seeking democratic, high-quality, and sustainable food—are burgeoning.

My past ethnographic research provides a good foundation for studying the contemporary alternative food sector in Cagliari. I did research in Bosa, Sardinia, in the late 1970s on the modernization of traditional foodways (Counihan 1981, 1984), and in the early 1980s in Florence on the evolution of family and gender relations revealed through people's food-centered life histories (Counihan 1988, 1999, 2004). In 2009 I began a study of food activism through interviews with leaders of several Slow Food chapters in diverse Italian regions, including Sardinia. In 2011 I was able to return to Cagliari to build on my past research on Sardinia and to study the alternative food sector holistically in one place.

I used the snowball method to recruit study participants, who varied in age from twenty-nine to sixty-eight and consisted of slightly more males than females.[4] I talked with people involved in two farmers' markets, the local Slow Food chapter, a vegetarian restaurant, farm-to-school programs, organic production and distribution, and a GAS (*gruppo d'acquisto solidale*)—a collective buying group.[5] People were enthusiastic participants in the research. Some I talked to briefly and informally, for example, while visiting the farmers' markets or Slow Food events. With others I carried out digitally recorded semistructured interviews. The men were more likely to have full-time jobs in the food sector, whereas the women were more likely to be volunteers or have part-time food jobs—a fact that reflected the wider societal division of labor and men's greater labor force participation.

Narratives of Women's Food Activism

The following stories of four female food activists in Cagliari show what they do, how they got into it, what it means to them, what challenges they face, and what forms of agency they display in their efforts to change the food system. The four are Anna Cossu, a lawyer and leader (*fiduciaria*) of the Slow Food Cagliari chapter; Alessandra Guigoni, a cultural anthropologist and member of Slow Food Cagliari; Teresa Piras, a retired teacher and leader of a grassroots women's group called Domusamigas; and Francesca Spiga, the owner and manager of an organic food store.

Anna Cossu

Anna Cossu was born in 1974 in Sardinia and proudly declared herself "sarda sarda" because both her parents are Sardinian. She earned law degrees from the University of Cagliari and worked as a consultant for European Union local development projects in Sardinia. When I interviewed her in 2011, she was in-between jobs due to the economic crisis and the paucity of funds for projects. She used this employment lull to throw herself into her new volunteer job as leader of Slow Food Cagliari. When I asked her what led her to work with Slow Food, she replied, "Well, fundamentally I am a lover of good food (*una buongustaia*). Luckily I come from a family in which there has always been attention to good food, and hence to the culture of good food and rural life, the importance of food in season, respect for biodiversity, and above all the preference for local food. This line of thought was implicitly transmitted to me from childhood.... Then I found myself saying yes, I love good food, but what is behind good food, what are the criteria to locate it? And so I approached Slow Food."

As for many Italian food activists (Counihan 2014), for Cossu love of good food was an important motivation to and strategy of action: "Taste is central.... I grew up here [in Sardinia], hence I am used to certain tastes, strong tastes that are characteristic of here, so when I travel to another region or another country, I suffer. I suffer because I am totally used to a high quality range of foods, and I realize that I seek strong tastes that are typical of a very sun-drenched land, of a land that is isolated and so also has certain products that are not available elsewhere."

In addition to being a powerful personal motivator for Cossu, taste was central to many activities organized by the Cagliari Slow Food chapter. For example, one of Cossu's first initiatives was a three-part beer program featuring a class on home-brewing, a tasting led by an expert beer master, and a delicious multicourse dinner centered on beer and appropriately paired foods. The goal was to expand the Slow Food network and to promote tasty local foods. The three events attracted diverse constituencies through taste education and commensality.

To learn more about the taste of local food, the chapter organized a visit to the S. Margherita di Pula Sapore di Sole tomato cooperative, about twenty miles from

Cagliari. The message, Cossu said, was "biodiversity that is transmitted at the table." The event mixed education and conviviality around one of Sardinia's principal crops and dietary staples. Twenty or thirty Slow Food members and friends gathered at the cooperative, where its male marketing director led us on a guided tour of the packing plant where male farmers delivered their tomatoes and female workers sorted and packed them for shipment. With two male scientists, we visited the experimental greenhouse where the tomato cooperative safeguards seeds and experiments with hybrids. The last event of the day was a festive dinner completely based around the tomato.

Cossu was the leader of the day's events, keeping things moving along and chatting with everyone, demonstrating her role as catalyst and facilitator, constantly working to connect people with one another and with Slow Food's commitment to "good, clean and fair food." This event reflected some of the complex gender dynamics in the food system. In the tomato cooperative, the men had the better-paying and more prestigious jobs of scientist and marketing director, and the more autonomous jobs as farmers. Women held precarious and low-paying jobs as tomato packers, earning approximately €9 per hour and working four to six hours a day from November through June. Cossu did not comment on the gendered division of labor, and she herself was not paid for her work organizing the visit, but nonetheless she had prestige as the Slow Food leader and agency in her ability to choose to do work she loved, to promote education about good food and its production, and to forge relationships between consumers and producers.

Slow Food fit Cossu well and provided a channel for doing work she had long been committed to. As she said, "In Slow Food I found written down all those principles that I already had in my mind, that I already practiced, so it was beautiful because I found an organization that functions for those objectives, giving them a systematic structure." She could step into and mold that structure to fit local Sardinian issues, interests, and realities. But she identified challenges in her work: first, in communicating the knowledge of local foods to young people who lacked ties with the land; second, in "giving voice to producers" to press for their economic interests and networks; and, third, in managing all the work there was to do as a volunteer without a salaried position. But she was able to operate with agency because she loved her work, promoted local food, strengthened the alternative food network, and advanced her goals and values in the public sphere.

Alessandra Guigoni

Alessandra Guigoni is a cultural anthropologist and active member of Slow Food Cagliari who was born in Genoa in 1968 and moved to Sardinia in 1993 because of her husband's work. She earned a BA in 1993 at the University of Genoa and a doctorate in 2004 in the joint PhD program of the Universities of Siena and Cagliari with a dissertation on the influences of American plants in Sardinia, which resulted in her book *Alla scoperta dell'America in Sardegna: Vegetali americani nell'alimentazione sarda* (Guigoni 2009). Due to the scarcity of academic positions in Italy and her husband's job near Cagliari, she has worked as an independent researcher, doing consulting and research about Sardinian foodways, publishing academic and popular articles and books, appearing on television and radio, and writing a lively blog.[6]

Guigoni joined Slow Food in 2009 when Cagliari chapter leader Giulia Annis invited her to take charge of cultural issues; she accepted because this was of anthropological interest. When Anna Cossu became the chapter leader in 2011, she asked Guigoni to take charge of developing "food communities" (*comunità del cibo*). The Slow Food website defines food communities as "those people involved in the production, transformation, and distribution of a particular food, who are closely linked to a geographic area either historically, socially, or culturally. Food community members are small producers who make high-quality products in a sustainable way" (Slow Food 2013; see Siniscalchi 2012, 2013). Supporting food communities both locally and worldwide is a key Slow Food strategy to promote cultural and biological diversity, and it fits Guigoni's similar commitment as an anthropologist.

While she is passionate about developing the food communities, Guigoni emphasizes that it is a challenging and complex undertaking because the producers are small and diffident. "It takes time, you have to talk a lot, sustain them, help them understand.... It's fieldwork." But she likes this work because it is a way "of putting into practice what I study, and doing something practical." She helped start the Slow Food "caper food community," revitalizing small-scale production of this historically important product in Selargius near Cagliari, and thinks it is wonderful because it brings economic benefits to struggling small farmers (see Guigoni 2010). She has also worked to establish a food community of the Gonnosfanadiga watermelon, a product unique to the Campidano plain surrounding Gonnosfanadiga, thirty-five miles northwest of Cagliari. Before she started this community work, Guigoni said, "I had been missing something."

When she was doing her PhD research, a farmer from Gavoi in central Sardinia gave her some seeds from a type of bean called *fagiolo trighine*, which he had developed over the years. Having no children to pass them on to, he feared the seeds would be lost when he died. For two years Guigoni kept them in her refrigerator until finally she came across a female agronomist from the University of Sassari who preserves Sardinian seeds and who was able to germinate them, to Guigoni's joy. She champions saving seeds to help local populations maintain their "historical and cultural memory." She likes working with the food communities because "they already exist. You help them emerge, find economic and cultural support, and you can bring an anthropological perspective to others."

I asked her if she considered herself an activist (*un'attivista*), and she replied, "I am an activist when it comes to small farmers, but I fear doing too much. I don't want to influence and impose upon others my view of what should be done. Informing others about the world of small farmers is already a lot. Their biggest challenge is survival. Politically, there is little awareness. Peasant culture is still seen as backward, as needing to be changed." She lamented that Italy does not have a biodiversity law nor a regional registry of indigenous plants, which are essential to safeguarding Italy's cultural and biological autonomy and diversity.

I saw Guigoni speaking several times for cultural and ecological sustainability on public panels and at Slow Food events. She was among the approximately fifty people at an open house in June 2011 at the AGRIS Bean Research Center in Uta, twelve miles northwest of Cagliari, which is preserving over 120 Sardinian bean varieties. The goal of the open house was to educate about the beans, the center's work, the possibility of acquiring seeds, and their economic and agricultural potential. After a visit to the green, lush bean fields, we had a question-and-answer session inside. When the scientists urged us to conserve beans, Guigoni intervened and said, "When you collect the beans, also collect the knowledge"—the traditions, colloquial names, planting routines, cultural habits, and recipes. She declared that time is running out, the custodians of seed knowledge are old, and "we cannot waste time." She urged people to support passage of the law on biodiversity to have the necessary teeth to safeguard Sardinian plants.

Getting involved in food activism enabled Guigoni to act dynamically by applying her anthropological skills to practical ends and making real changes in the world. It provided a forum for learning and teaching about traditional foods, farmers, and cultural traditions and was an outlet for her long-standing commitment to social and economic justice. It connected her with a wide range of other people who shared her goals, and it opened up work possibilities to her, important for an independent researcher. It was a meaningful way to express her agency and her capacity to effect change and transform her anthropological knowledge into immediate and concrete results.

Teresa Piras

Alessandra Guigoni introduced me to 68-year-old Teresa Piras at a book fair in Villamassargia, thirty miles from Cagliari. She and a group of women in the Sulcis-Iglesiente province west of Cagliari started the Center for Self-Development Experimentation (Centro di Sperimentazione Autosviluppo), also called "house of women friends," or Domusamigas.[7] Piras is a retired teacher and earned a pedagogy degree from the University of Cagliari with Aldo Capitini as her advisor, who was dedicated to nonviolence and introduced conscientious objection to Italy (Capitini 2000). Piras said, "He gave me the instruction and the heart" for activism. She has always had a teaching vocation, taught at a middle school for years, had a school garden at least fifteen years ago, and always worked in partnership with civil society institutions. From her teaching days, she already knew producers and had formed "a social fabric in the region—I already held many threads." When she retired and needed more to do, she used her networks to start Domusamigas. Through it she feels she is developing her "spiritual soul (*anima spirituale*)."

Piras said the goal of her group is to live as much as possible from products of the territory, working for "self-development" by creating links between consumers and producers from the region. One project is "olden furrows/*antichi solchi*" to support biodiversity through revitalization of threatened species. The members held a "grafting feast" inspired by one of their families who had many heirloom varieties of fruit trees. When the time was ripe, in the late winter, they gathered the scions (buds used in grafting), and about 100 people assembled to graft the diverse pear varieties onto wild pear trees along an abandoned rail line. While they were doing this, they ran into a shepherd who invited them to harvest the pears from his heirloom trees. They decided to turn it into "a feast of pears" where they harvested the fruit, used old recipes to make all kinds of cakes, and held a great commensal feast. I commented on how their work seemed like a snowball, and she said that "we women work like this in small steps."

In 2011 Piras and her group organized a class by Maurizio Fadda from Nuoro on how to build no-till raised bed gardens (*orti sinergici*) based on "self fertilization." Composed of organically rich soil and planted with a rotation of crops, these gardens maintain fertility and repel pests. Forty young men and women, mostly unemployed recent college graduates, signed up for the three-day class. The first day was "theory," and the second and third days were "practice"—preparing a garden on the land of a young farmer transitioning to organic production. This class was an example of how Piras's food activism fostered education, propagated alternative agriculture, and expanded her networks.

Piras's group has formed a "type of GAS"—a "solidarity buying group" to purchase fruit and vegetables directly from a local woman farmer who brings the orders to their weekly meetings. There they also provide fair trade coffee, tea, sugar, and chocolate for purchase "to support the concept of fair trade here in Sardinia." While a key goal of the group is to connect consumers with local producers, they purchase fair trade products from global suppliers because their work "is not a form of closure but of solidarity with all small producers.... We want to support the division of wealth."

Piras's food work gave her agency in several ways. It came from her own creative initiative and was meaningful and fulfilling. It enabled her to stay busy and connected with food-centered sociopolitical networks after retirement. She and a small group of other women transformed their market participation by purchasing collectively and directly from small farmers, benefiting both. They practiced food education of children and youth, and introduced people to and helped propagate local heirloom varieties, literally transforming the landscape with flowering pear trees and sustainable gardens and supplanting industrial products with local foods.

Francesca Spiga

Francesca Spiga owns and manages the Organic Food Emporium in Cagliari. She started the store with high hopes as a means to change her life and do meaningful work. She and her then husband opened the store in 2003 when she was forty-six; a few years later she and her husband divorced, which Spiga attributed in part to the many stresses of running the business:

> The store was born eight years ago with great anticipation and enthusiasm, to try to lead a different life, but naturally things were not that simple. It has become—I don't want to say a trap, but almost. In our Sardinian environment it is not so easy to propose new things—people are still very set in their ways. In Sardinia there is a huge concentration of shopping centers, more than in all of Italy relative to the population we have. Imagine the difficulty of working in an environment like this where people are considered sheep to bring to pasture in those places. It is not easy.
>
> I wanted to change my life with this work. I was not living here in Sardinia, I was in the Trentino [in northern Italy]. I wanted to return to Sardinia, to change my job. I was doing pharmaceutical research for a huge multinational company, imagine. I was truly convinced that this store was the right job to change my life completely. I was born in a village, in San Sperate [12 miles north of Cagliari], I still live in San Sperate. My return was also for this: here I have my land. We Sardinians should distance ourselves from this fixation, but that is just the way it is. We come back to suffer again in our land.

Spiga had become disillusioned by the food available in northern cities, where the links between producers and consumers had been broken, whereas in Sardinia it was still possible to get food locally, for example, "to get eggs from your neighbor's hens." I asked her if the senses were important in her store, and she replied,

> Yes. Yes. For people who eat organic, absolutely!... In the sense that you realize when you eat something, you can understand from the fragrance, even with your eyes closed, what food it is....But instead if you eat [industrial foods]—you can no longer tell one food from another....[Organic food] is less manipulated, it brings you back to nature. Nature rejoices in the variety of colors, the different greens. If man did not interfere, nature would take care of things—she knows what to do. Instead if man wants to, he intervenes in things almost like a laboratory and makes everything the same—everything the same color, all the same size, and there we lose completely—including the sense of grandeur.

She conceived of the store as an idealistic project to counter the agro-industrial food system and not only change her own life but also enable other people to change theirs by eating healthy food and maintaining close connections with producers and the local environment. She said, "I have always believed that our food should be as simple as possible, as natural as possible." Her store has organic produce, bread, wine, cookies, rice, pasta, legumes, makeup, soaps, shampoos, cleaning products, herbal medicines, tea, coffee, chocolate, cereal, yogurt, milk, soy products, hemp products, and books on cooking, ecodesign, yoga, the Dalai Lama, and many other topics.

Her clients are mainly teachers, state workers, clerks, and counterculture youth looking for organic products for various reasons—for example, because they have young children, have allergies, or are vegan. She estimated that 98 percent of her clients were female. Local doctors sent patients to Spiga's store for gluten-free, lactose-free, and other specialty food products. Spiga rented space in her store two days a week to the famers of the Terranuova cooperative from Siliqua, twenty miles northwest of Cagliari. They came twice a week with organic fruits and vegetables of their own and others' production. They enabled Spiga to provide good produce without increasing her already very heavy workload. After she split up with her husband she had to run the store herself with one part-time clerk because she could not afford to pay a regular full-time employee. She spent most days from 9 A.M. to 8 P.M. in the store and handled everything, including the Italian state bureaucracy and its regulations for small businesses. "From a fiscal point of view, the State kills us. I can't live. It is impossible. The taxation is impossible."

She faced many challenges in addition to high taxes. One was the failure of her alliance with an organic food chain that had initially seemed promising but turned out to be a "disaster," which she was reluctant to discuss. Another was competition from the large organic food cooperative S'Atra Sardigna, which had five organic food stores in Cagliari and left only a "little slice" of the market for her—"those who have food intolerances." Another was the "disastrous communication networks in Sardinia. I receive more quickly from the mainland than from Sardinia!" She tried to purchase eggs locally but could not get a farmer to supply her regularly, so she gave up and imported organic eggs from the mainland. She had a farmer come to her store and offer her Sardinian chickpeas to sell; she enthusiastically told him to bring her all he had, but she never saw him again. Ensuring a regular, dependable supply was a big problem for small purveyors like her who wanted to find a local source.

Another challenge was consumer interest and acceptance. There was a small part of the population who embraced her efforts to supply healthy organic food, but there was resistance on two fronts—first, because her goods were more expensive as they were organic and largely imported and, second, because many Sardinians, even city dwellers, did not need her store to supply local products because they had their own production: "Living on an island, we don't feel strongly the demands for the natural because everyone has a garden in their village. . . . If you go into central Italy, there are more problems of the environment, more pollution, but here we don't feel this oppression yet." So the relatively good environment of Sardinia and the persistence of local production worked against the success of her business. Spiga's perspective was widely shared by others trying to make a living in the alternative food sector who, in spite of their strong commitment, suffered obstacles and disappointments.

Conclusion

This chapter highlights the experiences of four women who are devoting time and energy to promoting good food and reveals how activism can take different forms that present different challenges and rewards. While Francesca Spiga effectively transformed the marketplace of food in Cagliari, she struggled to make a living and to deal with exhaustion, bureaucratic impediments, competition for a small market, and discouragement. But the other three women discussed here participated in food activism as a collateral activity and were not trying to survive from it. Their attitudes were understandably more idealistic and optimistic. All four saw changing the food system as a way of leading more fulfilling lives and changing society. They were able to express agency by choosing meaningful work that allowed them to live in accordance with their values. They expanded their own personal networks and contributed to constructing broader alliances between food producers and consumers in Cagliari. And they all made real changes, however small, in the world around them.

Stepping back from these women's mostly positive experiences as food activists, I would like to raise the question as to whether small personal actions by women like them can change the broader society. Although they and many other Italian women are expanding their socially allocated food roles into public political work, they are largely doing so through the same kinds of precarious jobs that typify women's work in general (Fantone 2007). And, so far, men have not come into the home in equal numbers to share the unpaid family labor, a reciprocity that is essential to more egalitarian gender relations.

Statistics indicate that the Italian home remains a zone of unequal division of labor whose "naturalness" is rarely questioned. Italian laws covering child care, old-age care, and pensions uphold women's responsibility for unpaid family work (Lombardo and Sangiuliano 2009; Saraceno 2011; Saraceno and Keck 2011). According to the Italian government's statistics office (ISTAT), women do 98 percent of domestic food-related work when they do not work outside the home, and 90 percent when they do (ISTAT 2010). Women's labor force participation is far behind men's—45.3 percent for women versus 69.7 percent for men, among the lowest in the European Union (Lombardo and Sangiuliano 2009).

Scholars of food activism note that an uncritical food politics can reproduce entrenched gender, class, and race hierarchies (DuPuis and Goodman 2005; Guthman 2008; Pilgeram 2012). Kathleen Schroeder (2006) found that community kitchens in Bolivia and Peru gave women a positive forum for becoming leaders and expressing agency but also normalized women's free labor for their families and community, isolated them from paid work, and freed men and the state from responsibility for food insecurity. Italian women's participation in food activism may successfully give them agency but may not subvert overriding gender inequalities without more explicit feminist goals and actions, particularly directed toward challenging the gendered division of labor around food at home and in the public.

Acknowledgments

Thanks to the University of Cagliari Visiting Professor Program, which hosted me while I was conducting research for this chapter. Thanks also to many colleagues and friends in Cagliari: Gabriella Da Re, Giovanna Caltagirone, Antonello Dessì, Felice Tiragallo, Filippo Zerilli, Benedetto Meloni, Franco Lai, Valeria Farigu, Giulio Angioni, Marinella Angioni, Benedetto Caltagirone, and especially the participants in the research project. Thanks to the University of Gastronomic Sciences for hosting me as a visiting professor since 2005. Thanks to Millersville University and its Faculty Grants Committee for invaluable support for twenty-five years. Special thanks to my husband, anthropologist Jim Taggart, who joined in the research, read several drafts of this chapter, and asked many good questions.

Notes

1. Some sources on food in Italian history and culture are Apergi and Bianco 1991; Black 2012; Capatti, De Bernardi, and Varni 1998; Capatti and Montanari 1999; Cavanaugh 2007; Conti 2008; Counihan 1981, 1984, 1988, 1999, 2004; Grasseni 2007; Harper and Faccioli 2010; Helstosky 2004; Leitch 2003; Montanari 2010; Parasecoli 2004; Sassatellli and Davolio 2010; Siniscalchi 2000, 2012; Sorcinelli 1998; and Vercelloni 1998.
2. Men seem to play a leading role in organized social movements like the French Confédération Paysanne (Heller 2001), La Via Campesina (Desmarais 2003), Slow Food (Siniscalchi 2010), and anti-GMO movements (Heller 2001; Schurman 2004), although women also operate in these organizations.
3. See Burresi 2002; Mileti, Prete, and Guido 2011; and Ministero dello Sviluppo Economico 2010. See also the supermarket industry website http://www.infocommercio.it/pagine/banche-dati/index_supermercati.php. Comparing Sardinia to other regions (Ministero dello Sviluppo Economico 2010: 245), the actual number of supermarkets is not particularly high, but the density is: Sardinia has 2,787 square feet of supermarket per 1,000 inhabitants, over 1,000 square feet per inhabitant more than the average for the South and Islands (1,706 square feet per person) and higher than the averages of the Center (1,922 square feet), Northeast (2.764 square feet), and Northwest (2,463 square feet). The number of supermarkets in the South and Islands has increased nearly tenfold between 1981 and 2010—from 289 in 1981 to 2,839 in 2010 (Ministero dello Sviluppo Economico 2010: 251).
4. This research project was approved by the Millersville University Institutional Review Board.
5. The GAS are loosely organized and diverse collective buying groups; there are more than 600 of them throughout Italy (Grasseni 2012, 2013).
6. Alessandra Guigoni's blog is at http://www.etnografia.it/.
7. See http://www.domusamigas.it.

References

Allen, P., and Sachs, C. (2007), "Women and Food Chains: The Gendered Politics of Food," *International Journal of Sociology of Food and Agriculture,* 15/1: 1–23.

Apergi, F., and Bianco, C. (1991), *La ricca cena: Famiglia mezzadrile e pratiche alimentari a Vicchio di Mugello,* Florence: Centro Editoriale Toscano.

Barndt, D. (ed.) (1999), *Women Working the NAFTA Food Chain: Women, Food and Globalization,* Toronto: Sumach.

Black, R. E. (2012), *Porta Palazzo: The Anthropology of an Italian Market,* Philadelphia: University of Pennsylvania Press.

Burresi, A. (ed.) (2002), *Il cambiamento della distribuzione in Toscana negli anni Novanta: verso nuovi profili di modernità.* Milano: Franco Angeli.

Capitini, A. (2000), "A Philosopher of Nonviolence: Excerpts from the Books *Scritti filosofici e religiosi,* and *La nonviolenza oggi,* " *Diogenes,* 48/4: 104–120.

Capatti, A., De Bernardi, A., and Varni, A. (eds.) (1998), *Storia d'Italia: L'alimentazione,* Annali 13, Turin: Einaudi.

Capatti, A., and Montanari, M. (1999), *La cucina italiana: Storia di una cultura,* Rome: Laterza.

Cavanaugh, J. R. (2007), "Making Salami, Producing Bergamo: The Production and Transformation of Value in Northern Italy," *Ethnos,* 72/2: 114–139.

Conti, P. C. (2008), *La leggenda del buon cibo italiano e altri miti alimentari contemporanei,* Lucca, Italy: Fazi.

Counihan, C. (1981), *Food, Culture and Political Economy: Changing Lifestyles in the Sardinian Town of Bosa,* PhD diss., University of Massachusetts, Amherst.

Counihan, C. (1984), "Bread as World: Food Habits and Social Relations in Modernizing Sardinia," *Anthropological Quarterly,* 57/2: 47–59.

Counihan, C. (1988), "Female Identity, Food, and Power in Contemporary Florence," *Anthropological Quarterly,* 61/2: 51–62.

Counihan, C. (1999), *The Anthropology of Food and Body: Gender, Meaning and Power,* New York: Routledge.

Counihan, C. (2004), *Around the Tuscan Table: Food, Family and Gender in Twentieth Century Florence,* New York: Routledge.

Counihan, C. (2014), "Cultural Heritage in Food Activism: Local and Global Tensions," in R. Brulotte and M. Di Giovine (eds.), *Edible Identities: Food and Foodways as Cultural Heritage,* Farnham, UK: Ashgate.

Desmarais, A. A. (2003), "The Via Campesina: Peasant Women on the Frontiers of Food Sovereignty," *Canadian Woman Studies,* 23/1: 140–145.

DuPuis, E. M., and Goodman, D. (2005), "Should We Go 'Home' to Eat? Toward a Reflexive Politics of Localism," *Journal of Rural Studies,* 21: 359–371.

Fantone, L. (2007), "Precarious Changes: Gender and Generational Politics in Contemporary Italy," *Feminist Review,* 87: 5–20.

Field, D. (1999), "Putting Food First: Women's Role in Creating a Grassroots Food System outside the Marketplace," in D. Barndt (ed.), *Women Working the NAFTA Food Chain: Women, Food and Globalization,* Toronto: Sumach, 193–208.

Gramsci, A. (1955), *Il materialismo storico e la filosofia di Benedetto Croce,* Turin: Einaudi.

Grasseni, C. (2007), *La reinvenzione del Cibo: Culture del gusto fra tradizione e globalizzazione ai piedi delle Alpi,* Verona: Qui Edit.

Grasseni, C. (2012), "Reinventing Food: The Ethics of Developing Local Food," in J. G. Carrier and P. G. Luetchford (eds.), *Ethical Consumption: Social Value and Economic Practice,* Oxford: Berghahn, 198–216.

Grasseni, C. (2013), *Beyond Alternative Food Networks: Italy's Solidarity Purchase Groups,* London: Bloomsbury.

Guigoni, A. (2009), *Alla scoperta dell'America in Sardegna: Vegetali americani nell'alimentazione sarda,* Cagliari, Italy: AM&D.

Guigoni, A. (2010), "Il cappero di Selargius: Aspetti storici e culturali di una pianta ultracentenaria," *Anthropos e Iatria,* 14/4: 8–13.

Guthman, J. (2008), "'If They Only Knew': Color Blindness and Universalism in California Alternative Food Institutions," *The Professional Geographer,* 60: 387–397.

Harper, D., and Faccioli, P. (2010), *The Italian Way: Food and Social Life,* Chicago: University of Chicago Press.

Hayes-Conroy, A., and Hayes-Conroy, J. (2010), "Visceral Difference: Variations in Feeling (Slow) Food," *Environment and Planning A,* 42: 2956–2971.

Heller, C. (2001), "From Risk to Globalization: Discursive Shifts in the French Debate on GMOs," *Medical Anthropology Quarterly,* 15/1: 25–28.

Helstosky, C. F. (2004), *Garlic and Oil: Politics of Food in Italy,* Oxford: Berg.

Istituto Nazionale di Statistica (ISTAT). (2010), La divisione dei ruoli nelle coppie, 2008–2009. Rome: Istituto Nazionale di Statistica. http://www3.istat.it/salastampa/comunicati/non_calendario/20101110_00/testointegrale20101110.pdf, accessed July 12, 2013.

Istituto Nazionale di Statistica (ISTAT). (2011), http://demo.istat.it/pop2011/index.html, accessed July 11, 2013.

Lang, T. (1999), "Food Policy for the 21st Century: Can It Be Both Radical and Reasonable?," in M. Koc, R. MacRae, L.J.A. Mougeot, and J. Welsh (eds.), *For Hunger-Proof Cities: Sustainable Urban Food Systems,* Ottawa: International Development Research Centre, 216–224.

Leitch, A. (2003), "Slow Food and the Politics of Pork Fat: Italian Food and European Identity," *Ethnos,* 68/4: 437–462.

Lombardo, E., and Sangiuliano, M. (2009), "'Gender and Employment' in the Italian Policy Debates: The Construction of 'Non Employed' Gendered Subjects," *Women's Studies International Forum,* 32/6: 445–452.

Mileti, A., Prete, M. I., Guido, G. (eds.) (2011), "The Role of New Retailing Formats in the Italian Local Development," *Chinese Business Review,* 10/8: 587–600.

Ministero dello Sviluppo Economico. (2010), "Rapporto sul sistema distributivo: Analisi economico-strutturale del commercio italiano," http://osservatoriocommercio.sviluppoeconomico.gov.it/Rapporto_2010_Web.pdf, accessed July 12, 2013.

Moffett, D., and Morgan, M. L. (1999), "Women as Organizers: Building Confidence and Community through Food," in D. Barndt (ed.), *Women Working the NAFTA Food Chain: Women, Food and Globalization,* Toronto: Sumach, 221–236.

Montanari, M. (2010), *Il formaggio con le pere: La storia in un proverbio,* Bari: Laterza.

Parasecoli, F. (2004), *Food Culture in Italy,* Westport, CT: Greenwood.

Pilgeram, R. (2012), "Social Sustainability and the White, Nuclear Family: Constructions of Gender, Race, and Class at a Northwest Farmers' Market," *Race, Gender & Class,* 19/1–2: 37–60.

Sacks, K. (1974), "Engels Revisited: Women, the Organization of Production, and Private Property," in M. Z. Rosaldo and L. Lamphere (eds.), *Women, Culture and Society,* Stanford, CA: Stanford University Press, 207–222.

Saraceno, C. (2011), "Beyond Care: The Persistent Invisibility of Unpaid Family Work," *Sociologica,* 1: 1–15.

Saraceno, C., and Keck, W. (2011), "Towards an Integrated Approach for the Analysis of Gender Equity in Policies Supporting Paid Work and Care Responsibilities," *Demographic Research,* 25: 371–405.

Sassatelli, R., and Davolio, F. (2010), "Consumption, Pleasure, and Politics: Slow Food and the Politico-aesthetic Problematization of Food," *Journal of Consumer Culture,* 10/2: 1–31.

Schroeder, K. (2006), "A Feminist Examination of Community Kitchens in Peru and Bolivia," *Gender, Place & Culture,* 13/6: 663–668.

Schurman, R. (2004), "Fighting 'Frankenfoods': Industry Opportunity Structures and the Efficacy of the Anti-biotech Movement in Western Europe," *Social Problems,* 51/2: 243–268.

Siniscalchi, V. (2000), "'Il dolce paese del torrone': Economia e storia in un paese dell'Italia del Sud," *Meridiana: Rivista di storia e scienze sociali,* 38/39: 199–222.

Siniscalchi, V. (2010), "Power and Gender inside the Italian Slow Food Movement," public lecture, Millersville University, November 15.

Siniscalchi, V. (2012), "Au delà de l'opposition slow-fast: L'économie morale d'un mouvement," *Lo Squaderno,* 26: 67–74.

Siniscalchi, V. (2013), "Slow versus Fast: Économie e écologie dans le mouvement Slow Food," *Terrain,* 60: 132–147.

Slow Food. (2013), "Terra Madre Network," http://www.terramadre.info/pagine/rete/?-session=terramadre:6C37508A04e913379Alw2E21E635, accessed February 1, 2013.

Sorcinelli, P. (1998), "Per una storia sociale dell'alimentazione: Dalla polenta ai crackers," in A. Capatti, A. De Bernardi, and A. Varni (eds.), *Storia d'Italia: L'alimentazione*, Annali 13, Turin: Einaudi, 453–493.

Vercelloni, L. (1998), "La modernità alimentare," in A. Capatti, A. De Bernardi, and A. Varni (eds.), *Storia d'Italia: L'alimentazione*, Annali 13, Turin: Einaudi, 951–1005.

Villagomez, M. D. (1999), "Grassroots Responses to Globalization: Mexican Rural and Urban Women's Collective Alternatives," in D. Barndt (ed.), *Women Working the NAFTA Food Chain: Women, Food and Globalization*, Toronto: Sumach, 209–219.

6

The Movement to Reinvigorate Local Food Culture in Kyoto, Japan

Greg de St. Maurice

Introduction

In 2010 the media corporation Food Channel compiled a list of food trends it expected to increase in popularity the following year. Number three on the list was a phenomenon called "Local Somewhere" that acknowledged both the widespread appeal the term *local* holds for consumers and the degree to which marketers attempt to manipulate this appeal. The article asserted that "local goes beyond a geographical definition"; that "if someone, somewhere, is personally growing and tending to this product, as opposed to packing and sorting on the assembly line, then it's local"; and that "if the product is closer to me philosophically, it is local. Somewhere" (Food Channel 2010). This was not satire. These statements illustrate the extent to which food and place can be affectively linked for consumers and more particularly how labeling or marketing a product as "local" can render it a value-added product.

As faraway places are becoming ever more interconnected and interdependent, food often travels great distances before it is consumed, and a variety of food movements have emerged to reassert the value of local food systems and traditions. It is arguably more important than ever to examine the role that "place" plays in contemporary food movements. David Harvey writes that "place has to be one of the most multi-layered and multi-purpose words in our language" (1993: 4). John Agnew (2005) identifies three dominant, overlapping meanings for place: (1) "a location or site in space" in which an activity or object may be situated—a kind of address, like a city or settlement; (2) a locale or setting for everyday action—a kind of stage, like the workplace, the home, or the playground; and (3) a "sense of place" where identity, group affiliation, and habitus emerge. Such a "sense of place" exists because places are meaningful in idiosyncratic ways; in the words of the geographer Yi-fu Tuan, "Place is an organized world of meaning" (1977: 179; see also Basso 1996).

This chapter focuses on the movement to revitalize local food culture and particularly heirloom vegetables in Kyoto, Japan. For local food activists, Kyoto serves as a place in each of the senses that Agnew describes. Yet there exist, in fact, multiple

"Kyotos." Kyoto Prefecture, occupying approximately 2,866 square miles in western Japan, is the thirty-first largest of Japan's forty-seven prefectures (Ministry of Internal Affairs and Communications, Statistics Bureau 2012). It has a population of about 2.6 million people. Kyoto City, the capital of Kyoto Prefecture, is approximately 514 square miles with a population of almost 1.5 million people (Kyoto City Industry and Tourism Bureau 2010). Kyoto City's distance from Kyoto Prefecture's fisheries has resulted in a food culture that has placed a great deal of importance on cooking with vegetables. Kyoto—Prefecture and City—certainly functions as site and setting. But the impact of Kyoto's "sense of place" on the movement to revive local food culture cannot be overemphasized. Kyoto conjures up a specific set of established feelings and associations. It is considered the mytho-historical birthplace of much of Japan's "traditional" culture—including its agricultural and culinary heritage (Brumann 2009, 2012; Hosking 1996; Rath 2010). Kyoto is called *Nihon no kokoro no furusato* (the Japanese heart/mind's hometown) for this reason, and one finds the national headquarters for most Buddhist sects and traditional Japanese arts and crafts associations in Kyoto (Brumann 2009). Furthermore, the cityscape itself—notable for architectural treasures that include Buddhist temples, Shinto shrines, imperial palaces, and *kyō machiya* (traditional "town houses")—was spared the bombing and destruction that other Japanese cities experienced during World War II. In fact, Kyoto's image is so recognizable that surveys have found that Kyoto had the second-strongest place-based brand out of the forty-seven Japanese prefectures (after Hokkaido; Brand Research Institute 2010; Nikkei Research 2011). This powerful sense of place and the notion of Kyoto's unique heritage have motivated local food activists and appealed to the consumer public.

This chapter first explains the cultural, political, economic, and historical context in which Kyoto's food activism takes place. Next, it describes the actions and strategies that chefs, farmers, bureaucrats, and members of nonprofit organizations have employed. The following section highlights what I argue may be labeled the political repercussions of this avowedly apolitical movement by applying the theoretical insights of Antonio Gramsci, Karl Polanyi, and Michel Foucault. In the final section, I consider the role that place can play in social movements and food activism. Kyoto's food activism shows that, on the one hand, a movement can be defined, delimited, invested with significance, and energized by the boundaries of place. Take CSAs and farmers' markets, for instance. Opportunities for interacting with farmers and other actors face-to-face make it easier for consumers to gauge the impact of their purchases, whether they are most interested in issues pertaining to social justice, health, or the environment. Forging boundaries that define the local can also motivate individuals to act via implicit or explicit appeals based on identity and relevancy. These appeals call on residents to work on the food system both because it is a part of their lives and because it is a kind of civic responsibility. On the other hand, place can restrict a movement, very literally limiting its impact. Spatial boundaries, particularly when compounded with class, ethnic, or cultural differences, may also be infused with xenophobic tensions, thereby undermining goals of food democracy, social justice, and multiculturalism. The boundaries created in the processes of place-making need not be rigid or xenophobic, however (Hinrichs 2003). Kyoto provides an example of how local agricultural and culinary traditions may be supported and exalted while welcoming the addition of things from outside, be they ingredients, cooking techniques, or even foreign cuisines.

This ethnography is based on fieldwork conducted in Kyoto in 2006–2008 and 2012–2013. One component of this work consists of archival research examining newspaper articles published at the movement's inception and prefectural, municipal, and regional documents about agricultural programs, such as the Kyō Brand and the Kyoto Seasonal Vegetable Program. This study is informed by many semistructured and informal interviews conducted with chefs, farmers, local government officials, local experts, members of nonprofit organizations, and consumers. This chapter draws heavily on recorded interviews with four chefs and three farmers who held prominence in the local food movement in its thirty-year evolution. Data on bureaucratic efforts to promote local food culture and the agrofood economy come from structured recorded interviews with seven officials serving in unelected positions in the regional, prefectural, and municipal governments and institutions. My understanding of Japanese consumers' perceptions of local food and Kyoto's food culture in particular derives from more than fifty informal, unstructured interviews and over thirty questionnaires. Respondents were selected to represent diversity in terms of place of residence, gender, and age. Data also come from participant observation at events celebrating Kyoto's agricultural and culinary traditions, such as farmers' markets, agricultural fairs, and more infrequent events such as 2012's first Kujō scallion festival or the yearly Shishigatani squash "mass" at Anrakuji temple.

Context for Action

Kyoto's food activism is local in orientation in that Kyoto is identified as the relevant place for action. In spite of this localism, this movement has been influenced by ideas, policies, and institutions well beyond its borders and those of the Japanese state. This is clear when one takes a look at international as well as national policies on agriculture and trade over the course of the past half century.

Neoliberal economic theory and policies and the emergence of a global agrofood industry have had a significant impact on Japanese agriculture. Efficiency, deregulation, and free trade are three key neoliberal tenets. Neoliberal economists and policymakers valorize the large-scale, capital-intensive, specialized farm as "the final and most advanced stage of individual holding in a mixed economy" (Todaro and Smith 2003: 448). Bureaucrats determining national agricultural policies in post–World War II Japan promoted modernization and industrialization in line with these neoliberal ideals in a drive to transform the country into an export-oriented "developed" economy (Nishiyama and Hirata Kimura 2005: 86). In 1956 Japan signed the General Agreement on Tariffs and Trade, which was replaced by the World Trade Organization in 1995. In the past few decades, meanwhile, the national government has pursued Economic Partnership Agreements with many countries, including Chile, India, Mexico, and those belonging to the Association for Southeast Asian Nations. As a result of these agreements, comparatively inexpensive produce grown abroad has made its way onto supermarket shelves and restaurant menus. These trends have had a direct impact on Japanese agriculture as a whole. By the mid-1960s the economic contribution of agriculture to the national economy had fallen to the point that only 15 percent of the population was engaged in farming, and the sector as a whole contributed only 8 percent to the net domestic product (Pempel 1998: 60). Today, Japan's agricultural sector consists of less than 4 percent of the nation's workforce and contributes little more than 1 percent to the gross domestic product (Central Intelligence Agency 2013). Its national self-sufficiency rate has fallen from 73 percent (calculated in calories) in 1965 to about 40 percent in recent years, the lowest of any developed country (Ministry of Internal Affairs and Communications, Statistics Bureau 2010: 62–64).

Under Prime Minister Shinzō Abe, Japan has entered into negotiations for the Trans-Pacific Partnership (TPP), a free trade agreement that could involve as many as eleven other countries, including New Zealand, Peru, Vietnam, the United States, Mexico, and Canada. Aurelia George Mulgan (2012) notes, "The MAFF [Ministry of Agriculture, Forestry and Fisheries] has made a trial calculation that if Japan were to sign on to the TPP, the value of domestic agricultural production would drop by approximately 4.1 trillion yen ($5.2 billion USD), almost half of the total production value, and the food self-sufficiency rate (calorie-based) would fall from the current 40 percent to 14 percent." Though Abe's Liberal Democratic Party is in favor of a free trade agreement, it also depends on the votes of farmers and citizens in rural areas, many of whom oppose the agreement, fearing that it would mean the demise of Japanese agriculture.

The average farmer in Kyoto Prefecture owns about half the land the average Japanese farmer does. This is especially significant considering that Japanese agriculture is itself relatively small-scale. Moreover, if one looks only at dry fields, thereby excluding rice paddies, the average farmer in Kyoto owns only about one-sixth the area the average Japanese farmer does (Kinki Regional Agricultural Administration Office 2006; Ministry of Agriculture, Forestry, and Fisheries 2005). This explains why the average Kyoto farmer obtains less income from agriculture than other Japanese farmers. On the other hand, Kyoto's farmers earn more for every ten acres of land they farm (Kinki Regional Agricultural Administration Office 2006).[1] Vegetable sales make up a much greater percentage of Kyoto's agricultural product than they do for the nation as a whole. Yet Kyoto's self-sufficiency rate for food has reached a low of 13 percent (Ministry of Agriculture, Forestry, and Fisheries 2012).

I conducted research on the "taste of Kyoto" as perceived by consumers from all over Japan via informal interviews and questionnaires. When I asked respondents to describe Kyoto's food culture, many of them immediately mentioned "Kyoto vegetables," or *kyō yasai* (de St. Maurice 2012). *Kyō yasai* and other terms used to categorize the various vegetables grown in Kyoto can be quite confusing. Several months into my first round of fieldwork in Kyoto, I brought a Chinese friend with me to buy vegetables from a farmer whose small truck made stops in my neighborhood. She asked the farmer, Y-san, if the sweet potatoes for sale were kyō yasai.[2] Y-san told her that they were not but that the Kamo eggplant and Takagamine green pepper were. Then, realizing my friend's confusion, she elaborated, explaining that all of the vegetables were grown in Kyoto City by her husband. From her point of view, vegetables such as the Kamo eggplant and Takagamine green pepper, whose seeds have been handed down for generations in Kyoto, are Kyoto vegetables, while others, like the sweet potatoes and corn she sells, are "merely" local. Y-san takes pride in growing and selling kyō yasai because they are a form of local heritage. Although some of the heirloom varieties have a "shallow" history of 100–200 years in the greater Kyoto area, the phrase "Kyoto vegetables" evokes images of the city over a thousand years ago.

The mytho-history of kyō yasai's origins mixes fact and fantasy but nonetheless resonates in the present. According to the Kyoto Prefectural University agronomist Takashima Shiro (2003: 12), it is said that high-quality vegetables were associated with Kyoto soon after the city became the populous cultural, political, and religious capital of Japan in the Heian era (794–1185 C.E.). Several interviewees—agricultural experts, food scholars, and food industry employees—claimed that at this time, the best foreign vegetables were brought to the capital for the emperor. Because the soil and climate are conducive to farming, these vegetables were grown successfully around the capital and adapted to local conditions. Prohibitions on eating meat (Ishige 2012: 57–61) as well as the capital's location—far from the coast—meant that these vegetables became the focus of local cuisines, from vegetarian temple cooking and domestic fare to Kyoto's haute cuisine, the refined multicourse *kaiseki.* In this mytho-historical context, Kyoto is considered the birthplace of "Japanese" foodways (Rath 2010: 21).

Surprisingly, many of the consumers I spoke with expressed views of Kyoto's food culture that anchored it in the Heian era, as though these traditions had changed very little until the past half century or so. Of course, recent changes in domestic life have meant that traditional vegetable varieties that involve a fair amount of preparation or that have a strong, distinctive taste are likely to be passed over. The vegetable varieties that are most acceptable to Japanese citizens from different regions with different preferences and that are well suited to large-scale cultivation and cross-country transport have become the standard. Consequently, by the 1960s farmers across Japan—including Kyoto—increasingly began buying F1 hybrid seeds from seed companies. With these first-generation hybrid seeds, farmers no longer had to go to the effort of harvesting seeds and were guaranteed a consistently uniform crop. Today the cultivation of F1 varieties is the norm. For example, the aokubi daikon, a variety of Japanese radish that is long, thick, and straight and possesses a mild flavor, has become ubiquitous throughout Japan. Not only is it comparatively easy to cultivate, harvest, and transport, but it is also easy to peel and prepare. In contrast, Kyoto's sharp-tasting karami daikon has become more difficult to obtain, and the Kōri daikon, a variety with a long, thin root that loops as it develops, has become extinct (Takashima 2003).

Reviving Heirloom Vegetable Varieties and Local Food Culture

By the 1980s many Kyoto chefs had become concerned that the vegetables available for purchase, especially for the average Japanese citizen, were standardized varieties that had been shipped from a distance and did not taste good. They worried that the decline of heirloom vegetables might continue to the point that these varieties could be found only in the fields of farmers paid to grow them for preservation purposes by Kyoto City or in Kyoto Prefecture's seed bank. I spoke with leaders of the Kyō ryōri Mebaekai, an active group of almost eighty chefs from local haute cuisine restaurants. My two main informants were Murata Yoshihiro of Kikunoi restaurant and Takahashi Eiichi of Hyōtei restaurant.[3] These informants spoke to the group's desire to nurture Kyoto's food culture not only in haute cuisine but also in society at large.

Mebaekai chefs decided to use their position as cultural elites and celebrities who appear on television and are household names to try to make tasty heirloom vegetables available to Kyoto's residents at reasonable prices. They hoped that if they could accomplish this in Kyoto, the movement to revive local agricultural traditions would catch fire and spread across Japan. The chefs set up contracts with local farmers, explaining what varieties they most needed at particular times of the year and promising to purchase all the heirloom vegetables the farmers could grow. Farmers interested in growing more heirloom varieties welcomed this assurance. In 1986 the group launched its first session of a series of symposia aimed at spreading awareness of heirloom vegetable varieties and getting the public interested in Kyoto's food culture. They organized cooking classes, food-tasting events, and opportunities for citizens to buy heirloom vegetables from local farmers. Kyō yasai were treated as a source of local identity and pride that could be integrated into daily life throughout the year. Chefs and farmers emphasized the link between local seasonal produce and health and explained the associations between vegetables and seasonal events and ceremonies. Sharing recipes enabled consumers both to see that these vegetables fit into local food culture and to understand how they could prepare and consume them today.

The popularity of the symposia is apparent in the newspaper coverage at the time. The *Nikkei Marketing Journal* reported a crowd of over 1,500 people at the second symposium in November 1987, with the 500 meals prepared only holding out until noon and the fifteen vegetable varieties available for purchase selling out by mid-morning (Nikkei Marketing Journal 1987).

The Mebaekai's activities began while Japan was experiencing its economic bubble and was in the midst of what has been called a "gourmet boom." Not long after, the media declared a "kyō yasai boom," and upscale department stores and large supermarket chains as far away as Tokyo became interested in creating "kyō yasai corners" (Yomiuri Shimbun 1989). Groups of chefs in other parts of Japan were inspired by the Kyoto Mebaekai's success and sought to accomplish the same for heirloom vegetables associated with their regions. Although demand for Kyoto vegetables exploded and production increased, there were unanticipated consequences to the success of Kyoto's food activists. Several informants claimed that the surge in demand resulted in sales of "Kyoto" vegetables actually grown in other places as well as Kyoto vegetables that were grown using far greater amounts of chemical fertilizers and pesticides than farmers had used before. Who could tell what kind of a Kyoto vegetable one was buying unless one bought it directly from the farmer? People worried that the distinctiveness and renewed reputation of Kyoto vegetables could now be threatened because of the varieties' rapid new appeal.

In response, in 1987 Kyoto Prefecture, Kyoto City, the Prefectural Central Union of Agricultural Cooperatives, and the Prefectural Economic Federation of Agricultural Cooperatives specifically defined *kyō no dentō yasai* ("traditional Kyoto vegetables") under the guidance of Takashima (Kyō no Furusato Sanpin Kyōkai 2010: 4). Those varieties inscribed on the list of traditional Kyoto vegetables met certain criteria: they were introduced and cultivated in parts of Kyoto Prefecture before the Meiji era (1868–1912 C.E.); bamboo shoots were included but not mushrooms; and varieties once grown as crops but now cultivated for preservation by local research institutions, as well as those that were extinct, were also included.[4] While this definition in and of itself could not prevent producers, distributors, and retailers from other parts of Japan from co-opting the term *Kyoto,* this move established a clear foundation for further action. It created a much clearer term than *Kyoto vegetables* to use to promote local heirloom vegetables, and a kind of geographic indication before a system for registering geographic indications existed in Japan. The term *traditional Kyoto vegetables* was inscribed as such in 2007 once such a national system had been developed. Today, farmers can use the term *traditional Kyoto vegetable* only on boxes for specific vegetables varieties grown within the current prefectural boundaries. Additionally, defining *traditional Kyoto vegetables* marked the varieties on the list as important prefectural cultural heritage.

Building on this, a committee that included representatives from the prefectural government, city and town governments, Kyoto Prefectural University, and local branches of the Japanese Agricultural Cooperatives decided to create a prefectural brand for vegetables, which overlaps with but differs from the list of traditional Kyoto vegetables. The Kyō Brand was born in 1989, with exports to Tokyo

"Kyoto seasonal vegetable"

Broccoli, sweet corn, etc.

"Kyoto vegetable"

Yahata burdock root, Kyō temari tomato, etc.

"Kyoto traditional vegetable"

Hatakena, sugikina, etc.

"Kyō" Brand produce

Horikawa burdock root, mizuna, etc.

Kintoki carrot, murasaki zukin (eda mame), etc.

Tōji turnip (extinct), Kōri daikon (extinct), etc.

Kyō Tango pear, Tamba chestnuts, etc.

occurring a year later. The Kyō Brand has been well received. The leafy green mizuna, which makes up about half of the brand's sales, sells for almost twice the price of that from Ibaraki prefecture, which produces 80 percent of the mizuna available at the Tokyo Central Wholesale Market.[5] The price difference appears to be true for both Kyō Brand vegetables and many nonbranded vegetables, implying that branding has benefited Kyoto's vegetable industry in general, a conclusion also reached by the Kyoto Prefectural Agricultural Research Institute (2007). This is seen as one reason Kyoto's annual gross product (total market value) for fruits and vegetables has suffered less than that of other prefectures in the Kinki region as Japan's borders have been opened to cheap agricultural imports by a dozen or so free trade agreements (Kyō no Furusato Sanpin Kyōkai 2010).

Following suit, in 1989 a group of farmers from Kyoto City's Kamigamo neighborhood formed the Kamigamo Heirloom Vegetable Research Group, creating a system for collectively harvesting seeds and branding their produce. They reasoned that if the Kamo eggplant had a recorded history of being grown in the area and had acquired the name of their neighborhood, then a brand would help protect their local agricultural heritage and economy. Less than a decade later, Kyoto City launched the Kyoto Seasonal Vegetable Program (Kyō no Kodawari Shun Yasai Purogurammu), supporting city smallholders like those living in the Kamigamo area, mainly by providing assistance with marketing and distribution. Through the program, Kyoto City has created a logo for produce grown by participating farmers, established stands selling local produce in places like subway stations, and disseminated information to consumers about places where they can purchase locally grown vegetables.

Today, schools and hospitals throughout Kyoto Prefecture serve food made with locally purveyed ingredients. Public schools teach about cooking with kyō yasai and the importance of Kyoto's food culture. Kyoto Prefecture publishes recipes and information on the nutritional value of kyō yasai in pamphlets and newsletters and on the Internet.[6] The prefectural newsletter, for example, delivered monthly to all households, always includes a recipe in which the main or secret ingredient is a Kyoto vegetable.

Although civil servants, farmers, and chefs have been at the forefront of Kyoto's local food movement, others not directly affiliated with the food economy have also been active. Participant observation with the Kyoto Food Culture Club[7] revealed to me some of the ways that other organizations seek to spread an appreciation of Kyoto's food culture. Community participation is a key characteristic of the club. What surprised me the first time I exchanged business cards after a working group meeting was the group's diversity. I met people employed in the cinema industry, the fine arts, and local nonprofit organizations. The club has links to local government, though not to elected officials, political parties, or policy platforms. Prefectural and municipal government employees have taken on several leadership positions, and the prefecture has subsidized group activities and covered budget shortfalls, providing marketing, equipment, and access to information and individuals that would otherwise have been more difficult to obtain. The organization has had multiple working groups that meet to discuss and plan different projects, and I participated in the meetings and activities for two of those groups regularly over the course of the past six years: the Seasonal Seminar Project and the Educating Consumers Project. The seminars have included lectures by college professors and farmers, cooking lessons, and themed lunches—all related to Kyoto's food culture. The latter project plans more frequent events that have included sessions on table manners, hands-on Kyoto-style cooking, and the traditional tableware used in Kyoto's more elaborate cuisines. Although the style of such events is more laid-back and less stylized than the activities organized by the Mebaekai, they share a belief that food culture is lived and incorporated into daily lives and bodies. Seasonal cooking classes, as a result, teach attendees not only about local foodstuffs and signature dishes but also about ways to create tasty meals that feature locally purveyed ingredients.

Food Activism with a Kyoto Flavor

Farmer lobbying efforts, consumer campaigns against genetically modified foods, and protests against rising food prices in the Global South are some of the most visible images of food activism today. Kyoto's food activism is of a more discreet variety and is characterized by an intentional lack of political activity. Interviews and archival research revealed no signs of lobbying, protest activity, or an "us-versus-them" mentality. Chefs and other activists did not wish to promote local vegetables at the expense of produce from other places. Ingredients and techniques from other parts of Japan and even the world have been intentionally *included* in local food culture. Thus, in Kyō ryōri restaurants bamboo shoots from southern areas of Japan serve as harbingers of spring in Kyoto and of its own harvest of prized shoots. Likewise, at Kyoto Food Culture Club events a cooking teacher includes ingredients like Dijon mustard, bacon, and olive oil in her recipes for seasonal Kyoto cuisine. "Things from foreign countries can also fit perfectly," she tells those who attend her classes.

The celebrity chefs who have participated in Kyoto's food activism may have fueled the movement, but they have not done so as political spokesmen. Takahashi Eiichi stressed that one of the Mebaekai's principles is that it will remain apolitical. Murata Yoshihiro commented that the problem they faced was not one that political activity was likely to solve. Takahashi Takuji of Kinobu restaurant described his position as one of "lighting fires" that generate positive change. These "fires" are not the fires of protest or overt political action. Instead, when he identifies something as lacking in popular food culture, he tries to incorporate it in his menu if he can and encourages the trend to spread. Thus, when the Mebaekai deemed that it had accomplished its goal of reviving local vegetables, it set a new goal: making high-quality salts available to the public at affordable prices.

Even government involvement has been apolitical and nonpartisan, largely conducted by nonelected officials through programs and microlevel tactical moves rather than political campaigns or radical laws. Examples include the formation of the Kyō Brand and support for schools and hospitals that serve meals with local produce. Such apoliticism is in line with trends for food activism throughout Japan; Aya Hirata Kimura and Mima Nishiyama inform us that within local food movements in contemporary Japan "political activism is rarely envisioned. [Participants] tend to focus on marketing activities and purchasing of local produce" (2008: 60).

Kyoto's food activists have consciously acted at the local level. They did not envision a grand transformation of the structures or processes at work in the globalization of food and agriculture. The Mebaekai's original goals were to increase the availability of tasty traditional vegetable varieties, diversify the diets of consumers, reinvigorate local food culture, and strengthen the local agro-economy. To do this, they held events locally and reached out to local institutions or the local branches of national institutions. Thus, although the *Nihon Keizai Shimbun* (particularly the regional edition) and other national media paid attention to the events they hosted, coverage predominantly occurred in the local newspaper, the *Kyoto Shimbun*. More recently, Kyō no Furusato Sanpin Kyōkai, the institution responsible for managing the Kyō Brand, has actively promoted the brand in places like Tokyo, but the vast majority of the brand's sales occur within Kyoto Prefecture.

Kyoto's food activism was culturally motivated. This certainly does not mean that economic factors were unimportant, but financial reasons are not enough to motivate people to become local food activists. This is particularly true of those individuals who choose to become farmers. Throughout Kyoto Prefecture, farmers continue to cultivate land passed down from their ancestors, even though they must find other sources of income to supplement their agricultural income. Hoping to support a continued existence on the land for them and generations to come, many lease portions of their land to companies that build parking lots or apartment buildings. Several told me they wanted to contribute to their local community. Tazuru Hitoshi, who has teamed up with the Mebaekai from its early days, has said that since it is common knowledge that fresh vegetables keep one healthy, farmers should be as respected as doctors. Another farmer indicated that he continues to grow an heirloom variety that does not sell because preserving culture is important to him. Yet another explained that he farms out of a sense of obligation to his ancestors. Indeed, one trend is for sons to work as "salarymen," only to take up farming when their fathers can no longer take care of the family plots alone.

Kyoto's local food movement is emphatically cultural and avowedly apolitical. Nevertheless, Steven Buechler argues that social movements possess an "inevitable duality" consisting of both cultural and political aspects and states that a social movement's political dimension may be located by identifying "some form of challenge to prevailing forms of authority" (2000: 211). Using *political* in this sense of the word enables us to probe the political dimensions and implications of a movement whose participants consciously avoid what they believe to be political activity.

Although Kyoto's food activists generally do not envision their actions as having an explicitly ideological dimension, I believe there are counterhegemonic aspects to the movement. Antonio Gramsci conceived of hegemony as the ideology promulgated by both the state and the institutions of civil society that establish legitimacy and procure consent (Gramsci 1971; Mittelman and Chin 2000). Gramsci defines counterhegemonic tactics as those that are employed in society at large to challenge the ideology of the prevailing political economic system. The World Trade Organization, the World Bank, think tanks, higher-education institutions, agribusiness corporations, and political parties exercise a type of contemporary hegemony when they advocate and disseminate neoliberal economic ideology. In a counterhegemonic fashion Kyoto's food activists have taken to educating people about the value of local produce and local foods. Murata-san said the Mebaekai wanted to get Japanese citizens to see "how amazing local things are"—not only things from Kyoto, but "it would be good if Kyoto served as an example." These chefs and farmers interact with the local media, go to schools, accept interns, and the like. The conspicuous incorporation of Kyoto vegetables in schools and hospitals dovetails with national-level policies of *chisan-chisho*, or "local production for local consumption,"[8] that clash with global hegemonic positions toward agriculture and have the potential to reverberate beyond Kyoto in counterhegemonic fashion.

Kyoto's food activists, for the most part, are not opposed to globalization. Nevertheless, on the whole they seek to temper the negative impacts of the globalization of food and agriculture. Karl Polanyi's concept of countermovements can be used to illuminate the ways Kyoto's food activism positions itself vis-à-vis its political economic context even if it does so without engaging in overt political action. In *The Great Transformation* (1975), Polanyi concluded that the development of free-market capitalism threatens society and catalyzes countermovements to re-embed markets in local social relations. Local food movements such as Kyoto's certainly resemble the double movements Polanyi describes (Pratt 2007: 289). Even as Japan continues to negotiate its way into regional and international trade agreements, actors from the MAFF down to local chefs work to anchor markets for agricultural goods within society and strengthen the local agrofood economy. The formation of the Kyō Brand was meant to alleviate the dislocation and hardship farmers were likely to encounter as the MAFF implemented policies discouraging the rice production that the prefecture's agricultural economy was dependent on. It is thus a kind of countermovement. Kyoto's food activists' emphasis on the value of Kyoto's local agricultural and culinary heritage, though not explicitly economic or political in orientation, may also be glossed as a type of countermovement. As one farmer told me, "Local production for local consumption makes for a better society because relationships are at the center."

Gramsci's and Polanyi's theoretical insights can be adapted to set in relief the ways in which the movement to revive Kyoto's heirloom vegetables has a context that is political, economic, and ideological in very specific ways. The movement engenders activism concerned with ideology and the place of markets in contemporary capitalist societies. Michel Foucault's notion of biopolitics and the microphysics of power may shed light on more ambiguous power relations, on the focus on the body and dietetics, and on the political dimension of social movements. Power is omnipresent, embodied, and productive as well as repressive (Foucault 1980). The production, distribution, regulation, marketing, preparation, and consumption of food occur at the intersection of various fields of power. In their quest to safeguard local heirloom varieties and reinvigorate local food culture, from a Foucauldian perspective Kyoto's food activists act within the capillary system of the social body to engage in activism that has consequences for both local identity politics and the political economy. As a result of their efforts, kyō yasai are recognized throughout the country (de St. Maurice 2012), and the prefecture's agricultural sector has successfully shifted away from its prior dependence on rice production, something nearby prefectures have had a more difficult time managing. Moreover, individuals in Kyoto and beyond have made choices about what to grow, sell, and eat that valorize the local and the traditional. Kyoto's food activists have nurtured a space in which farmers, chefs, and consumers have alternatives to conventional vegetable varieties, standardized foods, and neoliberal positions on food and agriculture.

Viewing Kyoto's local food movement through the theoretical lenses of counterhegemony, countermovements, and biopolitics/microresistance sets in relief the political implications and consequences of the movement. One must be careful, however, not to simply label this movement "resistance" or "opposition" to those actors, ideologies, and structures that exert power at various scales within the globalization of food and agriculture. Indeed, as I elaborate on in the following section, Kyoto's actors have sought to engage with the processes of globalization rather than to isolate themselves from them.

Keeping Kyoto Grounded in Place

Place-making involves the creation of boundaries. Discussions of local food systems, foodsheds, and food democracy thus invite questions about the processes for inclusion and exclusion and the management of boundaries and borders. For example, so-called locavores choose to eat only those foods grown within distinct geographic, ecological, or political boundaries up to a predetermined distance from their residence. Such locavores practice "defensive" localism. Foods outside their area of choice are excluded and deemed inappropriate. The localism I have observed in Kyoto is more cosmopolitan and inclusive. Nevertheless, the brands that have been formed in Kyoto create distinctions that have much to do with geopolitical boundaries. Borders separate neighbors, distinguishing Kyō Brand vegetables, for example, from vegetables grown in the next-door prefectures of Shiga, Osaka, and Hyogo. Vegetable farmers residing in those prefectures are not allowed to participate in the Kyō Brand even if they grow the same varieties as Kyō Brand farmers using the same methods.

Dangers lurk in territorial boundary creation. Movements that discriminate and exclude find in food a means of asserting collective exclusionary identity (McKinley 2010; Pratt 2007: 292). For example, in Japan, food from China is treated as suspicious and unsafe, although the Japanese companies that import it somehow retain an aura of trustworthiness (Rosenberger 2009). Defensive localism, with rigid and xenophobic boundaries, is not the only variety of localism, however (Hinrichs 2003). Many food activists display a tendency toward "diversity-embracing localism." Clare Hinrichs believes this "signifies a promising opening, where 'local' foodstuffs are combined in new ways reflecting the changing diversity of producers and consumers now living in the region" (2003: 42).

Inasmuch as Kyoto's food activism is linked to the globalization of food and agriculture, Kyoto's actors are not "anti-globalization." Globalization can be described as the set of processes that propel people, things, ideas, and capital across the world; the structures that enable these processes; and the changes that ensue from them (Murray 2006). Global connections can serve to bolster local traditions and foster localism (see Caldwell and Lozada 2007). The individuals and groups involved in Kyoto's local food movement have capitalized on globalization in order to accomplish locally oriented objectives. For instance, people from outside Kyoto and even Japan are invited to participate—as restaurant interns or employees, as customers, or in my case as participant-observer and interviewer. Furthermore, Kyoto's "local" foods incorporate foreign ingredients or techniques, as in Kamo eggplant jam and Shōgoin turnip with Parmesan cheese. Even the chefs who consider it their mission to safeguard local gastronomic heritage possess an understanding of Kyō ryōri that allows for flexibility and interpretation. In their study group meetings, I have heard these chefs discuss the lessons that various French, Italian, and Chinese cooking techniques hold for Kyō ryōri, which they wish to see evolve without losing its authenticity.

This incorporation of foreign ingredients into cooking that is viewed as "traditional" is true of household chefs as well. A group of Kyoto ladies whose website is dedicated to sharing advice on traditional living in Kyoto has one especially surprising recipe in their collection of obanzai home-cooking recipes: yogurt with raisins soaked in wine (Kyō no Machiya Kurashi no Ishō Kaigi 2010a). These women readily admit that the ingredients involved are not traditional in and of themselves. Why, then, is this recipe posted in the section for obanzai cuisine? For these ladies what is traditional is the way of thinking about everyday cooking, combining readily available ingredients in a manner that results in a practical, healthy, and delicious dish (Kyō no Machiya Kurashi no Ishō Kaigi 2010b).[9] According to them, it is perfectly feasible to create a "traditional" and "local" dish from ingredients that are modern additions to the Japanese diet. Such attitudes toward people, things, and ideas from outside illustrate that the efforts of actors in Kyoto to protect and strengthen local food culture are more akin to the "diversity-embracing" localism Hinrichs describes than the defensive variety. Locality—including both "place" and the "local"—has an affective dimension that can be deployed effectively in calls to action. This may in part explain why many food movements engage in the discourse of the local, although—as Laura DeLind (2006) argues—they may not be very grounded in any place at all.

The "local" in local food movements may be in danger of being appropriated or disappearing and becoming meaningless if the "local somewhere" trend the Food Channel identified develops further. Although the local may be impossible to pin down because it lacks scalar or geographic specificity, places like Champagne, Brooklyn, or Kyoto seem to offer refuge from ambiguity because they appear to be specific, singular entities. Harvey thus argues that "the elaboration of place-bound identities has become more rather than less important in a world of diminishing spatial barriers to exchange, movement and communication." In fact, he goes so far as to profess that "territorial place-based identity...is one of the most pervasive bases for both progressive political mobilization and reactionary exclusionary politics" (1993: 4).

The successes and failures of Kyoto's food movement are inextricably linked to the key role that Kyoto—as a site, setting, and "sense of place"—has played in the movement's evolution. When the local food movement was born, the vision of Kyoto's chefs and farmers was to inspire other movements to revive traditional vegetables all over Japan. This happened to a limited extent, as indicated by the emergence of brands like those for Kaga vegetables (Kanagawa Prefecture) and Naniwa traditional vegetables (Osaka Prefecture). Some of the farmers and chefs I interviewed, however, expressed disappointment that Japanese consumers have taken the message to be that

Kyoto vegetables are special and delicious, which has led those in other parts of Japan to overlook heirloom varieties closer to home. In other words, the result is open to the same criticism that Jeff Pratt applies to the Slow Food movement for contributing to the formation of a "patchwork of specialties" rather than a localized food system (2007: 292). When I surveyed the shelves of several grocery stores in Morioka City, Iwate Prefecture, I located one heirloom variety hailing from Iwate in a shopping mall's specialty grocery store, and many kinds of Kyō Brand vegetables in the grocery section of an upscale department store. Visiting a department store in Sendai, Miyagi Prefecture, I found several local varieties and a small section dedicated to an assortment of Kyoto vegetables, which recalled one chef's words: "A Tokyo supermarket should have a Tokyo vegetable corner before it organizes one for Kyoto vegetables."

Kyoto may thus offer more specificity than the term *local*, but it is also not without problems. One farmer told me the movement to revive Kyoto vegetables was problematic from the start due to its focus on the "Kyō" in kyō yasai. He wishes more people would understand that because places experience their own seasons on their own time, what is seasonal in one place is not what is most suited to people who live in another, distant place. He mused about whether the terms *jiyasai* (local vegetables) and *jimoto ni au yasai* (vegetables that fit/belong locally) might not have been more appropriate to the movement.

In an interdependent and interconnected world what one eats, how one eats it, and how much one pays for food are influenced by actors and events across the globe, making it critical to examine how food activists situate themselves. Some movements may define themselves in terms of ethical issues or political agendas that operate transnationally, while others hone in on smaller, more defined communities. Ethnographic accounts of social movements can widen our understanding of the ways societies seek to address contemporary problems.

Kyoto's food activism has been apolitical, culture oriented, led by elites, and focused on both Kyoto City and Kyoto Prefecture. Activists employed narrowly targeted, pragmatic, and incremental strategies for engendering change. As Neva Hassanein (2003) has argued, such movements have genuine transformative potential and should not be summarily dismissed as unambitious attempts to achieve negligible goals. The successes of movements like the one described in this chapter impact people's lives in tangible ways. Kyoto's food activism reinvigorated the local agricultural and culinary traditions, bolstered the local food system, and has what can be glossed as political repercussions. In the end, whatever the disappointments and setbacks, keeping "Kyoto" grounded in the face of the "local somewhere" phenomenon is no small feat.

Acknowledgements

I would like to thank Richard Scaglion, Chelsea Wentworth, and Ieva Tretjuka for insightful comments on early drafts. Thank you also to Carole Counihan and Valeria Siniscalchi for their peerless editorial work.

Notes

1. One hundred ares is equal to one hectare (approximately 2.5 acres).
2. I have either omitted or replaced the names of most farmers and chefs with pseudonyms to preserve anonymity. The only full names that appear are those of individuals who were active leaders of the movement in the public eye and whose names appear in archival documents.
3. The Mebaekai was one of several groups active at the time. I focus on it because its efforts were well documented, its influence obvious, and its leaders approachable.
4. The list includes thirty-seven varieties, including two that are extinct, with three additional varieties listed as subtraditional.
5. This was true even before the radiation leaks at the Fukushima Daiichi Nuclear Power Plant in the towns of Okuma and Futaba, Fukushima Prefecture, which led to consumer fears of radioactivity in produce from northern and eastern Japan.
6. See, for instance, Miyako no Ippin Kyōyasai, Kyoto Prefecture Department of Agriculture, Forestry, and Fisheries, Research and Brand Promotion Division, http://www.pref.kyoto.jp/brand/11700078.html (last accessed July 12, 2013).
7. This is a pseudonym.
8. For more on this, including criticism of the movement's failures, see Hirata Kimura and Nishiyama 2008.
9. Personal communication with Kinoshita Yuka, webmaster for the Kyō no Machiya group.

References

Agnew, J. (2005), "Space: Place," in P. J. Cloke and R. J. Johnston (eds.), *Spaces of Geographical Thought: Deconstructing Human Geography's Binaries*, London: Sage, 81–96.

Basso, K. H. (1996), *Wisdom Sits in Places: Landscape and Language among the Western Apache*, Albuquerque: University of New Mexico Press.

Brand Research Institute. (2010), "Chiiki Burando Chōsa 2010' Chōsa Kekka: Motto Mo Miryokutekina Shikuchōson ni Sapporoshi ga Kaerizaki! Todōfuken de ha Hokkaido ga 2 Nen Renzoku," http://tiiki.jp/corp_new/pressrelease/2010/20100908.html, accessed July 14, 2013.

Brumann, C. (2009), "Outside the Glass Case: The Social Life of Urban Heritage in Kyoto," *American Ethnologist*, 36/2: 276–299.

Brumann, C. (2012), *Tradition, Democracy and the Townscape of Kyoto: Claiming a Right to the Past*, New York: Routledge.

Buechler, S. (2000), *Social Movements in Advanced Capitalism: The Political Economy and Cultural Construction of Social Activism*, New York: Oxford University Press.

Caldwell, M. L., and Lozada, E. P., Jr. (2007), "The Fate of the Local," in G. Ritzer (ed.), *The Blackwell Companion to Globalization*, Malden, MA: Blackwell, 498–515.

Central Intelligence Agency. (2013), *World Factbook: Japan,* https://www.cia.gov/library/publications/the-world-factbook/geos/ja.html, accessed July 14, 2013.

DeLind, L. (2006), "Of Bodies, Place, and Culture: Re-situating Local Food," *Journal of Agricultural and Environmental Ethics,* 19/2: 121–146.

de St. Maurice, G. (2012), "Savoring Kyoto: Sensory Fieldwork on the Taste of Place," *Etnofoor,* 24/2: 107–122.

Food Channel. (2010), "#3 Food Trend for 2011: Local Somewhere," Food Channel [online article], http://www.foodchannel.com/articles/article/3-food-trend-2011-local-somewhere/, accessed December 12, 2010.

Foucault, M. (1980), *Power/Knowledge: Selected Interviews and Other Writings, 1972–1977,* ed. and trans. C. Gordon, New York: Pantheon.

Gramsci, A. (1971), *Selections from the Prison Notebooks of Antonio Gramsci,* ed. and trans. Q. Hoare and G. Nowell-Smith, New York: International.

Harvey, D. (1993), "From Space to Place and Back Again: Reflections on the Condition of Postmodernity," in J. Bird, B. Curtis, T. Putnam, G. Robertson, and L. Tickner (eds.), *Mapping the Futures: Local Cultures, Global Change,* London: Routledge, 3–29.

Hassanein, N. (2003), "Practicing Food Democracy: A Pragmatic Politics of Transformation," *Journal of Rural Studies,* 19: 77–86.

Hinrichs, C. C. (2003), "The Practice and Politics of Food System Localization," *Journal of Rural Studies,* 19: 33–45.

Hirata Kimura, A., and Nishiyama, M. (2008), "The *Chisan-Chisho* Movement: Japanese Local Food Movement and Its Challenges," *Agriculture and Human Values,* 25: 49–64.

Hosking, R. (1996), *A Dictionary of Japanese Food: Ingredients and Culture,* Rutland, VT: Charles E. Tuttle.

Ishige, N. (2012), *L'art Culinaire Au Japon,* Paris: Lucie Editions.

Kinki Regional Agricultural Administration Office. (2006), "Kinki Nōgyō No Gaiyō." Kinki Region: Kinki Regional Agricultural Administration Office.

Kyō no Furusato Sanpin Kyōkai. (2010), *Burando Suishin Jigyō 20 Nen No Ayumi.* Kyoto City: Kyō no Furusato Sanpin Kyōkai.

Kyō no Machiya Kurashi no Ishō Kaigi. (2010a). "Hoshibudō no Akawainzuke," http://www.kyo-kurashi.com/obanzai/recipe/vege135.html, accessed April 27, 2010.

Kyō no Machiya Kurashi no Ishō Kaigi. (2010b). "Kyoto no Obanzai ni tsuite," www.kyo-kurashi.com/obanzai/policy/, accessed April 27, 2010.

Kyoto City Industry and Tourism Bureau. (2010), "Kyōtoshi no Shuyō Keizai Shihyō," http://www.city.kyoto.lg.jp/sankan/cmsfiles/contents/0000126/126744/13.pdf, accessed July 13, 2013.

Kyoto Prefectural Agricultural Research Institute. (2007), "Kyōtofu Nōgyō Sōgō Kenkyūjo Shiken Kenkyū Seiseki Hōkokukai Hōkoku Yōshi." Kameoka City, Kyoto Prefecture: Kyoto Prefectural Agricultural Research Institute.

McKinley, L. (2010), Yes to Polenta, No to Couscous! Constructed Identities and Contested Boundaries between Local and Global in Northern Italy's Gastronomic

Landscape. Bachelor's honors thesis, Henry M. Jackson School of International Studies at the University of Washington, https://digital.lib.washington.edu/researchworks/bitstream/handle/1773/15916/lucas%20mckinley.pdf?sequence=1, accessed October 23, 2012.

Ministry of Agriculture, Forestry, and Fisheries. (2005), "2005 Nen Nōrinsuishansho Sensasu Nōrin Eigyōtai Chōsa Zenkoku Todōfuken Betsu Ichiranhyō," Tokyo: Ministry of Agriculture, Forestry, and Fisheries.

Ministry of Agriculture, Forestry, and Fisheries. (2012), "Heisei 22 Nendo (Gaisanne) Heisei 21 Nendo (Kakuteine) no Todōfuken Betsu Shokuryō Jikyūritsu," Tokyo: Ministry of Internal Affairs and Communications, Statistics Bureau.

Ministry of Internal Affairs and Communications, Statistics Bureau. (2010), *Statistical Handbook of Japan 2010.* Tokyo: Ministry of Internal Affairs and Communications, Statistics Bureau.

Ministry of Internal Affairs and Communications, Statistics Bureau. (2012), *Nihon no Tōkei 2012.* Tokyo: Ministry of Internal Affairs and Communications, Statistics Bureau.

Mittelman, J. H., and Chin, C. (2000), "Conceptualizing Resistance to Globalization," in J. H. Mittelman (ed.), *The Globalization Syndrome,* Princeton, NJ: Princeton University Press, 165–178.

Mulgan, A. G. (2012), "Interview by Laura Araki for the National Bureau of Asian Research. 21 June 2012," http: http://www.nbr.org/research/activity.aspx?id=257#.Ubx9jPahJ_w, accessed August 15, 2012.

Murray, W. E. (2006), *Geographies of Globalization,* London: Routledge.

Nikkei Marketing Journal. (1987), *Kyō Yasai Fukkatsu He Tenjikai, Ryōriten Wakate Keieisha Ga Kessoku,* (December 3), 13.

Nikkei Research. (2011), "2010 Chiiki Burando Sa-bei." Tokyo: Nikkei Research.

Nishiyama, M., and Hirata Kimura, A. (2005), "Alternative Agro-food Movement in Contemporary Japan," *Technical Bulletin for the Faculty of Horticulture of Chiba University,* 59: 85–96.

Pempel, T. J. (1998), *Regime Shift,* Ithaca, NY: Cornell University Press.

Polanyi, K. (1975), *The Great Transformation,* New York: Octagon.

Pratt, J. (2007), "Food Values: The Local and the Authentic," *Critique of Anthropology,* 27/3: 285–300.

Rath, E. C. (2010), *Food and Fantasy in Early Modern Japan,* Berkeley: University of California Press.

Rosenberger, N. (2009), "Global Food Terror in Japan: Media Shaping Risk Perception, the Nation, and Women," *Ecology of Food and Nutrition,* 48: 237–262.

Takashima, S. (2003), *Kyō no Dentō Yasai to Shun Yasai,* Osaka: Tombo.

Todaro, M. P., and Smith, S. C. (2003), *Economic Development,* Boston: Addison Wesley.

Tuan, Y.-F. (1977), *Space and Place: The Perspective of Experience,* Minneapolis: University of Minnesota Press.

Yomiuri Shimbun. (1989), *Kyō Yasai ni Kyakkō Kamo Nasu ya Mizuna… Usuaji de Satto Niru Honrai no Umami wo Taisetsu ni,* September 10: 14.

Part III

National Actions

7

French Biodynamic Viticulture:
Militancy or Market Niche?

Marie-France Garcia-Parpet

Social scientists working on food movements have mainly focused on the actions of consumers appearing on the political stage and using the way they consume to demonstrate their approval or disapproval of production ethics (Dubuisson-Quellier and Lamine 2004; Guthman 2008; Lamine 2008b; Siniscalchi 2013; Vidal 2011). The few authors who have studied the actions of producers emphasize the fact that the creation of voluntary standards has proven to be more of a marketing strategy to develop market niches than a way of promoting sustainable development and/or social justice (Potoski and Prakash 2005). The case of French organic and biodynamic wine production shows that there can be diverse motivations for promoting sustainable development, depending on the historical context and the possibility that these motivations can coexist. In this chapter I examine the standpoints and sociological profile of winegrowers who act in accordance with ethical values to change the agricultural system and I also consider the way in which they combine economic rationality with their ideological goals.

First, I look at how wine production became institutionalized in France. Under the cover of an image of "traditional" methods, French winegrowers have become major consumers of chemical products—even more so than the rest of the agricultural industry. I then examine how a certain number of winegrowers opposed this dominant model and adopted practices that are better for the environment and more independent of the institutions that govern this production. I explain how and why biodynamic producers, with their radical practices and vision of the world, who were once more stigmatized than organic producers, are today more successful in the context of market globalization that is calling the *appellation d'origine contrôlée* (AOC) model into question.[1]

For this chapter, I interviewed approximately thirty producers using biodynamic or organic methods between 1996 and 2011. These interviews build on earlier ones conducted with conventional producers for a book on transformations in French winemaking in the face of globalization (Garcia-Parpet 2009). During this period of field research, I was able to visit vineyards and observe cultivation practices and marketing methods, as well as conduct analyses of some producer websites.

AOCs and *Terroir*: A Traditional Production?

In France the 1935 viticulture legislation worked in favor of an artisanal production model and a natural conception of wine that opposed industrial winemaking, creating the AOCs. This was the label designating quality agricultural products tied to geographic zones which respect the specificities of the *terroir* (a term that denotes both the properties of the soil itself and the local winegrowing traditions).[2] The Institut National Appellation d'Origine (The National Institute of Designation of Origins) is the certifying organism under the French Ministry of Agriculture. The use of synthetic chemical products to fight cryptogamic diseases and insect attacks, which had grown significantly since the 1960s, was not covered in the 1935 legislation. Even while stressing the use of tradition as a source of specificity and nobility, wine producers in AOC zones adopted production methods using high doses of chemical products.

During the 1970s the majority of mixed-crop farms switched to single crops, and winegrowers who resisted this trend were marginalized by most consumers, who did not buy their wines, and by professional organizations, which did not elect them as representatives. At the same time, winegrowers were increasingly turning to enologists to manage their vineyards and perform their vinification, something that was often given a positive slant in the enological guides that came into general use in the 1980s.[3] In addition to the sulfur traditionally found in vinification, synthetic products were used to preserve the wines, with chemical yeasts adding flavors. The sale of wine, which had previously been one component of family income, along with cereals and/or livestock, became vital to the successful operation of the business, and the use of chemical products became even more popular in that it significantly reduced the labor required and helped to secure the harvest. Winegrowers began valorizing their production by doing their own bottling and direct selling. They wanted to be part of a prestigious and distinct competition, building an aristocratic image of their wines, adopting a wine estate name or even a *château* name,[4] valorizing the number of generations that their vineyards had existed, and thus breaking away from the peasant-farmer identity that had inspired the policies of the Third Republic. Vineyards introduced tasting rooms for visitors, set up displays to demonstrate their traditions and reputation, and systematically listed awards and provided press releases about their production.

Production That Went against Current Trends

During the 1970s some winegrowers and farmers decided to ignore the prevailing trend of the technical, economic, and symbolic construction of their profession and to run their vineyards in a completely different manner. These growers rejected the dominant mode of farming for a variety of reasons. One was in response to health problems caused by chemical products and their dangers for the environment. Another was the rejection of the domination of the profession by the bureaucracy of the Institut National des Appellations d'Origine. Most of these winegrowers who adopted organic or biodynamic methods first joined the Lemaire & Boucher or Nature et Progrès movements and, later on, Rudolf Steiner's biodynamic movement.[5] They met and were inspired by small groups of followers of Steiner or by personal reading: the Maison de l'Agriculture Bio-dynamique had a bookshop and its own publications of the works of the master and his disciples, along with practical guides. From these writings, winegrowers gleaned both ethical principles and practical advice that affected how they ran their vineyards.

While organic producers really differ from conventional growers only in that they do not use chemicals, biodynamic practices are embedded in a vision of the world inspired by Steiner, in which the evolution of nature is an integral part of the evolution of the cosmos. Biodynamic farmers adopted a calendar that indicated propitious dates for planting and for treatments to overcome the degeneration of the soil, in relation to their plant life cycles and those of the stars; they also used preparations made from plants, silica, and cow dung used in homeopathic doses, diluted in water (energized), and sprayed throughout the vineyards. The winegrowers focused on vine growing and care for the soil; vinification was secondary, with grape quality defined as the essential element governing wine quality. This way of working was in total opposition to the increasing importance of enology in France and abroad, which made it possible, within the boundaries of existing legislation, to correct any "defects" of a wine during the vinification process. Biodynamic winegrowers focused on the vicissitudes of the farming cycle and on the quality of the soil. They worked their fields (a practice almost entirely abandoned in conventional winegrowing due to the use of weed killers) and partially replaced machines with manual work and with draft horses.

Biodynamic winegrowers have revalorized the mixed-crop practices so characteristic of peasant farmers. Many of them breed cows and smaller farmyard animals and have one or more draft horses for working in the vineyards; in addition, they may also grow wheat, make their own bread, and have a vegetable garden. For researchers who are used to visiting vineyards that practice so-called conventional winegrowing, biodynamic establishments are something of a surprise, with courtyards having an unkempt appearance, filled with weeds and machinery.

Adepts of organic farming were generally seen by most consumers and producers as "dropouts" or as backward members of France's "generation of '68." Farmers who used biodynamic methods were marginalized even further. Among other things, biodynamic growers' use of cow dung stored in a cow's horn and buried for a period of time in order to "reenergize" it shocked people by its irrationality. A winegrower from the Champagne region who adopted this method explained how when his colleagues saw him heading into his vineyards, they would say, "There goes the druid again, off to tend his vines." The biodynamic winegrowers' negative attitude toward the scientific and economic institutions that dominated the farming industry, and their perception of the products of science as a source of death rather than of progress, led to them being rejected by the majority of farmers, who considered them members of a sect and unsuitable representatives of professional organizations. The creation of their own networks among biodynamic winemakers thus became crucial to the marketing of their wines. One of the pioneers of biodynamic farming in relation to winegrowing wrote in the preface to his book (Bouchet 2003) that during his first meeting with farmers who used this method, he believed them to be "somewhat deranged." Nowadays, although there are only a few such producers producing over a small area,[6] the quality of their wine is highly valued.

The peasant-farmer identity is frequently brought to the fore by biodynamic winegrowers, be it during conversations, on advertising brochures, or in books aimed at the public. For example, the film *L'esprit du vin, le réveil des terroirs (The Spirit of Wine: "The Re-Awakening of Local Traditions")*, made by Bordeaux winegrowers (Minvielle and Minvielle 2011), features a photo of the wife of the owner of Coulée de Serrant, the leading biodynamic vineyard, which has about 49.421 acres of vines, a well-known appellation, and a small *château.* The legend under the photo reads: "Coralie Joly, peasant." The film is intended as a defense of terroirs through biodynamics, showing how these methods have gained recognition with regard to sustainable development and gustatory excellence. There are interviews with biodynamic producers, personalities from the world of gastronomy, and academics. It is a militant film, judging by the debates raging in professional, ministerial, and parliamentary circles regarding the future of AOCs.

Marc Angeli, another Val de Loire producer who is at the forefront of the biodynamic movement, rejects any use of the wine estate's name in the presentation of his vineyard, preferring to refer to it as a "farm" on his advertising brochures and listing his non-winemaking activities—flour production and poultry raising. While it is out of the question for the majority of wine estates with highly renowned vines to convert part of their vineyards into farmland or grazing pastures, we did find three that had gone into partnership with livestock farms in order to recreate a complementarity between the different products.

Instead of methods dictated by science and directed at ad hoc problems (diseases or insects), biodynamic producers tend to prefer observation and comparison, in an attempt to develop a vision of overall balance. They also demand independence from synthetic products, believing that they can find most of the inputs they need in nature itself. Practically speaking, not having suitable products at hand, or not having the time to gather and prepare them, a fair proportion of these producers buy their products from distributors specializing in such preparations. They heap varying degrees of scathing criticism on "classic" schools of agriculture for being "bringers of death"[7] or acting as "marketers for the phytosanitary industry" (Joly 2007: 36), and they are reluctant to heed the advice of "overpaid bureaucrats," chambers of agriculture, or the French National Institute for Agriculture Research, preferring to trust their intuition rather than rely on logical reasoning. They rely on their colleagues who have used the same methods, and they use private consultants outside of official teaching and research organizations. Their relationship with these people is not one of submission to a relatively benevolent authority[8] but rather a business relationship where there are shared beliefs with mutual respect or even admiration. They also attend courses in biodynamic farming offered by the Maison de l'Agriculture Bio-dynamique or by the Syndicat International des Vignerons en culture bio-dynamique (International Union of Winegrowers in Biodynamic) and by the École du Vin et des Terroirs (Wine and Terroirs School) recently created in Burgundy. A market for biodynamic training and consultancy has thus developed, along with a market for specific preparations.

In addition to being an alternative technique, biodynamics serves to assert the possession of knowledge and the autonomy of thought. An Alsace biodynamic wine-grower voiced a widely shared opinion: "We are not underlings, we don't apply what other people have discovered, we are involved, we can experiment, we ask ourselves questions. There's no magic formula…that makes farmers autonomous and we are autonomous.… Biodynamics allow people to evolve; it's not just the land and crops which will change, but you yourself, you'll ask yourself questions, you'll meet other people." This spirit of independence which is part of this kind of farming is also a source of critical thinking regarding new technologies (genetically modified organisms [GMOs], nanotechnology, nuclear energy, etc.) and the environment, and leads biodynamic producers toward diverse militant networks and causes, turning some of them into activists. For some winegrowers who adopted these methods during the twentieth century, this critical perception of the world simply leads to a way of life that integrates these "alternative" values. Some of them even hesitated a long time before announcing their use of biodynamic methods that their customers might have felt to be compromising. "It took us ten years to put it on the label; it's discreet, we didn't do it to attract new customers," explains a Val de Loire winegrower who has taken over his father's vineyard and is determined not to lose the hard-won cli-entele of an appellation that still remains relatively unknown in wine's social hierar-chy. One winegrower from the Champagne region, who comes from a milieu where organic farming was the byword, did not anticipate any negative reaction from con-sumers; when he first went to the marketplace, he proudly declared his biodynamic production methods and caused consumers to flee to the other side of the road so as not to have to walk past his stand, terrified by the presence of what they considered to be a sect. This experience led him to rely solely on the quality of his wines (which he asserts to be superior) rather than on their biodynamic production to make sales.

Other winegrowers mark their difference from the norm by focusing on their personal relations with visitors and potential customers, spending as much time as needed to explain their methods and way of life, and to criticize the viticulture recommended by the AOCs. Such is the case of a man with a "generation of '68" ponytail, the son of an engineer, who sailed around the world before taking over his grandfather's vineyard in the Val de Loire. He set aside the "traditional" presentation of the estate on the Internet. He does not display press cuttings and the flattering classifications of wine critics, preferring to provide a fuss-free personal welcome, inviting us to visit his vineyards, to see how the draft horses are used and the benefits for the soil, and to discover the farmyard animals and sheep. At the picnic organized for my visit, we were joined by the estate's workers, a journalist, and a couple of winegrowers looking for information on techniques for working with draft horses. Punctuating the visit and demonstrating a different frame of reference were extensive commentaries on the techniques used in relation to the state of the soil and the vines, scorn heaped on the AOC bureaucracy and enology, and comments on the attitude of his neighbors—conventional winemakers who over recent decades have adopted sophisticated machinery.

Others have traded their tasting-room exhibitions of awards and press cuttings for provocative documents concerning the established standards of excellence: a violent criticism of conventional winemaking and a call for a society that is more concerned about nature and more socially inclusive (rewarding small farms). This is the case for an Anjou winegrower from the south of France, with a degree in chemistry, who presents his wines in a brochure entitled "The Wrath of Grapes," combining descriptions of his wines and methods with criticisms of conventional viticulture. For some winemakers, taking a stance and participating in public debates on winegrowing and environmental issues and on inequalities between the Northern and Southern Hemispheres constitutes the logical conclusion of the invitation to think for oneself that is found in Steiner's work, leading some winegrowers to become activists.

The search for products in harmony with nature undermines the rigidity of the conception of typical characteristics laid down by the Institut National des Appellations d'Origine. Wines produced using indigenous yeasts, little sulfite, no chaptalization (the adding of sugar), and no artificial fertilizers (thus with a far lower yield than conventional wines) do not have the same taste. They are often refused the AOC label, which is awarded by a jury composed of conventional winegrowers: this makes them harder to sell and deprives them of the higher awards that take the appellation into account when making comparisons (the Mâcon award, the Vignerons Indépendants award), because the winning wine must "represent" the appellation.

"Militant Commercialization" Methods

How can winegrowers live from their work, that is, sell their wines, in a context where production and producers would appear to be in conflict with established norms? In wine regions where there are fine-wine merchants, it is possible to sell one's wines when demand is high, but biodynamic production does not procure any added value to pay for the extra work and the risks. It is therefore easy to see the importance of the networks established by producers to extend their contacts and sell their stock.

Their militancy is two-pronged, and their strategies help to develop commercial networks and media awareness that benefit their causes and enhance the reputation of the winegrowers. Does this simply serve to challenge the dominant models, or does it bring together individuals with similar views, thus constituting a potential demand for these "unconventional" products? The press, with its tendency to sensationalism (Champagne 1991), has become a precious promotional force and helps to compensate for these growers' exclusion from the more conservative institution of awards given in accordance with AOC values. One Alsace winemaker who had contributed to the institutionalization of *grand crus*[9] in the Alsace region mentioned the press's interest in nontraditional biodynamic methods of production. Another producer from the same region said that his methods and stances on environmental issues had attracted media attention and that his more traditional colleagues were furious to see "heretics" being courted more than other winegrowers. While in the tasting rooms of conventional winegrowers visitors might find leaflets with information on local tourist sites, several of the biodynamic producers we interviewed exhibit publications that challenge not only conventional viticulture but also nuclear energy and animal exploitation, along with others promoting an ethical, socially inclusive ecological heritage. The producers' Internet sites also constitute a popular way of presenting wines and draw consumer attention to the debate on the dangers of pesticides.

The creation of the Alsace Eco-Bio Fair in Rouffach, which began in 1982 to bring together producers of organic products (bread, cheese, and wine) from France, Germany, and Switzerland, is another example of the ambivalent nature of the economic and political institutions put in place by these supporters of a different environmental and economic regulation. At its head is Pierre Frick, a biodynamic producer who belongs to the peasant confederation and is a regional adviser for the French Green Party; he has a strong personality and a talent for rallying people to a cause. Determined to find an outlet for these little-known products, and backed by a group of producers who shared his ideas, he had the idea of creating a fair where organic producers could exhibit their products and save themselves from marginality and anonymity. While remaining a festive event, the fair has enabled producers to valorize their products by allowing visitors to taste them and by holding annual conferences to inform both them and winegrowers from other regions. Making the most of his contacts as former regional chairman of the Lemaire & Boucher association, this winemaker has turned the fair into a national producer network that promotes the organic sector and the militant vocation of the producers. Conferences and debates on nuclear issues, GMOs, and the North-South relationship bring together well-known speakers and cover burning issues.

Organic Wine: "Good Business"

Since the 1990s we have seen changes in both producers' and consumers' perceptions of organic and biodynamic production methods, making them "good business."

Following the mad cow crisis and increasing concern for the environment, people are paying more attention to product quality and the production process. The consumption of organic foodstuffs has developed just as much through personal relations and associations for the preservation of peasant farming (Association pour le maintien de l'agriculture paysanne, AMAP)[10] (Dubuisson-Quellier and Lamine 2004; Lamine 2008a, 2008b; Oudraougo 1998) as through the increasing number of specialist shops and chains (Biocoop, Naturalia, Bio-génération) and large-scale retailers (Sylvander 2000). The subsidies granted by public authorities to organic farming from 1998 on have contributed toward its legitimization and, by extension, to that of biodynamics. The consumption of organic products has seen spectacular growth, even attracting major food companies looking for guaranteed profits as well as multinationals in the organic product certification market (Baqué 2011; Garcia-Parpet 2012). The organic wine sector has become one of the most dynamic agricultural sectors in France. Its growth accelerated at the turn of the century, especially from 2006, with an annual growth of 20 percent, reaching a record 30 percent in 2009.[11] This staggering growth in the number of producers went hand in hand with a change in the sociological profile of new growers. Up until the 1980s, organic and biodynamic winemakers were essentially neorurals from France and elsewhere; they were producers who were generally better known for their attachment to these methods than for their reputation in the world of wine. Since the 1990s a relatively important number of producers from well-known appellations making *grands crus,* notably in Burgundy and Alsace, declared themselves to be part of the organic and above all biodynamic sector. In 1993 "Millésime bio," the first international exhibition for organic wine professionals and amateurs, occurred in Montpellier, followed by a large number of smaller local and regional exhibitions. More recently, with organic products becoming an attractive niche, traditional exhibitions have opened their doors to these avant-garde winegrowers, in contrast to the reluctance demonstrated by exhibition organizers a few years previously. On February 4, 2011, an article in *Le Monde* newspaper entitled "Du vin de pays aux grands crus, la viticulture bio séduit de plus en plus de producteurs et de consommateurs" (From Country Wines to *Grands Crus,* Organic Viticulture Wins over an Increasing Number of Winegrowers and Consumers)[12] mentioned the very high score given by Robert Parker, the most famous of wine critics, to an organic winemaker in Anjou. This demonstrated a new recognition of the quality of organic wines.

A number of organic winemaker associations have emerged since the 1990s to introduce and gain recognition for vinification specifications and/or to promote wines among professionals and consumers. In 1998 the Fédération Nationale Interprofessionnelle des Vins de l'Agriculture Biologique (National Interprofessional Federation of Organic Wines) was created. With fifty or so members, including producers and merchants spread unevenly throughout the winegrowing regions, it has set itself the task of achieving official recognition for the concept of "organic wine" in Europe. Faced with the impossibility of regulating the manufacture of wine, these winemakers and merchants have mobilized to develop a private law charter that sets out the rules for vinification, aging, and processing, excluding in particular the overuse of sulfites and other products used to stabilize wines, as well as the use of GMOs. Other smaller associations have also emerged. The Association des Vins Naturels (Association for Natural Wines) was created by a group of friends who met one another through the Paris wine bars they supply; they defend organic growing and the reduction or banning of chemicals in vinification. The year 2008 saw the creation of the *Ceps et charrue, l'association des vignerons bios du Beaujolais* ("vine and plows, the Beaujolais organic growers association"), bringing together organic winegrowers of the Beaujolais region to promote their wines. There is also the Couleur Bio association, a group of eight producers from the Entre-Deux-Mers region, working together to market their wines.

But the "organizations" (*groupements* in French) that have been created around biodynamics are "the most successful" movements (the expression used by one of the protagonists); members of these organizations have many well-known wine estates that attract winemakers and consumers, and according to certain producers I interviewed, they are so successful that many of them want to be biodynamic more than they want to be organic (the prerequisite for becoming biodynamic).

In 1996 the Syndicat International des Vignerons en culture bio-dynamique was created, which in turn created the Biodyvin label, more distinctive than the organic label because of the reputation of its members: a dozen owners of well-known wine estates in the Alsace, Burgundy, Val de Loire, and Bordeaux regions who had converted to biodynamics after learning about its beneficial effects on soil and grape quality from a biodynamics adviser and who met one another through him. These new followers rewarded the technical aspect of biodynamics rather than the philosophical one. The idea was to work together to distribute the method, to discuss techniques, to provide customers with traceability for practices (the label is certified by Ecocert, the certifying organization with the greatest level of legitimacy regarding care for the environment), and to promote their wines, particularly by organizing tastings for both amateurs and professionals—a practice that one of them had started back in the 1980s and that had proven to be very effective.

According to the Alsace winegrower who started this movement, these producers were "doing advanced research, looking to take things a step further, but not in terms of philosophy." He himself, when he considered that he was making no technical progress, had talked to geologists in order to understand the differences in taste. "We were looking, but we kept hitting a dead end, there was something missing." A Burgundy winemaker who had offered him a wine tasting put him in touch with a biodynamics consultant.

I did some tests on a hectare of land, and the following year I converted my entire vineyard to biodynamics. I did the preparations just any old how. It's only afterwards that I started to think about it. At first, I read Steiner and found it impossible to understand. The creators of Biodyvin are not followers of Steiner, their mindset is more to do with the continuity of the family estates. The anthroposophical philosophy came about because there were concerns, you take care with the soil, with the products, you want a wine that will benefit human beings...these people are not anthroposophists.

Another winemaker who is a member of the Syndicat International des Vignerons en culture bio-dynamique and who returned to the family estate with his partner, explained how he became involved in biodynamics:

> I remembered methods from the old days, from the past, it was a very emotional thing. My "dear neighbors" were using phito products and I wondered why they were doing that. While I was looking for people to talk to, I came across the Renaissance des Appellations[13] association and discovered biodynamics. At first, I thought it was all a bit crazy, but it's a sort of management of the heritage of practices, re-thought, re-theorized—it's also a treatise on good practices, but I don't like that term.

Members of the union of biodynamic viniculture considered the biodynamic farmers' union (Demeter) brand to be very sectarian and took these winegrowers to be rich men. "We were the black sheep of biodynamics and the membership fees were very expensive for winemakers and Demeter didn't accept single-crop production," said one of the Syndicat International des Vignerons en culture bio-dynamique founders. "At the time, people were anthroposophical, they said they practiced biodynamics, they didn't make any preparations." So it was practicality that drew these wine estate owners into biodynamics: "it was the only solution." This did not prevent them from immediately displaying biodynamics alongside the "history of the estate," "press articles," and "the estate's wines" on the front page of their Internet sites, in a section titled "Biodynamics" or "The Spirit of the Estate." If Steiner's name was used, it was in relation to the method and principle he had defined (preparations, calendar, etc.) and "the biodynamic winemaker's purpose, through the growing of vines, is to produce high-quality wine with its own specific characteristics created by the unique quality and traditions of each individual estate. The wine will be the result of this, because the local qualities and traditions will be respected."[14] These methods of production proved to be even more attractive because they were valorized by demand from abroad, Japan in particular, at a time when competition from so-called New World countries was in full swing and was undermining the French producers who had for so long dominated the market.[15]

The quality of the members has meant that membership in the union has become a mark of prestige, with excellent opportunities for selling wine. "They organize wonderful promotional events and they have all the right people...like the Renaissance des Appellations association, and what I like, is both the serious nature of biodynamics, the serious-mindedness of the producers...there are a lot of good wine estates and I like that," said one winegrower with a small appellation from the Val de Loire. A real commercial success is encouraging a large number of producers to adopt biodynamic methods and thus benefit from the market opening created by recent globalization and the receptiveness of foreign countries.

From "Organic Wine" to the "Full Expression of AOC Wines"

At the turn of the twenty-first century, another biodynamic association saw the light of day: La Renaissance des Appellations. Most of the members of this group have a solid reputation in the world of wine, and many of them belong to prestigious appellations such as Burgundy and Alsace, producing *grands crus* and/or holding leading positions in movements fighting for sustainable development.[16] As a biodynamics specialist pointed out, while the group does organize a certain number of meetings with a technical bent, it wants to be and is considered a "club where winemakers come together to market" their produce. Of course, environmental concerns have not been forgotten, but the solid communication skills of the leaders have made it possible to transform these methods—which had previously been considered esoteric—into politically correct practices. It is headed by the son of a surgeon who owns an estate in another well-known appellation in the Val de Loire. Nicolas Joly, a man with a great deal of charisma and an MBA from Columbia University, had first worked in finance before returning to a family estate that was losing money. The property is a former monastery, listed among France's "historical monuments"; it is surrounded by a vineyard constituted by an appellation that bears the name of Joly's wine estate and that currently enjoys an excellent reputation among French and foreign wine critics.[17] He told us how, when he took over the estate, he had been surprised by the extent to which the use of weed killers had caused soil erosion throughout the property, and by the scarcity of the birds that filled his boyhood memories; he talked about how he had returned to traditional methods and adopted biodynamics. All of the winegrowers, whether they belonged to the association or not, and all of the wine professionals we spoke to about the group highlighted its promotional effectiveness through the creation of professional exhibitions, in Angers in particular, and through the organization of tastings in various parts of the world, along with the publication of two books on biodynamics, which have been translated into ten languages (Joly 2007).

Other members are by no means lacking in communication skills. A former professor at the Conservatoire des Arts et Métiers, Yvon Minvielle, and his partner, owners of Château Lagarette, Gault & Millau's revelation of the year for Bordeaux Gault & Millau, made the film *L'esprit du vin: Le réveil des terroirs.* It is presented as a complement to *Mondovino,* John Nossiter's documentary on the globalization of the wine industry and the increasing use of chemicals in the winemaking process, which was very successful in public cinemas.

Indeed, at the turn of the century, the hegemony of French wines was under considerable threat from a change in the social makeup of the demand for wine. It is the middle classes in foreign countries who now constitute the dominant element. Unfamiliar with French culture and gastronomy, they have difficulty understanding classifications that are based on origin and are overly complex. They find it much easier to understand the classifications based on grape variety, as used by "outsiders"—that is, the producers of "New World" wines. This new market structure has severely undermined France's long-standing hegemony in the fine-wines market (Garcia-Parpet 2009).

In May 2006 the Institut National des Appellations d'Origine put forward a reform of the appellations, proposing a way of straightening out a heterogeneous production system that satisfied neither those who supported AOCs and their restrictive rules nor those who refused to be constrained, who ignored the defined zones, and who used whatever techniques and grape varieties they wished. The fact that the leaders of the biodynamics trend take the environmental aspect into consideration is vital to a debate where the need to tighten the criteria for appellation quality is clear but the bases on which this should be done had no satisfactory foundations. According to those who practice biodynamics, the "sustainable development" criterion is legitimate for defining the qualities required for a proper definition of techniques and traditions. The debates that raged in France's professional wine milieus in the 1990s concerned the comparison between "vins de terroirs" and "technological" wines, and related to the opposition between France and New World countries. Today the opposition is between groups of French producers: organic/biodynamic versus conventional.

Joly highlighted the fact that the AOC spirit had been completely changed by the use of synthetic products that had ruined the soil or the terroir, considering that "the land's footprint has been erased.... The ultimate goal of AOCs is a true taste; our objective is to grasp the land and the climate, to return to that true taste." Biodynamics may lead people to think about health, but it is really a question of taste for many wine producers. During the opening speech at the 2011 biodynamic winegrowing congress in Dijon, capital of the Côte d'Or region, a *grand cru* owner and member of the Renaissance des Appellations bureau asserted that "winegrowers who use fertilizers and other synthetic products should have their AOC certification withdrawn. It is only by once again giving the soil a bacterial and microbial life that we can return to the wines with individual characteristics: a concept which is at the root of AOC specificity and which distinguishes AOCs from technological wines which can be reproduced in all aspects." In addition, Joly stated that the reason for the increasing number of major winemakers throughout the world (almost half of the group's members come from countries other than France)[18] is essentially due to the gustatory results obtained.

We can clearly see here that concern for the environment is still present but that it is a means to access the organoleptic excellence that has been negatively impacted by synthetic products. Biodynamics is a way of elevating the production of excellence, and it was the eulogy to biodynamics by Michel Bettane, a renowned French wine critic, as "having the capacity to express a *terroir*" that was repeated at the first biodynamic winegrowing congress. Members of the Renaissance des Appellations fight to once again give AOCs their full meaning. We see here a fundamental difference between the traditional conception of French AOCs and that of these newcomers, who define land by the quality of the soil and the ways in which it is worked, regardless of the nationality. What is certain is that at the present time producers using biodynamic methods, whether they joined the movement because they were convinced of the superiority of methods that respected nature or because they wanted to rediscover distinctive organoleptic qualities, have now won over a large number of customers; far from triggering ridicule and criticism from the press and consumers, they have clearly succeeded in finding economic outlets, especially abroad, for the notion of "revisited" terroirs.

Conclusion

This chapter has examined French biodynamic wine producers as an interesting case for those studying food activism. Starting as a fringe movement inspired by Steiner's philosophy and aiming for ethical, sustainable production, biodynamics encountered skepticism among enologists and the general public alike. It gained approval when reputed winegrowers joined this movement and created networks and organizations among biodynamic producers, gaining attention from the press, designing attractive websites and promotional materials, mobilizing the public against industrial production, and producing high-quality wines appreciated by experts and traders on the international market. Biodynamic wine producers opened the way to a kind of subtle activism able to mesh ethics, sustainability, and economics to create a successful alternative to conventional wine production.

Notes

1. AOC is the dominant model based on geographic delimitation.
2. For an analysis of the institutionalization of AOCs, see Jacquet and Laferté 2006.
3. Enological guides, which first developed in the United States and Great Britain in the 1960s and became popular in France in the 1980s, made word of mouth less important (Garcia-Parpet 2009).
4. The term *château* designates wine estates that were highly successful in the Gironde region in the nineteenth century. With the prosperity that reigned during the Second Empire, buildings were constructed for the development and storage of wines, and residences were embellished, especially in Burgundy. A certain number of cooperatives producing quality wines recently began using the term on their labels to give added value to the wines.
5. For an analysis of these movements see Cadiou et al. 1978. The Austrian "philosopher" Rudolf Steiner was the founder of anthroposophy, a school of thought that aims to restore the connection between humans and the spiritual worlds. In 1924 he held conferences attended by farmers, veterinarians, and scientists who were worried about the intensified use of chemical products in farming, during which he explained his philosophical principles and gave practical advice.
6. The Syndicat International des Vignerons en culture bio-dynamique (International Union of Winegrowers in Biodynamic) covers fifty-nine vineyards for

a total of 3,978 acres. Organic wine production involves 4,692 vineyards over 58,887 acres. The number of highly renowned vineyards is higher among biodynamic producers.

7. "La colère des raisins," a wine brochure prepared and distributed by Marc Angeli, who has been producing wine in the Angevin region since 2004.

8. In her article "Déqualifier le paysan, introniser l'agronome, France 1840–1914," Nathalie Jas (2005) shows how agronomists came to have authority over peasants as far back as the nineteenth century in Germany but also in France, where agronomists described peasant farmers as uneducated and incapable of running a modern farm or using scientific methods, especially with regard to fertilizers, and thus requiring agronomists to take action outside of their laboratories.

9. The highest distinction in the AOC.

10. The Association pour le maintien de l'agriculture paysanne (AMAP) is a French association that links consumers and producers for the provisioning of vegetables.

11. The regions with the highest growth are Languedoc-Roussillon (with 20,601 acres of organic vineyards), Provence Côte d'Azur (16,491 acres), and Aquitaine (9,298 acres). These three regions represent two-thirds of the surface area for certified vines (Agence Bio 2011).

12. "*Vin de pays*" (country wine) is a category distinct from the high-quality *grands crus* category. It was developed to valorize the production of wine without an "origin denomination" (AOC).

13. Rebirth of Appellations.

14. This sentence, which appears on one vineyard's Internet site, is taken from the brochure of the Syndicat International des Vignerons en culture bio-dynamique.

15. Cf. Garcia-Parpet, 2009. Regarding exports, we only have figures relating to organic wines: 70 percent of these were exported in 2009.

16. In particular, Pierre Frick, regional adviser for the French Green Party, and Dominique Techer, chairman of the Bio-cohérence brand, a winegrower representing the network of the Fédération des Vins Issus de l'Agriculture Biologique (organic wines federation).

17. Bettan and Desseauve, 2012; see also the interventions of Jancis Robinson on *Financial Times*: http://www.ft.com/life-arts/jancis-robinson accessed July 23, 2013.

18. Particularly from the United States, Italy, and Slovenia.

References

Agence Bio. (2011), L'agriculture biologique. Chiffres clés, Les chiffres de la bio en 2010, Agence Bio, http://www.agencebio.org/la-bio-en-france, accessed July 23, 2013.

Baqué, P. (2011), "Florissante industrie de l'agriculture biologique," *Le Monde diplomatique* (February): 20–21, http://www.monde-diplomatique.fr/2011/02/BAQUE/20129, accessed July 23, 2013.

Bettan, M., and Desseauve, T. (2012), *Le grand guide des vins de France*, Paris: Editions de la Martinière.

Bouchet, F. (2003), *Cinquante ans de pratique et d'enseignement de l'agriculture bio-dynamique*, Romeyer, France: Éditions deux versants.

Cadiou, P., Lefebvre, A., Le Pape, Y., Mathieu-Gaudrot, F., and Oriol, S. (1978), *L'agriculture biologique en France: Écologie ou mythologie*, Grenoble, France: Presses universiatires de Grenoble.

Champagne, P. (1991), "La construction médiatique des malaises sociaux," *Actes de la recherche en sciences sociales*, 90: 64–76.

Dubuisson-Quellier, S., and Lamine, C. (2004), "Faire le marché autrement: L'abonnement à un panier de fruits et de légumes comme forme d'engagement politique des consommateurs," *Sciences de la Société*, 62: 144–167.

Garcia-Parpet, M. F. (2009), *Le marché de l'excellence: Les grands crus à l'épreuve de la mondialisation*, Paris: Seuil.

Garcia-Parpet, M. F. (2012), "Le marché des certificateurs de l'agriculture bio-logique," in L. Bonnaud and N. Joly (eds.), *L'alimentation sous contrôle, tracer, auditer, conseiller*, Versailles: Editions Quae Educagri.

Guthman, J. (2008), "Bringing Good Food to Others: Investigating the Subjects of Alternative Food Practice," *Cultural Geographies*, 15: 431.

Jacquet, O., and Laferté, G. (2006), "Le contrôle républicain du marché: Vignerons et négociants sous la troisième République," *Annales: Histoire, Sciences Sociales*, 5: 1147–1170.

Jas, N. (2005), "Déqualifier le paysan, introniser l'agronome, France 1840–1914," *Ecologie et Politique*, 31: 1–11.

Joly, N. (2007), *Le vin, la vigne et la biodynamie*, Paris: Éditions Sang de la terre.

Lamine, C. (2008a), *Les AMAP: Un nouveau pacte entre producteurs et consommateurs?* Gap, France: Yves Michel.

Lamine, C. (2008b), *Les intermittents du bio. Pour une sociologie pragmatique des choix alimentaires émergents*, Paris: Quae.

Minvielle, O., and Minvielle, Y. (2011), *L'esprit du vin, le réveil des terroirs*, Paris: Production Anemos.

Oudraougo, A. P. (1998), "Manger 'naturel', les consommateurs de produits bio-logiques," *Journal des Anthropologues*, 74: 13–27.

Potoski, M., and Prakash, A. (2005), "Green Clubs and Voluntary Governance: ISO 14001 and Firms' Regulatory Compliance," *American Journal of Political Sciences*, 49/2: 235–248.

Siniscalchi, V. (2013), "Slow versus Fast: Économie et écologie dans le mouvement Slow Food," *Terrain*, 60: 132–147.

Sylvander, B. (2000), "Les tendances de la consommation de produits biologiques en France et en Europe: Consequences sur les perspectives d'évolution du secteur," in G. Allard, C. David, and J. C. Henning (eds.), *L'agriculture biologique face à son développement - Les enjeux du futur.* Versailles: Institut national de la recherche agronomique editions, 193–212.

Vidal, M. (2011), "Manger et acheter local: Vers une économie de la proximité au service de l'environnement?" in S. Barrey and E. Kessous (eds.), *Consommer et protéger l'environnement, oppositon ou convergence?* Paris: Harmattan.

8

Food Activism and Antimafia Cooperatives in Contemporary Sicily

Theodoros Rakopoulos

Economic Democracy, Cooperatives, and Food Activism

By 2012 there were, around Italy, eight agrarian cooperatives (and two associations) working land that the state had confiscated from the mafia in the late 1990s. Four of these cooperatives operate (the oldest since 1999) in the valley of Alto Belice, in Western Sicily.[1] Along with many journalists, Libera, a nationwide nongovernmental organization (NGO) that organizes activism against the mafia,[2] claims that the area has been "liberated from the mafia" (Libera 2009a,b, 2010; Morelli 2003) and that economic processes are free of the control of *mafiosi.* These agrarian cooperatives produce organic food and wine, distributed through consumer cooperatives across Italy; their policies simultaneously promote organic cultivation and the struggle against the mafia (Frigerio and Pati 2006). Activist claims made by work groups and production organizations such as these cooperatives need to be evaluated because they encompass people from a variety of class and experiential backgrounds, who define and enact diverse conceptualizations of activism.

This chapter, therefore, focusing on the antimafia cooperatives in contemporary Sicily, asks, how are ideas on antimafia activism, associated with food and wine production and circulation, deployed? I shall particularly explore democracy in the food activism of these Sicilian work organizations, which promote antimafia principles and food activism in one breath. This is particularly urgent if we recall that food activism is often deployed in circumstances of ethical economic activity registered as a globalized movement for the solidarity economy, linked to eradicating social inequality (Laville 2010) or to a "human" economy, that is, economic activity of actors striving for economic democracy (Hart, Laville, and Cattani 2010). The idea of democracy here holds a twofold meaning: at once a process of democratic participation in economic activity and a fairer distribution of and access to resources. The solidarity economy stands between forms of activism and a means of guaranteeing resources and has been proposed as a route to sustainable development (Dacheux and Goujon 2012).

This chapter aims to elucidate how food activism processes are framed by the antimafia cooperatives of Sicily. I will suggest that an anthropological discussion of cooperatives' promotion of food activism necessitates paying attention to the diverse subjective degrees of identification with such claims, which can vary for the different work groups developed within such organizations, especially between a "production" and a "consumption/distribution" team. In fact, the broader argument I propose is that food activism claims are part of what makes divisions of labor within cooperatives more pronounced, in stark contrast with cases where democracy is the most central aim, at a local and global level, for food activists, and indeed contradicting the very meaning of cooperativism as industrial democracy (Holmström 1989; Kasmir 1996; Zamagni and Zamagni 2008). I will show, first, that in ethical production-oriented cooperatives, internal stratifications go well beyond systems of voting and reflect divisions among the workforce in terms of remuneration and ideology; second, that food activism can be a set of principles that cooperative administrators identify with more than workers do; and third, that a group's area of responsibility—production or consumption—influences the degree to which they claim to partake in "food activism."

To trace the local situatedness of food activism ethics, that is, the ethical configurations accompanying people's commitment to collective mobilization around issues related to food, it is necessary to discuss the character of the confiscation process as well as the cooperatives' organization of labor. To that end, the chapter will scrutinize the cooperatives, describing what they do, how they are organized, what the important roles are, what the relations are between members, and whether and how they carry out food activism.

Confiscations, Cooperatives, and Legality

The antimafia cooperatives cultivate land that has been confiscated from significant Alto Belice *mafiosi* by the Italian state. The law 646/82, passed in Parliament in 1982 (proposed by the Communist Party member of Parliament Pio La Torre, who was assassinated, for this reason, by the mafia), was elaborated into a more encompassing legislation with law 105/96, which mandated that the confiscated assets be given to social cooperatives and associations. When the assets included land—as they most often did—they were assigned to agrarian cooperatives for organic production of cereals, legumes, and wine, in order to establish a "project based on purity" (Consorzio Sviluppo e Legalità 2001). During twelve months of fieldwork in Alto Belice, based in the village of San Giovanni, I conducted participant observation among the members of these cooperatives with people, mainly men, from Alto Belice villages and Palermo.

The three cooperatives I studied (named Falcone, Borsellino, and Lavoroealtro) were allocated around 1,483 acres of vineyards and cereal farms and employed, as members and day laborers, a number of local manual laborers as well as a few administrators. Their administrative team members overwhelmingly came from Palermo and worked in the cooperatives' offices in San Giovanni; many of the administrators were also members of Libera.[3] The cooperatives, moreover, had the usufruct of two beautiful nineteenth-century Alto Belice *masserie* (farmhouses), both confiscated from the *mafioso* Giovanni Brusca and turned into establishments for agricultural tourism (*agriturismi*) where organic food was served to Italian and foreign tourists interested in the history of the antimafia movement (Santino 2000). The cooperatives' activities are organized around this antimafia mobilization, constantly referring to it and being inspired by it. Since the early 1990s the connection of civil society in Italy, and in Sicily in particular, with social mobilization, ethical issues, and identity politics (Cento Bull and Giorgio 2005; Ginsborg 2003) developed a branch of urban educated antimafia activism (Jamieson 2000), which interacted with and incorporated broader social concerns with food ethics. The fact that the most successful project of allocating confiscated mafia assets to cooperatives took place in Alto Belice, the cradle of Cosa Nostra,[4] was highly symbolic.

The antimafia cooperatives make explicit references to a political struggle waged against the mafia. "Legality," an activist and ethical embracing of the law, was members' constant point of reference. The term stems from the history of the antimafia movement and has been unrelated to other food ethics claims so far—despite having been a central tenet of the production of "democratic" public discourse in Italy (Ginsborg 2003: 145; Rakopoulos 2011; Santino 2002; Schneider and Schneider 2003, 2005) and potentially associated with a vocal civil society (Pizzini-Gambetta 2006). Their organic produce, small in production volumes[5] but highly valued and priced, quickly established the cooperatives as niche exporters of quality food from the island to northern Italy and a number of foreign countries and attracted the attention of many, often international, food reviews and magazines. Journalists noted, in a leitmotif phrase, the "combination of nature and culture" represented by the organic foodstuffs cultivated on confiscated land (e.g., Self 2009).

Through the discussion of the cooperatives' social composition below, I will elucidate how, first, internal divisions impeded democratic cooperative arrangements and associated food activist claims with administrators more than with workers; and second, how these divisions were, to an extent, the outcome of food activism commitments. In that respect, I aim to show how cooperatives' food activism goals often do not necessarily abide by or nurture industrial democracy (i.e., horizontal internal relations among cooperative workers; Holmström 1989) but indeed hinder it. In the case of the antimafia cooperatives this process was conveyed in a two-tiered organization, whereby administrators embraced food activist principles more than workers did.

Divisions of Labor: Fissures over Food

The cooperatives' labor force was organized into "administrators" (mostly from Palermo) and "workers" (peasants from the villages of the Alto Belice valley).

Disseminating the co-ops' reputation, distributing the produce, and promoting consumption were the work of administrators. As with many politicized movements, historicity matters (Gledhill 2000): using websites, leaflets, and newsletters, Libera endorsed what Lino, a co-op administrator, described to me as "the continuation of the antimafia movement's history." Many administrators were Libera members, and therefore Libera influenced the administration's collective decisions substantially. The food and wine produced, as Checco, the cooperatives' 30-year-old public relations manager, once told me, symbolized "a sense of purity: being the fruit of both organic agriculture *and* legality processes." Checco noted many times in our interlocutions that awareness of food ethics and antimafia awareness were two sides of the same coin for the cooperatives. Libera, whose Palermitan branch was most active in the cooperatives' marketing, called the cooperatives' foodstuffs and wine "pure" and "ethical." Giampiero, the 32-year-old vice president of Libera Palermo and a member of the Borsellino cooperative, told me that "*because* of this twofold approach" (antimafia and organic), buying their produce implied "ethical consumption."

My informants among Palermitan administrators, who were also members of Libera, stressed the "purity" (*purezza*) of their produce. They argued, in different circumstances, that the foodstuffs they produced participated in a "virtuous economic circle": the foods and wine were "the products of legality in all respects." Specifically, the administrators underlined that the foods the cooperatives produced were cultivated on legally expropriated land using organic agriculture, which guaranteed that their production was socially and environmentally fair. Moreover, distribution took place through consumer cooperatives as well as through outlets organized by Addiopizzo.[6] Piero, the Borsellino cooperative's agronomist, told me once that this fact was a way to establish the "coming full circle" of their food ethics and politics. "It is legality all the way," Luca, the Falcone cooperative's president, noted in an interview.[7]

Cooperative administrators promoted in a series of leaflets and newsletters, and explained in interviews, the idea that their products (organic wine, pasta, and legumes) embodied—in a play on words—"the fairness/the taste of Sicily" (*Il g(i)usto di Sicilia*). It is significant to acknowledge that this articulation of nature and culture emphasizes the incarnation in the landscape of the antimafia activism. Linking nature and culture in presenting food activist claims is a central tenet of some associations, such as Slow Food (Petrini 2007: 8). Recent studies have explored and problematized Slow Food's interacting principles of economy/ecology (Siniscalchi 2013). The choice to cultivate organic foods (one not necessarily shared by workers) is, in that sense, the outcome of a series of interlocked conditions: it appears as "fair" and "alternative" (to the dominant system of food distribution, as well as to the hegemonic mafia influence in Sicily), but, eventually, it serves a marketing logic. The commercial recognition of this choice is supported by a system of northern Italian consumer cooperatives and by Addiopizzo, an anti-racketeering association, in ways that underline how the negotiation of the antimafia legality claims contributes significantly to the branding of the cooperatives' products.

In addition to the administrators, other cooperative members were manual workers, handling production. Giampiero spoke to me at length in an interview about the changes that wage employment in the cooperatives had brought about locally, for peasants who cultivated conventional grain and vines but were employed by the cooperatives. He suggested that Libera and the administrators of Borsellino

> had managed to convince the peasants using only the wallet [*col portafoglio solo*]: we ask them how much the *mafioso* pays them, they tell us, "he pays 30 euro a day" [*iddu mi paga 30 euro a jurna*]....OK, we tell them; last year the daily pay according to the law, the daily contract for agriculture was 51.62 euros....So, come to us!...This is how much they get, legally. It's the norm [*È la normalità*]. And so, imagine Theo, for the Borsellino co-op there were 300 applications for *braccianti* positions! People realized that their interests were with the legality, the normality.

The peasants of the cooperatives that Giampiero referred to were the people in the manual workforce who were either members of the cooperatives or day laborers; alongside their cooperative employment, they were also smallholders. They earned wages from the cooperatives by working in the confiscated land plots and also worked on their own land tracts (*pezzi di terra*), mostly vineyards.[8] One such case was Pippo Pitrè, a 58-year-old from San Giovanni, who used to be a member of the Borsellino cooperative but had resigned a few months before I met him. (His resignation was due to conflicts with the administration over the fact that, as a member-worker, he did not receive a monthly wage, over a misunderstanding about work they thought he did voluntarily, helping out another co-op, but for which he retrospectively demanded wages.) He eventually decided to go back to work as a daily worker for the Falcone, as he needed the money. I rented the apartment he owned at the center of the village. Pippo's family lived in a farmhouse 1.2 miles outside the village, as they preferred the tranquility of that area. Maria, his wife, sixteen years his junior, did not work outside the home; they had a seventeen-year-old daughter, Elena.

As I had become good friends with Pippo, the Pitrè family often invited me for dinner. Regularly, after a day of work in the vineyards of the cooperatives, Pippo asked me to join him in his house for a warm dish of pasta with vegetables from his garden, cooked by Maria. As we sat gathered around the table, he boasted that we were enjoying his "own wine," comparing it to the cooperative's: "the cooperative wine is too commercial," while the wine from his vineyard was "authentic and pure." He was proud that he cultivated the red Nero D'Avola variety at 2,200 feet above sea level, as it was very difficult to grow red grapes at such a high altitude. "That's the heroism, that's what's really difficult," he said, "not just co-op activism." Pippo was also proud of the fact that he matured the wine in what he called his cellar (in fact, the garage). Like other daily cooperative workers, he thought homemade conventional wine was qualitatively superior to the organic wine made at the cooperatives' winery. For him, the only advantage of the cooperative production of bottled organic wine was that they produced it on a larger scale; in terms of quality, "his wine" was superior. Pippo, like many other peasants working in the cooperatives but also maintaining their own—conventional, not organic—vineyards and farms, could not conceive why organic produce was any better than "the local, traditional one," as he put it. Tano, another worker, emphasized to me that while he enjoyed working in the co-ops' vineyards, he much preferred his own: "there is more meaning in working my own land, despite what people [administrators] say about organic agriculture and activism. My own product is better."

While all the workers I spent time around insisted that organic agriculture and antimafia activism were not their primary concerns, the middle-class antimafia cooperative administrators constantly negotiated the discourse of legality, in ways that matched current food marketing needs. Their activity made leisure and work converge, as they often met outside work on occasions such as the Addiopizzo feast or film evenings organized by Libera; several of their friends worked at these events. In the words of Checco, attending such events was not only political socialization but also an "ethical obligation vis-à-vis their social allies" (such as the Addiopizzo and the consumer co-ops that distributed their products). It involved the promotion of their products, in stands that also showcased Libera leaflets that informed the public on antimafia initiatives, such as demonstrations and talks in schools.

As Ernesto, a Falcone administrator, told me once, their work entailed "a mission" to link food with antimafia ideas: this was their "cultural project." In order to explore this cultural project in Palermo and San Giovanni, I organized focus groups in which the administrators of the cooperatives participated. In these meetings, Ernesto solemnly stated that the administrators "embodied" civil society principles for San Giovanni, as well as the "mission" to develop organic agriculture in Alto Belice, an asset underestimated by local peasants. Their mission to produce organically on the confiscated land entailed negotiating a balance between the northern Italian consumer cooperatives that were their business collaborators and the local peasants working as manual laborers for the antimafia cooperatives. In the negotiation of food activism among antimafia cooperative members, fissures did not arise as to whether activism should be focused on production (more associated with manual workers) or consumption (the task of administrators), as the administrators, who liaised with consumer cooperatives of northern Italy, monopolized the cooperatives' strategic production of discourse on marketing and on food activism. The local peasants of Alto Belice, working in the cooperatives in working-class posts, were viewed as outsiders to this process. Giampiero, in an interview, admitted that "the wallet" was not always enough to "shift ideas":

As regards the peasants of San Giovanni, those under contract labor from the cooperatives, our member-workers [*i dipendenti delle cooperative*], I can tell you frankly that they are not antimafia [*loro non sono antimafia*].... They haven't been able to listen to the antimafia. We have managed to convince them only using the wallet [*col portafoglio solo*], but there is still work to do [...] to convince them about organic cultivation, about antimafia principles.

This critique of the "ideas" of the peasants often resonated with the negotiation of the co-ops' food policies, as set by the administrators. Once, Mina, Falcone's vice president, had invited Flavio, a representative of CoopTirreno, a left-wing consumer cooperative from Bologna, to come to San Giovanni to liaise with people from the cooperatives as a business partner, because CoopTirreno had just signed a business agreement to distribute the antimafia cooperatives' produce in Bologna. This was a success, as it sealed links between northern Italian consumer co-ops and the antimafia cooperatives. I accompanied some of my research interlocutors, who fetched Flavio from Trapani airport. As we approached the village in the car, Flavio said to me that San Giovanni looked like a zoo, and the locals ("imbued with mafia," he commented) were the animals in the zoo. He imagined that it must take a lot of effort to collaborate with the locals and even suggested that I should call myself not an ethnologist (anthropologist) but an ethologist.

Later the same day, at an interview arranged in advance, Luca, the president of Falcone, was somewhat embarrassed and apologetic toward me regarding the bigoted remark of their business partner. He wished to clarify that the cooperatives' activity, at once original in terms of food and antimafia activism, had a specific role in the area, often not understood either by locals or by their Bolognese partners:

> Here [in San Giovanni] we find ourselves [he spells each syllable out clearly and raises his voice] in an *unevolved* society [*una società non-evoluta*]—not only due to the presence of the mafia but also due to the fact that income, culture and social status are in such a condition that the only thing, when it comes to food, that matters to people is the price [of the produce]. That's it. It is not important *how* something, a foodstuff, is produced—the only thing that matters is its price, nothing else. And since I work in San Giovanni and not in Bologna, I have an eye open for all the world market but I pay attention to how to impose change on this reality. And this is done through attention to legality in the making and distributing of food and wine, which is organic—although people here cannot appreciate it and I should hence look towards Bologna. There, such efforts, to produce organic, or to do antimafia, will be appreciated. (emphasis added)

The vignette above, as well as Luca's words, point to a theme often acknowledged in the relevant literature (Pratt 2009): that food ethics do not mean the same thing across classes and that the negotiation of a past that constructs a retrospective genealogy of ethical food production associated with peasant struggles, and that constitutes current food production as part of a broader activism, is also informed by class. The relative distance, in the above quotations, between the different work groups of the cooperatives underlines that conceptualizations of agrarian change should take class dynamics seriously (Bernstein 2010).

This is influenced by the administrators' participation in the values of the recent antimafia movement, in which Libera plays a crucial role. The managerial roles of certain people (like Mina, Ernesto, and Luca) in associations such as the NGO Libera on the one hand and the cooperatives on the other are central to the merging of two parallel types of discourse (the antimafia movement and food ethics). At the same time, local workers, more focused on their own farms' produce, were absent from this configuration. This was reflected in the two-tiered organization of the cooperatives.

Table 8.1 Pay and Membership Status in the Alto Belice Cooperatives' Workforce.

	Cooperative members[a]		Contractual ("day") laborers	
	Administrative workforce	Manual workforce	Administrative workforce	Manual workforce
Liberanima	2 members, with a monthly wage of ca. €500	3 members (receiving daily pay[b])	—	1 seasonal[c] worker (man)
Borsellino	5 administrators, with a monthly wage ranging from €1200 (Salvo, president) to €940 (Niko, administrator)	12 members (all of them receiving daily pay)	—	4 seasonal workers (men)
Falcone	7 office-based administrators, with a monthly wage ranging from €1230 (Luca, president) to €1030 (Manlio, administrator)	10 worker-members 4 on monthly-wage contracts, 6 on contracts based on daily pay	2 office-based administrators, on annual renewable contracts (ca. €900 monthly)	11 seasonal workers (men, on daily-pay contracts); amassing €700 monthly 4 seasonal workers (men) in other capacities (tourism), receiving daily pay 5 seasonal workers (women), receiving daily pay
Lavoroealtro	3 administrators with a monthly wage ranging from €1100 (Vito, president) to €800 (Mario, administrator)	12 member-workers receiving daily pay	—	4 seasonal workers (men), receiving daily pay

[a] All members were on permanent contracts. All figures denote gross pay.
[b] Daily pay implied, in 2009, €51.62—the daily pay established by law for agricultural labor.
[c] For workers in agricultural labor posts, this implied about 90–120 days per year, mostly during January, April, and August–September. For seasonal workers in other capacities, the overall number of workdays per year was considerably less.

Concerns over Food and Internal Cooperative Democracy

While all of the peasants working in the co-ops thought of their jobs there as valid but not sufficient for their livelihoods, not all of them were members of the co-ops. One difference between members and other "daily" workers was, first of all, contracts: members had permanent contracts, although there were important distinctions between administrator-members and worker-members concerning levels of remuneration and timing of payment, as well as periods of actual work. While administrator-members harnessing food activism with antimafia activism enjoyed professional terms of continuous work, the permanent contracts of member-workers provided actual work and pay *only* for the agricultural season; only three worker-members had a monthly wage, with most being paid on a daily basis. The second key feature marking out members was democratic participation, meaning that all members sat on the Members' Assembly, which met annually. By contrast, nonmember-workers signed three-month contracts for seasonal agrarian work, being paid on a daily basis, and had no rights to democratic participation.

It would be misleading, however, to highlight the issue of democracy within the cooperatives as a member/non-member distinction. The daily workers' lack of voting and participation rights was not much of an issue for them; the mechanics of voting and "collective" decision making were not disputed, and during fieldwork I heard only a handful of complaints about this issue. The main dichotomy people perceived within the co-ops was rather the division between those (member- and non-member workers alike) doing production and those doing distribution (administrators, all of whom were co-op members).

In all three co-ops, democratic arrangements were set in two decision-making bodies: the Administration Council, meeting monthly, and the Members' Assembly, meeting annually, where all members had a vote. I observed Administration Council meetings in the three co-ops. In 2009 all decisions by the councils were approved with a 100 percent majority, including the councils' annual plans and the previous year's budget (*bilancio*). The Members' Assembly also elected the members for the next year's council, always reflecting the views of the Consortium[9] and Libera in electing a majority of administrator-members over worker-members (thus, for each cooperative, three administrator-members and two worker-members). As for the significance of the Members' Assembly as "democratic participation" and control, it suffices to quote the opinion of Mina, which she confided to me just after one of the co-op's annual Assembly meetings: "Well yes, the Assembly is important, but too much democracy can be a waste of time when deciding cooperative issues; we need organization and quick decisions to promote our principles about food and wine."

Mina, Giampiero, Luca, and several other administrators insisted, in several interviews, that in order to support food ethics, and to guarantee the distribution of their *g(i)usto* product and the dissemination of antimafia activism alongside and through the produce, hierarchical principles of labor should be applied to the cooperatives. Mina was one of the administrators who was more involved with promoting the cooperatives as ethical food and wine producers. Part of her job was to nurture and develop the business partnership of two Alto Belice cooperatives (Falcone and Borsellino) with consumer co-ops in northern Italy, where their produce was distributed. This work often raised issues of prioritizing a politicized marketing of the products, often by downplaying equal work relations and particularly democracy within the co-ops. For example, in one of her visits to Sicily, Erica, the 55-year-old Bolognese leading member of the Consiglio Sindacale[10] of the cooperatives Falcone, Borsellino, and Liberanima, once told me, "Well yes, the Assembly is important or whatever, but democracy can be a waste of time when it comes to deciding things corporate."

On the one hand, worker-members and daily workers had much in common despite the (undeniably significant) difference between stable employment and short-term contractual work. Worker-members' work (and hence pay) was as seasonal as that of most daily workers. Due to their similar pay, work, and living conditions, the situation of the daily workers was similar to that of the permanent worker-members, with whom they identified, as they equally considered themselves "parts of the co-operative" (see Table 8.1). On the other hand, there were crucial differences *among members,* between the administrators and worker-members. In that respect, diverging from a marked tendency in the anthropology of work to distinguish between workers in stable employment and contractual workers,[11] here the distinct stratification is *within* those in stable employment, driven by the administrators and Libera, who saw the cooperatives as an initiative of food activism. The two-tiered organization of all Alto Belice cooperatives is a salient issue, with repercussions in terms of class and the overall meaning of food ethics for members.

In fact, although bereft of voting rights in the cooperatives, daily workers' commonalities and shared values with worker-members rendered their experience and status similar. In addition, worker-members, as members, had the burden of sharing potential losses in the cooperative. An employee's voice in the co-ops, associated with membership and recurring stable employment, did not mark out a broad stratification along the lines of membership/nonmembership as much as the issue of identifying with food activism principles did. In order to understand internal divisions within cooperatives, we need to move, both methodologically and analytically, beyond a focus on schemes of decision making (Zamagni and Zamagni 2010). Governance itself, however, *can* be dictated by principles such as food activism, with which administrators identify and producers/workers do not.

It is telling to juxtapose with cooperatives' "participatory democracy" the fact that Falcone, Borsellino, and Lavoroealtro all had similar modes of collective management whereby the ideas of the administrative teams dictated the overall planning. The main actors in the cooperatives' decision making, the Palermitan administrators, engulfed a food activism by way of democratic politics: fusing the ideology of a pure political system (free from mafia) with the idea of a pure system of consuming ethical, organic foods. Doing this, however, comes with costs for internal democracy within the cooperatives.

Conclusion: Diverse Identification with Food Activism across the Organization of Labor

My chapter has briefly situated the actors of Sicilian antimafia food activism in specific divisions of labor; it underlined the issue of subjectivity in discussing economic organization and food ethics. Specifically, I have suggested that it is impossible to conceptualize cooperatives as united, cohesive actors in democratic mobilization over food concerns. On the contrary, claims about food ethics can often underline already existing internal divisions of labor. The positions of workers and administrators (the latter being the real actors of food activism in Sicily, rather than the "cooperatives" they compose) are influenced, among other issues, by their positionality vis-à-vis food ethics and values, where often a distance between local and "authentic" is present (Pratt 2008). In this case, the distance is present across divisions of labor and co-op members' overall viewpoints on organic production as well as their commitment to antimafia and legality principles.

I have explored the tensions within the division of labor in antimafia cooperatives. The idiom "legality" informs conceptualizations of food ethics and activism in contemporary Italy. The class-situatedness of this ethics, and the associated political activism from which it derives, is the key point for conceptualizing antimafia food activism in Sicily today. Administrators stress the discourse on organic production and on antimafia principles, while their co-members, the local workers, are less interested in framing their activity in these terms. It is important to conceptualize food activism as a classed element of cooperative ideology. Administrators are invested in shaping the cooperatives toward ethical consumption, while producers (local worker-members) identify much less with these proclaimed characteristics. This is identified both in how workers think of their activity (prioritizing their own produce over the cooperatives') and in how administrators think of their colleagues' commitment (which they see as relatively low).

Internal democracy in cooperatives draws from the ideological interaction of food activism and legality activism, wherein the administrators "guide" the co-ops in their mastering of the food ethics and antimafia discourses. Although I acknowledge the need to integrate the anthropological analysis of production and consumption, as underlined elsewhere (e.g., Goodman 2002; Goodman and DuPuis 2001; Klein and West 2012), the obvious two-tiered organization of labor in the agrarian antimafia cooperatives of Sicily tells a different story. The production of food and wine is mostly associated with local workers who care little about identifying with antimafia and/or food activism principles and who most often prioritize, in terms of their sense of selfhood and pride, their own private production of wine. The strict separation of consumption and production into different teams within a sharp division of labor is rooted in, and informed by, a series of other disconnections between producers and managers of distribution/consumption, including personal origin (respectively, rural Alto Belice and urban Palermo), ethical stance, and other sources of income (private farming).

Seeing political movements as moral politics cannot fully account for the agrarian moral economies they inspire (Edelman 2001); the antimafia agrarian cooperatives' discourse, conveyed by their administrators, explicitly attempted to merge moral claims regarding food production with a politicized discourse (around legality). The idealized notion and image of the peasant, so often traced in ethnographies of ethical food production (Edelman 2005), are entangled here in the discourse on food production.

Rethinking food activism in terms of agrarian cooperatives can help revisit participatory economics, or solidarity economies, when one considers schemes pertaining to the outside world of politicized cooperatives, which indicate a superficial cohesiveness concerning their members' viewpoints. The solidarity or "human" economy's principles are rooted in economic democracy (Hart 2013) and often draw on political commitment; cooperatives can reflect this. However, in the case of Sicily's antimafia cooperatives, principles of food activism are followed only by some members—a condition that emphasizes the challenges of achieving internal cohesiveness and democratic organization.

Notes

1. The co-ops and associations outside Alto Belice were situated in the southern regions of (eastern) Sicily, Campania, Puglia, and Calabria, as well as in the central region of Lazio.
2. Libera is an "umbrella NGO," the largest in Italy, to which 1,500 organizations belong (see http://www.libera.it). There are Libera branches in approximately fifty Italian cities. It caters for "the antimafia struggle," promoting "the restitution of land" (Libera 2009a) and "the eradication of mafias from Italian social life" (Libera 2009b: 12).
3. I divided my fieldwork between offices and farms, following the activities of the members of the manual workforce and the administration teams and voluntarily working alongside them as an agrarian laborer in the fields and as an assistant in the offices.
4. Totò Riina and Giovanni Brusca, today imprisoned for life, led Cosa Nostra's heroin trafficking from the mid-1980s to the mid-1990s, when Alto Belice *mafiosi* controlled the largest share of the world's circulation of the drug (Arlacchi 1986). Brusca lived almost all his life in San Giovanni. His nicknames speak to his fierce activity: *u verru* (the pig) and *u scannacristiani* (the slayer).
5. For example, in 2008 the cooperatives, combined, produced 3,178 tons of wine, 5,215 tons of grain, 542 tons of peas, and 147 tons of lentils.
6. Addiopizzo is the name of a Sicilian civil society association that presents itself as a movement, catering to the horizontal organization of retailers who adopt an "anti-racketeering" policy, that is, shopkeepers who refuse to pay racketeering

money to the mafia. Today, the association has NGO status, and 300 retailers sub-scribe to its principles. Even so, it is estimated that 70 percent of Sicily's retailers still pay the mafia's "racket" (Commissione Parlamentare Antimafia 2013).

7. This alleged "virtuous" economy, interestingly, echoes the claims of Slow Food, as problematized by Alison Leitch (2009).

8. The co-articulation of wage labor and land cultivation meant that informants were at the same time workers and independent peasant producers. There is a vast literature on people whose livelihoods combine peasant and worker sta-tuses, including ethnographies of Italy (e.g., Pratt 1994). This experience has been identified as a "mixed" one according to the Portici school of sociology; in Emilia the combination of farmer and laborer identities was incorporated within broader development plans (Mingione 1994). In Sicily it has been linked with household subsistence but not as contributing to broader growth (Centorrino, Spina, and Signorino 1999). Instead, this "mixed" mode has remained in place as a way of sustaining the livelihood of local households.

9. The land they cultivated was administered by an overarching state apparatus, the Alto Belice Consortium.

10. The Consiglio Sindacale is an apparatus external to the cooperative by definition; it oversees the flow of logistics, the incoming and outgoing capital of the co-op, and its general economics.

11. Of course, this is an older discussion, often highlighting gendered stratifications (for example, Goddard 1996). Recent anthropological research on industrial set-tings (Parry 2007) where there is a consistent divide between fixed and (sub) contracted workers takes the discussion further. The line of argument is that those in stable employment, unlike contractual workers, are privileged ("em-bourgeoised," as Parry has it) by comparison. The debate on precariousness and genealogical differences among workers is also akin to this discussion (Procoli 2004; Standing 2011).

References

Arlacchi, P. (1986), *Mafia Business: The Mafia Ethic and the Spirit of Capitalism*, London: Verso.

Bernstein, H. (2010), *Class Dynamics of Agrarian Change*, Halifax, NS: Fernwood.

Cento Bull, A., and Giorgio, A. (eds.) (2005), *Speaking Out and Silencing: Culture, Society and Politics in Italy in the 1970s*, Oxford: Legenda.

Centorrino, M., Spina, A. L., and Signorino, G. (1999), *Il Nodo Gordiano: Criminal-ità mafiosa e sviluppo nel Mezzogiorno*, Rome: Laterza.

Commissione Parlamentare Antimafia (2013), "Sportello Scuola e Università: Racket," Parlamento italiano, http://www.camera.it/_bicamerali/leg15/commbicantimafia/documentazionetematica/32/schedabase.asp, accessed August 17, 2013.

Consorzio Sviluppo e Legalità (Development and Legality Consortium) (2001), "Focus sul progetto pilota 'sviluppo e legalità,'" Consortium website, http://www.sviluppolegalita.it.

Dacheux, E., and Goujon, D. (2012), "The Solidarity Economy: An Alternative Development Strategy?" *International Social Science Journal*, 63/203–204: 205–215.

Edelman, M. (2001), "Social Movements: Changing Paradigms and Forms of Politics," *Annual Review of Anthropology*, 30/1: 285–317.

Edelman, M. (2005), "Bringing the Moral Economy Back In…to the Study of 21st-Century Transnational Peasant Movements," *American Anthropologist*, 107/3: 331–345.

Frigerio, L., and Pati, D. (2006), *L'uso sociale dei beni confiscati: La dimensione etica e culturale, le opportunità di sviluppo economic, il ruolo delle istituzioni e degli enti locali*, Book Formativo, Ministero dell'Interno, Dipartimento della Pubblica Sicurezza, con il cofinanziamento dell'Unione Europea, Programma Operativo Nazionale "Sicurezza per lo Sviluppo del Mezzogiorno d'Italia," 2000–2006. (Report).

Ginsborg, P. (2003), *A History of Contemporary Italy: Society and Politics*, New York: Palgrave MacMillan.

Gledhill, J. (2000), *Power and Its Disguises: Anthropological Perspectives on Politics*, London: Pluto.

Goddard, V. (1996), *Gender, Family, and Work in Naples*, Oxford: Berg.

Goodman, D. (2002), "Rethinking Food Production-Consumption: Integrative Perspectives," *Sociologia Ruralis*, 42/4: 271–279.

Goodman, D., and DuPuis, M. (2001), "Knowing and Growing Food: Beyond the Production-Consumption Debate in the Sociology of Agriculture," *Sociologia Ruralis*, 42/4: 6–23.

Hart, K. (2013), "Manifesto for a Human Economy," *The Memory Bank*, January 20, 2013, http://thememorybank.co.uk/2013/01/20/object-methods-and-principles-of-human-economy/, accessed January 21, 2013.

Hart, K., Laville, J.-L., and Cattani, A. D. (2010), *The Human Economy: A Citizen's Guide*, Cambridge, UK: Polity.

Holmström, M. (1989), *Industrial Democracy in Italy: Workers' Co-Ops and the Self-Management Debate*, Aldershot, UK: Avebury.

Jamieson, A. (2000), *The Antimafia: Italy's Fight against Organised Crime*, London: Macmillan.

Kasmir, S. (1996), *The Myth of Mondragón: Cooperatives, Politics, and Working-Class Life in a Basque Town*, Albany: State University of New York Press.

Klein, J. A., and West, H. (2012), "New Directions in the Anthropology of Food," in R. Fardon, O. Harris, T.H.J. Marchand, M. Nuttall, C. Shore, V. Strang, and R. A. Wilson (eds.), *The Sage Handbook of Social Anthropology*, London: Sage, 293–302.

Laville, J.-L. (2010), "The Solidarity Economy: An International Movement," *RCCS Annual Review* [online journal], 2, http://rccsar.revues.org/202, accessed January 25, 2013.

Leitch, A. (2009), "Slow Food and the Politics of 'Virtuous Globalization,'" in D. Inglis and D. Gimlin (eds.), *The Globalization of Food*, Oxford: Berg, 45–64.

Libera (2009a), "La Carovana Onda Libera" [leaflet].

Libera (2009b), "La via Libera," March.

Libera (2010), "Liberiamo un altro futuro" [leaflet].

Mingione, E. (1994), "Family Strategies and Social Development in Northern and Southern Italy," in H. Lustiger-Thaler and D. Salée (eds.), *Artful Practices: The Political Economy of Everyday Life*, Montreal: Black Rose.

Morelli, V. (2003), La rivincita della legalità. Polizia Moderna n. 1.

Parry, J. (2007), "The 'Embourgeoisement' of a Proletarian Vanguard?," Exploring the Middle Classes in South Asia conference, University of Sussex, July, http://www.fieldtofactory.lse.ac.uk/parry/parry.htm, accessed November 11, 2012.

Petrini, C. (2007), *Slow Food Nation: Why Our Food Should Be Good, Clean and Fair*, New York: Rizzoli Ex Libris.

Pizzini-Gambetta, V. (2006), "'Becoming Visible': Did the Emancipation of Women Reach the Sicilian Mafia?" in A. Giorgio and A. Cento Bull (eds.), *Speaking Out and Silencing: Culture, Society and Politics in Italy in the 1970s*, Oxford: Legenda.

Pratt, J. (1994), *The Rationality of Rural Life: Economic and Cultural Change in Tuscany*, Chur, Switzerland: Harwood Academic.

Pratt, J. (2008), "Food Values: The Local and the Authentic," *Research in Economic Anthropology*, 28: 53–70.

Pratt, J. (2009), "Incorporation and Resistance: Analytical Issues in the Conventionalization Debate and Alternative Food Chains," *Journal of Agrarian Change*, 9/2: 155–174.

Procoli, A. (2004), "Introduction," in A. Procoli (ed.), *Workers and Narratives of Survival in Europe: The Management of Precariousness at the End of the Twentieth Century*, Albany: State University of New York Press.

Rakopoulos, T. (2011), "From the 'Moral Question' of the Communists to '*Legalità*' of the NGOs: Transparency and Anti-mafia Rhetoric in Contemporary Italian Activism," in "Contested Transparencies," special issue, *Re-Public*, 11, http://www.re-public.gr/en/?p=4260, accessed October 21, 2012.

Santino, U. (2000), *Storia del Movimento Antimafia: Dalla Lotta di Classe all'Impegno Civile*, Rome: Editori Riuniti.

Santino, U. (2002), *Oltre la legalità: Appunti per un programma di lavoro in terra di mafie*, Palermo: Centro Siciliano di Documentazione Giuseppe Impastato.

Schneider, J., and Schneider, P. (2003), *Reversible Destiny: Mafia, Antimafia, and the Struggle for Palermo*, Berkeley: University of California Press.

Schneider, J., and Schneider, P. (2005). "Mafia, Antimafia, and the Plural Cultures of Sicily," *Current Anthropology*, 46/4: 501–520.

Self, W. (2009), "Heaven with a Cross to Bear," *The Times*, February 9.

Sider, G., and Smith, G. (eds.) (1997), *Between History and Histories: Silences and Commemorations*, Toronto: University of Toronto Press.

Siniscalchi, V. (2013), "Slow versus Fast: Économie et écologie dans le mouvement Slow Food," *Terrain* 60: 132–147.

Standing, G. (2011), *The Precariat: The New Dangerous Class*, London: Bloomsbury Academic.

Zamagni, S., and Zamagni, V. (2008), *La Cooperazione*, Bologna: Il Mulino.

Zamagni, S., and Zamagni, V. (2010), *Cooperative Enterprise: Facing the Challenge of Globalisation*, Cheltenham, UK: Edward Elgar.

–9–

The Canadian Wheat Board Struggle: Taking Freedom and Democracy to Market

Birgit Müller

Food activism in Canada today attempts "to reshape farming through links across a cultural as well as spatial divide between cities and countryside, all against the tide of corporate pressures to homogenize landscapes and crops" (Friedmann 2012). Corporate control over the food chain is a common target of all food activists; however, a division exists between farmer activists on the grain-producing western prairies and consumers and farmers in the urbanized regions of eastern Canada. While food activists in the eastern cities establish direct personal links with engaged producers of the fruits, vegetables, meat, and eggs they consumed (Friedmann 2007), activists on the western Canadian prairies—mostly family farmers producing wheat, barley, and durum for the eastern Canadian market and for export—wage a struggle against corporate market domination that hardly caught the attention of eastern food activists. The challenge that western activists address is, how can the struggle for food sovereignty be scaled up beyond the direct personal link between producer and consumer to include exchange relations that are impersonal and transpire across long distances, and nevertheless retain elements of fairness and solidarity?

A central issue of western food activism was the defense of single-desk selling[1] by the Canadian Wheat Board (CWB). The Wheat Board gave farmers a collective monopoly to sell all wheat and barley from western Canada through the single desk on the national and international market. This collective marketing structure—guaranteed by the state and governed by ten farmer-elected directors and five government-appointed ones—was able to maximize profits that would otherwise have been captured by large grain companies. It pooled the returns and distributed them back to the farmers. In 2006 Prime Minister Harper made it his personal mission to dismantle the Wheat Board in the name of "marketing freedom." Collective marketing that had been innovative and largely consensual in the middle of the twentieth century became residual (Williams 1973) and a threat to prevailing market liberalism at the onset of the twenty-first century. The battle was lost on August 1, 2012, when the Harper government ended single-desk selling and removed the elected directors.

This chapter looks at how the Wheat Board conflict came to be rephrased in terms of a struggle for food sovereignty, defined by the Via Campesina movement as a fight about the "right of peoples to define their agricultural and food policy" (Magnan 2011: 115). It analyzes the mobilizations in western Canada that endeavored to keep this marketing instrument in the hands of farmers against the onslaught of grain companies, a neoliberal government, and a strong minority of farmers who opposed single-desk selling and endorsed the Harper-government ideology of "marketing freedom." Where did the struggles for food sovereignty in western Canada converge with the objectives of food activists in the urbanized regions in the east? To what extent did these mobilizations defending achievements of the past address a blind spot of the emergent food activism in the cities? Where did the interests of food activists in eastern Canada clearly diverge from those of their counterparts in the west, making common strategic action hard to achieve?

This chapter examines these questions, based on interviews with western Canadian farmers, participant observation of the campaign for electing farmer representatives to the Wheat Board, and analysis of Internet and archival material. The first part of the chapter examines the clash of ideas about market freedom, justice, and democracy among farmers in western Canada. The second part looks at the particular types of mobilization around legal rights and due process that farmer activists used when defending the single-desk selling and orderly marketing of the Wheat Board. It shows that the laws and processes instituting the regulatory power of the Wheat Board and the mobilizations using them are part of a residual form of political culture that in Raymond Williams's (1973) sense became increasingly oppositional when from the 1980s "marketing freedom" emerged as a hegemonic cultural and political discourse. The hegemonic discourse of marketing freedom was, however, not strong enough to make a majority of farmers voluntarily forgo the economic advantage of using a collective marketing structure. Marketing freedom thus had to be imposed and forced on them. In the third part, I look at how urban consumer activists in the East and farmer activists in the West, far from the urban centers, converged in a fight for democracy and control over food production but not in a common movement.

Clashes of Worldviews

The Canadian Wheat Board was a collective marketing structure backed by government, and since 1998, it has been co-managed by farmers. It operated successfully for almost seventy years on the world market for wheat and barley and reined in the power of a handful of multinational grain companies over Canadian producers. Earlier agrarian movements, led by farmers in western Canada a century ago, had been able to count on a certain degree of urban support when they fought to develop cooperative structures and obtain government protection against the overwhelming power of a few large grain corporations and the railways. Parliament created the

Wheat Board in 1943 to act as an effective shield against excessive speculation on the grain market. The Wheat Board was created at a historical moment when the interests of government, citizens, farmers, and to some extent grain companies were converging (Boehm 2001) after the economic disasters of the Depression, the ecological catastrophe of the 1930s Dust Bowl, and the onset of World War II (Morris 1987). The unity of the nation and the future of the Canadian West were understood to be at stake and farming had to be protected.

The Wheat Board increased the marketing power of tens of thousands of farmers through a sales monopoly on all wheat, durum, and malting barley produced in western Canada. It worked hand in hand with the Canadian Grain Commission to guarantee a consistent quality of Canadian grain to its national and international customers, and fair grading and weighing to farmers. With its high protein content and excellent milling qualities, Canadian wheat served a niche in the international market and fetched premium prices.

By pooling their products, the farmers collectively became sufficiently powerful to negotiate a price and no longer had to take any price the grain companies offered. As Vernon Fowke explained it, "For the competitive producer, market price is a given fact, quite independent of the marketing decision of any individual. For the monopolist that condition does not prevail, and market price is not independent of the producer's sales policy" (1957: 222). When small individual producers compete with one another to sell to big grain companies, the farmers are obliged to take the market price. In contrast, a big central seller like the Wheat Board, whose product is desired by the buyers, is able to negotiate prices that are more favorable (Measner 2007). The seller becomes to some extent a "price maker" and can treat each customer differently (Gray 2007). Once the board marketed all the wheat and barley, farmers no longer dealt individually with the grain exchange, nor did they have to look for customers. This structure, which offered a clear economic advantage, worked only because it was also a constraint. Farmers were obliged by law to sell all their wheat and malting barley to the board. A majority of farmers perceived this as an advantage: a minority, however, resented the constraint as incompatible with their individual market freedom.

Underlying these oppositions was a clash of worldviews and ideologies that went beyond the Wheat Board struggle. Two conceptions of the world encountered each other: the remnants of a culture that emphasized the need for small producers to defend themselves collectively against the powers of corporations were pitted against ideas of economic merit and market opportunity. These contrasting viewpoints are evident when comparing an August 2011 opinion editorial written by the president of the National Farmers Union, Terry Boehm, to a February 2012 letter written by the minister of agriculture, Gerry Ritz. While Boehm asserts that the Wheat Board is owned by farmers, outside the reach of government, and incurs no cost through its existence, Ritz describes the board as a creation of Parliament whose liabilities are backed by government. What elected Parliamentarians have created they can also undo. The unionist demands to maintain the Wheat Board because it is "an institution that allows Western farmers some form of economic justice for the fruit of their labor." In contrast, the minister sees its abolition as an opportunity for the "farmer entrepreneurs", "eager to market their wheat and barley in the way that makes more sense to their farms."

The classic Lockean argument grounds the farmers' right to their property in the labor power they put into the land and the crop (Macfarlane 1998). This argument encounters here, however, the pure neoliberal figure of the farmer as his or her own entrepreneur (Foucault 2004), destined to be the master of his or her own success without need for the solidarity of others or the constraint posed by the state. The farm union leaders arguing in favor of the single desk stresses that the Wheat Board gives farmers market power in an international grain trade that is dominated by a handful of multinational grain companies. For the farmer, the board is an effective shield against oppression. The minister, on the other hand, emphasizes that the monopoly aspect of the Wheat Board was imposed on farmers without an effective vote during World War II. Farmers are thus oppressed by a board they have not chosen. The farmers' leader states that the strength of the Wheat Board lies in the orderly marketing of the farmers' grain. Farmers are strong if they are united. In contrast, the minister sees it as an advantage that the individual farmers can contract with maltsters, millers, and pasta plants on both sides of the U.S.–Canadian border, assuming that the individual can perfectly know and play the market.

Until the 1970s Canadian governments acknowledged, and to some extent actively supported, the discourse of the farmer as a laborer of the land whose fruits of labor may be stolen by grain companies if they do not unite to defend the value of their crops. After World War II, no foreign grain company set up business in the Canadian West until Cargill bought its first Canadian grain elevator in 1974. Since the 1980s this discourse has been gradually replaced in government publications and the media by the figure of the farmer entrepreneur. As partners of the grain companies, the farmer entrepreneurs are supposed to seize their opportunities on the open market, and the government should interfere as little as possible in their business (Müller 2008). Despite the fact that western Canadian prairie farmers are currently confronted, as they were in the beginning of the twentieth century, with five foreign grain companies and two railways that market and transport their grain, the second discourse has become increasingly hegemonic in Antonio Gramsci's sense. A hegemonic culture propagates its values and norms so that they become the commonsense values of all.

Williams, refining Gramsci's definition, sees a hegemony not only as an abstract system of meanings and values but as something that is organized and lived. "It is a whole body of practices and expectations; our assignment of energy, our ordinary understanding of the nature of man and of his world. It is a set of meanings and values which as they are experienced as practices, appear as reciprocally confirming"

(1973: 7). Williams does not see a hegemony as a static system but rather as the outcome of real social processes of incorporation, on which it depends. There always exists the possibility of opposition or alternatives that have their source in practices, meanings, and values that are not part of the effective dominant culture and cannot be expressed within it. As Williams (1973: 10–11) discusses, these can be "residual," "practiced on the basis of a residue—cultural as well as social—of some previous social formation," or "emergent," based on new meanings and values that are continually created.

The struggle for the Wheat Board was based on such residual values, meanings, and practices that were still institutionalized in the Wheat Board legislation and the Canada Grain Act. These residual elements were now in opposition, however, to the dominant culture and economic relationships. The vast majority of older farmers remained strongly attached to the Wheat Board, while—as opinion polls showed—the younger generation took the benefits it was bringing them for granted and thought its values were backward. A Wheat Board employee explained their disinterest in terms of political apathy born out of an affluent life. This argument, however, does not seem to fit the economic realities younger farmers confronted when starting their operations in the 1980s and 1990s. From 1985 to 2007, when prices for wheat and barley were generally low on the world market, most younger farmers were heavily in debt and were able to just make out. Farming was a high-risk gamble with the weather and the market, and many farmers lost their farms during that time period. As margins were small, farm size tended to increase, and more successful or lucky farmers tended to buy up the land of their less successful neighbors. The premiums achieved by the Wheat Board helped but did not make up for this loss of income in wheat and barley. Interest in the Wheat Board grew when the prices for wheat and barely improved on the world market and when after 1998 farmer elected directors introduced more flexible marketing programs.

The controversies however continued. Farmers who defended single-desk selling were accused of being backward, risk adverse, "political," and simply not astute enough to survive in the open market. As the activists recognized that their values were in conflict with the dominant culture, they tried to translate their defense of the Wheat Board into the terms of their opponents. One of the slogans most often used in the campaign was "Our Board—Our Business." Pro-Board activists tried to argue that the Wheat Board was not a political institution but made economic sense. A seventy-year-old grain farmer in Saskatchewan phrased it in the following way: "If your political outlook is different from Conservatives' that's what they would like to think that you're just being political about it, but I think it's the Conservative government that's being political in the fact that they have tried to destroy the board through political means." For him the open market was not an innovative system: "In my way of thinking the open market system of pricing food stuffs and grain, is an archaic way of doing it. I think a negotiated price, which the Board can do, makes much more sense than a fifteen second flurry of bidding at the Commodity Exchange....They talk about the Wheat Board as being archaic and not changing well. How much has the Commodity Exchange changed?" (interview, 2008).

In theory, today a farmer could go on the Internet to trade in barley, wheat, and canola futures and options to hedge his sales contracts with the grain companies. For most farmers, however, this is not a very realistic option, and those who tried it admitted that they mostly lost more money than they gained. However, the possibility of playing the market still served as an argument for the opponents of single-desk selling. One of the anti-single-desk candidates in the director elections explained, "I think the reason that we need the Wheat Board is that there are a lot of producers who don't want to take the time to market their own grain....When you are talking about an open market system there is always a high and a low, so if you are one of the farmers that have hit the high, well then the Wheat Board is not an advantage to you because you've hit the high" (interview, 2008).

For another opponent to single-desk selling, it did not in fact matter whether he made more money selling through the single desk; what he resented was that through the Wheat Board everybody got the same price. He considered himself more astute than others and wanted to profit from his astuteness and from the fact that he had built lots of storage for his grain. "If the other farmers are too stupid, too bad for them. As a citizen of a free country I want to have the freedom to sell when I want at the price I can get. Anything else is against my convictions!" He considered it unfair that a farmer who had a lot to sell would have the same say as a farmer who was farming very little and had a second job. Indeed, the old cooperative principle of an equal say for all farmers, big or small, rich or poor, was one of the principles laid out in the Wheat Board legislation. This contrasts sharply with the voting principles of shareholder boards, where big owners have more say according to the amount of shares they hold.

Some farmers even resented that the Wheat Board had government loan guarantees and could thus borrow at favorable rates. They endorsed the analysis of Barry Cooper, a political scientist from the University of Calgary, who wrote on the website of the Ministry of Agriculture that the Wheat Board "[has] no financial interest in the grain it purchases; it is never at risk. It has no bottom line because only farmer-participants in regulated pool accounts are financially exposed or are beneficiaries depending on how the market and the Board perform" (Cooper 2008). The Wheat Board was thus accused of not operating for its own benefit but behaving like an inflexible bureaucracy indifferent to the profits and losses of its members. In a point-by-point refutation, the Wheat Board countered that consistently maximizing returns for farmers was its primary goal.

The defenders of single-desk selling used economic statistics and accounts to convince their opponents that per year the board brought on average $500 million (Canadian) of additional economic gain to all the farmers and to the Canadian economy (Pugh 2007). In contrast, the protagonists of marketing freedom made highly emotional pleas for "freedom," the right to inequality, and distinction. The employee of the Wheat Board mentioned above commented in 2008, "In the last two years we have gone backwards in terms of the whole discussion being polarized and it's become more politicized. They aren't really looking: 'does this make sense to my business?'" (interview, 2008). In spite of the effort to reorganize the board and make the sales programs more flexible, the surveys ordered by the Wheat Board showed that many farmers still regarded the board as a government agency, not as controlled by farmers. "They say, it's bureaucratic, it's top-down and it's not receptive to the needs of their business and some of that's justified" (interview, 2008).

The Wheat Board employees could not explain to them the advantages of their organization because they were under a gag order from the agriculture minister. In contrast, the corporations successfully used customer service and branding to make farmers believe that their farming interests coincided with the objectives of the corporations.

> They [the corporations] hire farm kids right out of college that have good people skills and that can identify with the farmers and they throw a pile of resources at their staffing in the country....It is very, very service oriented. And then of course you roll in all the marketing, packaging and providing, selling them their seed, arranging the trucking off farm....And farmers like most of us in society they are susceptible to flattery that they are treated like they are big business people and their operations are significant. The bigger farms they will fly them down to Vegas for customer appreciation. (Interview, 2008)

Corporations thus had an important role to play in the incorporation of the ideology of the farmer entrepreneur. They were, however, unsuccessful in turning the majority of farmers against the single desk. When the Wheat Board consulted procurers in 2011, 62 percent were in favor of maintaining the single desk for wheat, and 51 percent supported maintaining the single desk for barley.

Defending Due Process and the Rule of Law

> When government does not comply with the law, this is not merely non-compliance with a particular law, it is an affront to the rule of law itself.
>
> —Justice Douglas R. Campbell (2011)

This sentence is part of the judgment condemning agriculture minister Gerry Ritz for "non-respect of the law" when in 2011 he introduced Bill C-18, an act to reorganize the Wheat Board into a Parliament controlled by a strong conservative majority. The minister failed, according to the judge, in his statutory duty (pursuant to section 47,1 of the Wheat Board Bill C-4 of 1998) to consult with the board of directors and to hold a plebiscite among producers prior to introducing the bill in October 2011. The government appealed the judgment of the federal court, and the appeals court decided on June 18, 2012, that there was nothing in the law of 1998 that would "restrain the minister from proposing to Parliament legislation fundamentally modifying or repealing the Wheat Board Act." The farmers' organizations opposing the minister countered by announcing that they would take the case to the Supreme Court.

The forms of activism that western Canadian farmers and their supporters deployed to defend their central selling agency show an extraordinary focus on the rule of law and the democratic process. They protested outside government offices; lobbied senators; issued radio ads; held innumerable press conferences; wrote press releases; set up websites dedicated to the struggle with hundreds of documents and direct links to court material, legal provisions, and press coverage; produced videos on YouTube and Facebook; and raised thousands of dollars in support of their court actions. At the center of these mobilizations was the conviction that the Wheat Board legitimately belonged to farmers and that they were going "to use democratic process to reclaim what is legitimately ours," as a former Wheat Board director expressed it.

In an interview for a small alternative television station, a member of the National Farmers Union explained:

> Let's consider the CWB to be a company that is owned by Western Canadian Farmers. Let's consider that the Canadian farmers are shareholders of that company. We employ 450 people here in Winnipeg. Those people market our grain to over 80 countries around the world. Through their efforts we earn 500 million CAD more than would be available on the open market system. Then we have a federal government. Prime Minister Stephen Harper came along and said: "we are removing the most valuable asset that you have—the single desk—and by the way we are removing the right to vote to determine the structure of your company. We are ordering the directors that you elected....And we are doing this because we are giving farmers freedom." We are moving to Orwellian times of opposition.

This statement raises several interesting questions about ideas regarding the legality and legitimacy of the ownership that Canadian farmers claimed over "their" agency. The Wheat Board distinguished itself from a private company, as it did not make a profit for itself but rather provided a service to the farmers on a not-for-profit basis. Farmers supervised the Wheat Board—as shareholders would supervise their company—so that it acted in and adapted to their interests. However, the Wheat Board also constrained the farmers to act as a group to their own economic advantage. By law, their individual interests were subsumed under the interest of the community. This constraint—the single desk—was at the same time their most valuable asset. It could be lifted if a majority of farmers were in favor, but it definitely constrained the minority to submit to the will of the majority. This rule drew much of its legitimacy from the democratic process set up by the Wheat Board law of 1998.

Paragraph 47.1 of Bill C-4 reforming the governance of the Wheat Board in 1998 stipulated, "The minister cannot introduce a bill into Parliament to exclude or add a crop from/to the single desk without the agreement of the farmers' elected board of Directors and the consent of the grain producers." By comparing the Wheat Board with a shareholding company, the union leader mentioned previously argued that the functions of both entities were based on social convention and legal backing. He posited that there was no legitimate reason why recognition of, and respect for, the legal form of a shareholding company should prevail over the legal form of the Wheat Board.

When Harper decided to abolish single-desk selling, he did so by overriding the stipulations of the 1998 law and the expectations the farmers had developed based on its provisions. In a speech in October 2011 before the new law was voted on, he said, "It's time for the Wheat Board and others who have been standing in the way to realize that this train is barreling down a prairie track. You're much better to get on it than to lie on the tracks because this is going ahead" (CBC News 2011). He made it clear that the law of 1998 was nothing but a cultural residue (Williams 1973) and that the relations of political power were against it. Sweeping away the legal arguments his opponents had made all throughout their campaign, he affirmed that elected government and Parliament ruled supreme.

However, even though his decision was upheld by the Supreme Court of Canada, it was not deemed legitimate by most farmers. According to their sense of justice, minister Ritz introduced the law (Bill C-18) in disrespect of the law (Bill C-4) that required the minister to obtain their prior consent before making substantive changes to the structure of the Wheat Board. The legal norm was here reduced to an order by the legislator, which means, as Jürgen Habermas (1992) pointed out, that justice dissolves into politics. This dissolves the idea of the political itself. The same consequence occurs if the law draws its autonomy from its own power, rather than from overriding moral reference to aspects of justice (Habermas 1992). In this way, even though the Supreme Court ruled that Ritz had the legal right to introduce Bill C-18 to end single-desk selling, his action was considered immoral and illegitimate by the farmers claiming ownership of "their Wheat Board."

The farmers responded to the introduction of Bill C-18 with their only illegal action. Wheat Board Directors, farm union leaders, and a crowd of determined farmers blocked the Canadian Pacific Railway Line by stationing a combine across the tracks. The railway line was shut down for the day. Police came and monitored the event, but nobody was arrested. One of the Wheat Board directors lay down on the tracks and declared, "Canadians just like me from all over the country need to stand up against this government or there will not be any democracy left." The action was filmed by the activists, put on their websites, and widely commented on. Many of those who had participated in the event felt great satisfaction and thought they should replicate the action all over the country. But the small number of committed activists was unable to move more farmers to engage in radical illegal action and struggled to draw the attention of the wider public.

Convergence of Food Activisms

When Ritz introduced legislation on October 18, 2011, to dismantle single-desk selling through the Wheat Board, the National Farmers Union launched a call to "non-farmer Canadian citizens" and their organizations to help protect the Wheat Board and thus "our food supply, sovereignty, economy, and democracy." As a national farmers' organization and member of the Via Campesina, the National Farmers Union had a long tradition dating back to the 1970s of emphasizing food as a catalyst for social and environmental change (National Farmers Union 1975). The organization represented large grain farmers in the West, as well as small farmers and fruit and vegetable growers in the East. The union argued that protecting the Wheat Board was affirming national sovereignty because it pushed back the "Americanization of our grain and food system" by reining in foreign corporate control over the wheat and barley marketing system. They advocated the Wheat Board as "a good example of Food Sovereignty in action: a democratic agency controlled by food producers and citizens." They called on the solidarity of all citizens to fight the antidemocratic methods of the Canadian government, "ramming legislation through parliament, using cloture to limit debate, refusing to let the agriculture committee hear the bill and instead setting up an ad hoc committee to review the bill, but limiting that committee to just 5 minutes per section." They argued, "If these anti-democratic tactics are not challenged, they will be repeated." Finally, they recalled the fact that it was only thanks to the Wheat Board's opposition that the introduction of transgenic wheat had been stopped. They called on Canadians to write to the prime minister and the Canadian senators and urge them to use due process and to enact policies that fostered food sovereignty and a strong Canadian nation.

A few weeks before the Canadian Parliament decided to abolish single-desk selling through the Wheat Board with a vote on December 16, 2011, some prominent activists representing consumer groups and citizen organizations entered the struggle on the side of the protesting farmers. Maude Barlow, the chairperson of the Council of Canadians, declared at a Wheat Board rally in Winnipeg that the government-imposed demise of the Wheat Board—this "pillar of democracy in a world of unregulated corporate food control"—was putting the individual over the collective interest and individual egoism over the common good. The Council of Canadians took up the letter-writing campaign of the National Farmers Union and incited their members to join in. The United Food and Commercial Workers Canada and the Agriculture Workers Alliance also called for an immediate stop to the Harper government's ideological attack on the Wheat Board. In a letter to Harper published on their web-site, their president argued, "Ending the single desk authority of the Wheat Board would throw western agriculture into turmoil and would transfer wealth created by Canadian farmers to big private, often foreign-owned grain companies instead of being returned to farmers and spent in their communities." Food Secure Canada, the newsletter of the Canadian food movement, put a note on its website informing its membership about the Wheat Board struggle.

The civil society organizations and trade unions defending the Wheat Board argued in terms of a fight against corporate control, against the loss of democratic rights, and for the national interest. These arguments, however compelling, did not touch the nerve of the food movements in eastern cities. As Harriet Friedmann has pointed out, what rallied food activists and councilors in the cities and served as an "emergent frame for interstitial change" was the issue of health. Linking the quality of food to health provided a "hinge through which politicians and public could agree across political divides" (Friedmann 2012). While the Wheat Board saw itself as defending the quality of Canadian wheat—striving for a consistent milling quality and high protein level—these were not concerns that health-conscious consumers cared about. They were instead important for the industrial production of bread, in particular for the baking of white, bloated toast bread in the Anglo-Saxon tradition. When the Wheat Board successfully stopped the authorization of genetically en-gineered wheat for production in Canada, it did not argue based on protecting the health of Canadians but based on the danger of the loss of markets in Europe and Asia. It also did not address the popular practice among conventional Western farm-ers of spraying glyphosate on the ripening wheat crop just before harvest, which is also a major health risk linked to large-scale wheat production. The Wheat Board did not impose a ban on this practice, nor did it commission studies of the consequences for human health and the environment (Magnan 2010). The Wheat Board's neglect of health issues was one reason it failed to mobilize popular interest in its activities and thus support.

In the Wheat Board's exercise of farmer control, the value of the single desk was framed primarily in terms of economic rationality—as a way of obtaining greater economic rents from an uneven global market (Magnan 2011). The board had been able to slow down the trends in the global agrifood industry, including the growing concentration of farms into ever larger units. The board had also reduced the corpo-ratization of all aspects of the agrifood system, from farm inputs, technology, ma-chinery, seeds, fertilizers, and herbicides to the processing, retailing, and marketing of food (Fridell 2012), but it had not been able to reverse it. While looking for allies to fight corporate control, few Wheat Board activists explicitly shared the objec-tives of the emergent food movements in the cities, which emphasized the sensorial relationship to food and the experience of caring for the soil, the seeds, and thus ultimately the food they produced for others.

Conclusion

In this chapter I showed how the controversies around the Wheat Board are at the center of three political cultures: first, a residual political culture that defends cooperation and regulation; second, the hegemonic political culture of individualism and inequality; and, third, the emergent political culture that emphasizes sharing food and caring for the soil, plants, and other humans. The residual culture is still dominant among western farmers. It conceives of economic power relations not as the outcome of the play of quasi-natural market forces but as the result of social conventions and political struggles. This way of thinking which was stronger in the past, was inscribed until recently in legal provisions and structures that challenged the current neoliberal government and the multinational corporations. Activism by western Canadian farmers was thus strongly legalistic, emphasizing the rule of law and due process. Most prairie farmers felt that the government had confiscated their "most precious asset," the single desk. What was less clear to them, however, was that by establishing the single desk, the state had also protected them from their own divisions and short-sighted egoisms, as it made the minority of farmers comply with the will of the majority.

By dismantling the Wheat Board, the current Canadian government strives to impose the hegemonic culture of market liberalism, putting the individual and individual egoism over the collective interest. This act amounts to the "reduction of legal norms to orders by the legislator" (Habermas 1992), undermining democratic governance and changing the moral foundations of the Canadian state. The loss of the Wheat Board is a serious one for food activists in cities, as it removed the last bastion against corporate control in the grain-growing West and eliminated an old institution that had been able over the previous fourteen years to adapt in a regulated fashion to changing producer and consumer demands. One can speculate that under a different federal government, one that would have appointed consumer representatives and environmental activists to the five government-appointed director positions of the Wheat Board, it might have been possible to redefine quality not only in terms of adaptability to industrial processes but also in terms of health. This would have reconnected the consumers in the eastern cities with the farmers out West, thus introducing elements of care for the environment and for other humans into the culture of the producers of staple foods. These efforts could have bridged the spatial and cultural gap that separates producers from consumers.

As this manuscript was being revised, the farmers organized as Friends of the Canadian Wheat Board lost their most recent legal battle. On January 17, 2013, the Supreme Court of Canada refused to hear an appeal for a constitutional and class-action lawsuit, which contained provisions to restore the single-desk Wheat Board and to seek damages of approximately $17 billion from the federal government. The demise of the Wheat Board also deals a further blow to the few remaining state marketing structures, especially those in developing countries that are under constant threat from structural adjustment programs and the World Trade Organization. There is still time, however, for the emergent food movements in the cities to join forces with the residual forces of old farmers in the Canadian West, whose critique of the corporate control of the food system is as pertinent as theirs.

Note

1. Single-desk selling is the selling of all western Canadian milling-quality wheat and malting-quality barley through a single agency, a "single desk."

References

Boehm, T. (2001), Keynote address at the National Convention of the National Farmers' Union, Regina, Saskatchewan, November.

Campbell, D. (2011), Judgment of the Federal Court, Friends of the Canadian Wheat Board vs. Minister of Agriculture Jerry Ritz, Winnipeg, Manitoba, Docket T-1057-11, December 7.

CBC News (2011), "Wheat Board Monopoly Will End, PM Vows," October 7, http://www.cbc.ca/news/politics/story/2011/10/07/sk-stephen-harper-visits-regina111007.html, accessed August 9, 2012.

Cooper, B. (2008), "The CWB Should Not Have Any Role in Marketing Barley," from AAFC Online - Newsroom - Information for Producers (October 31), http://www.agr.gc.ca/cb/index_e.php?s1=ip&page=ip60908a_q3, accessed August 14, 2012.

Foucault, M. (2004), *Sécurité, Territoire, Population: Cours au Collège de France, 1977–78*, Paris: Gallimard/Seuil.

Fowke, V. C. (1957), *The National Policy and the Wheat Economy*, Toronto: University of Toronto Press.

Fridell, G. (2012), "The Day the Wheat Board Died," *The Bullet* [e-bulletin of the Socialist Project], 671, July 27.

Friedmann, H. (2007), "Scaling Up: Bringing Public Institutions and Food Service Corporations into the Project for a Local, Sustainable Food System in Ontario," *Agriculture and Human Values*, 24/3: 389–398.

Friedmann, H. (2012), "Reinhabiting Our Earthly Home: Ways to Reshape an Urban Foodshed," American Sociological Association Annual Meeting, Denver, Colorado, August.

Gray, R. (2007), "The Economic Impact of the Canadian Wheat Board," in T. Pugh and D. McLaughlin (eds.), *Our Board Our Business: Why Farmers Support the Canadian Wheat Board*, Halifax, NS: Fernwood.

Habermas, J. (1992), "Wie ist Legitimität durch Legalität möglich?" in J. Habermas, *Faktizität und Geltung*, Frankfurt am Main: Suhrkamp, 541–570.

Macfarlane, A. (1998), "The Mystery of Property: Inheritance and Industrialization in England and Japan," in C. M. Hann (ed.), *Property Relation: Renewing the Anthropological Tradition*, Cambridge: Cambridge University Press.

Magnan, A. (2010), "The Canadian Wheat Board and the Creative Re-constitution of the Canada-UK Wheat Trade: Wheat and Bread in Food Regime History," PhD thesis, University of Toronto.

Magnan, A. (2011), "The Limits of Farmer-Control: Food Sovereignty and Conflicts over the Canadian Wheat Board," in H. Wittman, A. A. Desmarais, and N. Wiebe (eds.), *Food Sovereignty in Canada*, Winnipeg: Fernwood.

Measner, A. (2007), "The Global Trade and the Canadian Wheat Board," in T. Pugh and D. McLaughlin (eds.), *Our Board Our Business: Why Farmers Support the Canadian Wheat Board*, Halifax, NS: Fernwood.

Morris, W. (1987), *Chosen Instrument: A History of the Canadian Wheat Board: The McIvor Years*, Edmonton, AB: Reidmore Books.

Müller, B. (2008), "Still Feeding the World? The Political Ecology of Canadian Prairie Farmers," *Anthropologica: The Journal of the Canadian Anthropology Society*, 50/2: 389–407.

National Farmers Union (1975), *Nature Feeds Us: The Food System from Soil to Table*, Saskatoon, SK: Modern Press.

Pugh, T. (2007), "What Is at Stake If the CWB Marketing Advantage Is Sacrificed?" in T. Pugh and D. McLaughlin (eds.), *Our Board Our Business: Why Farmers Support the Canadian Wheat Board*, Halifax, NS: Fernwood, 108–111.

Williams, R. (1973), "Base and Superstructure in Marxist Cultural Theory," *New Left Review* 1/82 (November–December): 3–16.

–10–

Brothers in Faith: Islamic Food Activism in Egypt

Nefissa Naguib

Food, Faith, and Activism

The Society of the Muslim Brotherhood is the oldest and largest Islamist movement in Egypt. It was established in 1928 by Hassan al-Banna, a primary school teacher. From the start Hassan al-Banna demanded from Egyptians stronger commitment to the welfare of their community and awareness of those less fortunate (Davis and Robinson 2012; Naguib 1996). While the movement has always had a steady flow of recruits in rural areas, in its more recent history it has experienced increasingly active involvement by young urban and university-educated men with deep concerns about the arrogance and corruption of those in power (Singerman 2004). The young Brothers became particularly visible during Egypt's "Friday day of rage," January 28, 2011, when activists used Facebook, YouTube, and text messages to organize protests against rising food prices, police brutality, and government corruption. Although this was not the first time Egyptians had protested these ills, the rage of these demonstrations managed to oust President Hosni Mubarak and his government. Tahrir Square in Cairo became the epicenter for people's demands for bread, dignity, and justice. I watched as Muslim Brotherhood youth surrounded the square, under the slogan "religion is for God; the country is for all." They ensured that food, especially bread, as well as water and bandages, reached protesters.

This chapter is about the youth branch of the Brotherhood and its prospects for social change through food. It is an inquiry into the Brothers' social efforts regarding food activism and the ways they make their influence felt in society's fabric. I knew about the Brotherhood's social service efforts from my own anthropological research on its business ethics and welfare involvements. In my first attempt to research Arab Muslim male lives and aspirations, I studied the philanthropic and economic lives of the most successful Brotherhood businessmen, calling them "men of commitment" (Naguib 1996). But that was in the 1990s. With the rising global commodity prices and food riots across the world in 2007 and 2008, I decided to return to Egypt to study the food protests. I wondered whether Brotherhood businessmen were involved in food welfare programs. As with my previous research on the Brotherhood, I was fortunate to gain ethnographic access to the group's social work. I became interested in their food justice vision and efforts when one of my previous interlocutors, a doctor and member of the Brotherhood whom I have known for close to fifteen years, suggested I look more closely at the group's food activities. He acknowledged that he had never really thought about the "food question" until starting to work in the clinic, where many of his patients suffer from nutritional deficiencies and can afford only "to fill up their calories with bad quality subsidized bread."

I had no idea how to go about researching Brotherhood food projects except by asking around, like one who asks for street directions. In the fall of 2008, with the help of the doctor and his sister, I met with two young Brothers, Ahmad Tawil and Hussein Maher,[1] who were working in one of the group's low-cost food markets. They described themselves as Muslim men with an aim to help the needy in their everyday struggles. I asked them whether they compare themselves to global food movements that campaign for food welfare. The young Brothers liked my comparison. Ahmad looked down at my notebook, saying, "Write that ours is Islam-based." "Was this *activism*?" I asked using the English word. Hussein responded teasingly in Arabic and English, "Why not, it makes us modern. But remember write down Islam-based food activism." Hence, in this chapter I use the terms *activism* and *activist* to describe the Brotherhood's range of food provisions and outreach. Ahmad and Hussein became the first in a long chain of Brothers who, over the years, have led me to different corners of Cairo in search of Islamic food schemes. In this chapter I particularly use ethnographic data gathered during the revolution of 2011 and the following two years after the ousting of the Mubarak regime. I draw on a core group of Brothers between the ages of twenty and forty who come from lower- and middle-class backgrounds: for the most part, students or well-educated professionals such as doctors, engineers, teachers, lawyers, and bureaucrats. They were highly motivated and accomplished, proud to be among the best and brightest students in their class. It was also important for them to let me know that despite their family connections and urban mannerisms, their achievements come from God and devoted work. These men not only recounted their own beginnings as food activists but also relayed stories about older generations of food activists. They brought me along on regular visits to poor households where they distributed food, showed me bakeries and grocery stores that are administrated or sponsored by the Brotherhood, and took me to their food market stalls that are basically fruit and vegetable carts parked in different lower-income neighborhoods. I was allowed to take general pictures without identifying the Brothers; otherwise, I watched and listened to their daily routine. I always carried a notebook openly and wrote notes regularly. Occasionally, when I was not writing, they worried I was protecting them, assuring me that they "have nothing to hide."

In this piece, I refer to *how* and *why* the youth branch of the Brotherhood started questioning why people struggle for food and what they started to do about it. The *why* was the beginning of an analysis of the failure of food markets—that is, the absence of food in some people's everyday life. The *what* was faith-based activism: religiously based ideas and actions expressed individually and collectively about personal and societal life, about being a Muslim, about being a Brother—in short, about being an activist in its totality and plurality of meanings—about moral cosmologies, food, and action.

From the very start of the Brotherhood it insisted that active practical efforts to heal society are required for a good Islamic society (Lia 1998). The Brotherhood advocates social justice, coupled with a critique of greed, waste, and the lack of restraint (Munson 2001). The Brothers talked about the need to improve redistribution and the moral obligation to help those in need. These aims are religiously driven practices, and they invite questions regarding how the individual performance of activism intersects with everyday spiritual life in Egypt, as well as with broader economic and political concerns.

My conversations and observations attend to the particulars of individual Brothers as they engage in morally driven practices. These particulars undermine attempts to generalize, about either the Brotherhood, Islam, or activism. There are patterns, for instance, economic philosophies, but they cannot fully define Islam or typify the Brotherhood. Indeed, the ethnographic approach I outline in this piece foregrounds the range of morality that surrounds the economy and Islamic food activism. The moral economy is defined here as the capacity to forge relationships based on faith, practice, and moral order. To this end many relationships that are organized around finding food for the deprived are also moral relations that go beyond Islamic doctrine. My argument is that theology and pragmatism are intertwined in food. Neither religious codification nor nonorthodox practices totally define outreach and activism. Hence, the emerging agency of the young Brothers is in their actions and practices of making concrete efforts to democratize food access in communities, while also displaying their religious sensibilities. Religion, like economics and politics, involves morality, practice, controversy, and conventions—notions that are not always classified as religious.

I suggest that the Muslim Brotherhood's food justice activism is born of a politics of silence and exposure. As Carrie Rosefsky Wickham argues in her ethnography on outreach among young Brotherhood members in the 1980s, "The social embeddedness of Islamic networks also permitted a certain amount of flexibility and experimentation, enabling graduates to 'try out' different levels and forms of participation without initiating a break from their social circles" (2004: 233). My ethnographic focus is on 2008 and the uprising in 2011, a stretch when I observed and listened to a growing quest among the young Brothers to challenge the authority of not only the state but also older members of the Brotherhood.

Although the ways the young members recounted and engaged in activism produced a certain degree of normative behavior and sustained Islamic standards, their accounts and practices chipped away at established norms. Their challenge to the

Brotherhood establishment may be related to activist currents that converge in how individuals perform particular practices. Although these human actions are inspired by Islamic values, they transcend and sometimes bypass religious doctrine. I propose to call these morally directed, economically driven, and deeply paradoxical religious sentiments in food activism "Islamic food activism." Hence Islamic food activism is a set of activist interventions to promote food democracy embedded in Islamic religious beliefs and actions. It serves both to enable young members of the Egyptian Society of the Muslim Brotherhood to act out their religious faith in concrete practices promoting more equitable food access and to propagate a positive picture of their religion to Egyptian citizens outside the Society.

With Islamic food activism I introduce the activists' reconceptualization of faith as a set of interactions in process, examining how faith as "devotion" or "space" enables political action for social change. In what ways does piety drive the Brotherhood's food activism? Where is the social life of Islamic food activism?

Food Is a Life Trial

Two weeks before Egypt's first free parliamentary elections in November 2011 and a few days before the traditional Islamic rituals for the Feast of Sacrifice in Cairo, Muslim Brotherhood youth gathered outside mosques in poor neighborhoods; they stood under the banner "Know Us, Join Us," yelling out prices on discounted green beans, potatoes, onions, and other vegetables. Critics called it vote buying, yet another attempt by the Brotherhood to win over the hearts and souls of the poor (Tadros 2012). The specific distribution of bread and meat to the poor have been, throughout the Brotherhood's history in Egypt, among the most potent political efforts in their claim for legitimacy among ordinary Egyptians (Naguib 1996). In 2011 I observed the Brotherhood in Cairo responding to their critics in the media by arguing that food justice was a continuation of their outreach to all Egyptians.

Nancy J. Davis and Robert Robinson argue "The Brotherhood's work among professionals, students, and unemployed graduates was crucial in winning over those who became the most active and successful recruiters for the movement and in increasing its legitimacy with the broader public" (2012: 47). Since the establishment of the movement in 1928, the Muslim Brotherhood has continued its activities by bypassing the state and establishing far-reaching networks that engage in public service projects—the construction of mosques, clinics, schools, legal aid, day care centers, discount grocery stores, bread outlets, sports programs, and much more (see Burgat 2002; Davis and Robinson 2012; Zahid 2012).

While I do not go as far as François Burgat (2002), who suggests that the society of the Muslim Brotherhood in Egypt serves as the most legitimate and democratic expression of mass-based social activism, my ethnography considers that the youth branch's sense of political democracy, economic justice, moral obligation, and religious identity lends it a populist authenticity. It is worth noting that the Brotherhood is not the only youth movement demanding democracy in Egypt; the April 6 youth movement played a significant role in the protests that led to the occupation of Tahrir Square on January 25, 2011. However, the youth branch of the Muslim Brotherhood has been arguably the steadiest force in civil society by either legitimate or illegitimate means (see Zahid 2012).

Two striking features puzzled me during my research among Brotherhood food activists. First, they do not want to be categorized as mere members of a political social movement with close links to the headquarters but rather as those who purposely reach out. The argument, as expressed by a young activist, is that "the older generation is inward-looking and only concerned with building the Brotherhood, while we are outward-looking." He explained how the old guard only communicates with each other, while the young branch interacts online with other young people outside the Brotherhood.

Another feature is that although each of my interlocutors clearly felt affinities to the Brotherhood's Islamic guidelines, they were not prepared to let themselves be mobilized into actions they did not believe in. I thus found a dynamic range of variation, beyond religion, linked to other features of organization and identity. The young Brothers had protested several times prior to the popular revolution in 2011. They want a greater role for themselves, as individuals, in the Brotherhood (see also Davis and Robinson 2012; Tadros 2012). A young activist explained his personal wishes for more independent mobilization outside the constraints of the headquarters:

> The old men have to develop an up-to-date approach to world realities. They act like fathers in old times. These times are passed. We have faith just like them. We are also bound to God in a lasting relationship. But we use what God taught us proactively as the world is changing around us. There are people out there who don't have food. I want to be out there helping them. I am inspired by Islam to do good. I combine my Muslim faith and my energy in mobilizing against food injustice and for food sovereignty. The old men in the Brotherhood are happy with the state of affairs. They don't understand that this is a mobilization for democratic control over food production and food distribution. I do what I do because I care about the last people in the food chain. Those who are left out and come to the door.

This statement includes a number of interesting elements: personal aspirations established through food activism, the intensity of commitment to people who "come to the door," and, as I argue, a demonstration that Islamic activism, albeit in varying degrees and ways, straddles the boundaries between orthodoxy and nonconformity, the traditional and the modern, the old and the young, and the local and the global. But its immediate point is to show that religion can be progressive. We find complex religious clues in the sense that, rather than discussing difference and doctrine, the Brothers talk about themselves as committed to a morally driven economy, justice, and democracy.

The moral economy has particular significance in moments of upheaval, in which the imaginary and agency are likely to be intensified. This is manifested in the unfolding dramas of longer bread queues that allowed me to observe the Brothers during a contemporary period of economic disarray and food crisis. Although Brotherhood food activists act "for the love of God," they are visible in the Egyptian social welfare landscape and thus seemingly demand to be heard, not only by Brotherhood elders, but also by society at large. By accepting the Brotherhood's offering of food safety nets, individuals are bound to reciprocate through some sort of commitment to the Brotherhood. For them there is no incompatibility between Islam and the democratic structures of a compassionate society, commerce, and government.

When my interlocutors wanted to stress their claims for food justice, they referred to Qur'anic verses that speak of how the here is only transitory and how the hereafter is the "better and more lasting." What they do in this life to help others has consequences in the next. Accordingly, although the morality of food activism and its economic activity are clearly aimed "for God," it is carried out among "our brothers and sisters." Driven by faith, theirs is a help "that looks adversity right in the eye and deals with it," said Sherif Hassan, a young Brother with a degree in economics from the American University of Cairo.

Sherif always explained his actions with references to Qur'anic verses that highlight his argument about the links between Islamic economic activity and divine authority. He was one of my first interlocutors in 2008, and over the years he has talked to me about how religion urges all Muslims to honor the dignity of others and to distribute food in God's way. Underlying the notion of distributing food in God's way is the idea that all food belongs to God and that He is "the decider." This goodness from God must be managed in accordance with His sanctions by balancing the earthly with the heavenly, as well as the individual with the communal. As a valued human need, food is also a life trial. Sherif talked about how people who have too much are easily corrupted by plenty and "plunge" into excess. "Islamic activity is about telling everybody that a Muslim's wealth is governed by communal obligations that stress the rights of the needy, poor, orphaned, and drifters." As a "believing" activist, Sherif is motivated by a desire to "to do more" and actively contribute to voluntary work, "like distributing food and collecting charity to be able to sell good quality food at affordable prices."

The upshot of this strong basis for their food justice activism is the primacy of social justice within what my interlocutors talked about as "the Islamic and moral solution." Drawing on comparative studies on food riots, such as those of eighteenth-century England, E. P. Thompson (1991) argues that moral economy is not simply about regular access to food at a certain price and particular moment in history. Instead, food bears deep cultural, as well as economic, importance. Moreover, religion becomes equated with subjective states of faith, and ritual with symbolic action. If we take food and practices of everyday spirituality as contributing not only to people's needs but also to the young Brothers' identity and aspirations, then Islamic food activism may be analyzed as practices in which connections between those receiving food and Brothers providing food are established. Islamic food activism falls into this realm of societal relationships and issues, which inform adaptable faith-based processes, with all their potentialities and contradictions.

"Field of Struggle"

In *Life within Limits: Well-Being in a World of Want,* Michael D. Jackson uses the phrase "field of struggle" to point to emotional and physical spaces that make life livable in a harsh and cruel world (2011: ix). I borrow "field of struggle" to think about faith-driven activities and spaces created by the economy of food. Jackson's interlocutors in Sierra Leone talked not about what they got out of life but about how they should bear their loads. Jackson learns from his long conversations in the field that this thought cannot be separated from relational obligations and the needs of others.

I find Jackson's work helpful when reflecting on my observations and conversations with my interlocutors while they were doing activism in the field of struggle. For example, on a cold December day in 2011, I was sitting on a bench outside a subsidized bread outlet in a Cairo suburb with Karim Nasser, a member of the Muslim Brotherhood youth movement. Karim was studying law and placed a pile of papers and books on the bench between us. The uppermost caught my eye: several writings on genetically modified foods, climate change, and food security and a book on the life of the Prophet Muhammad. We sat and chatted about his activities within the Brotherhood over tea from the nearby coffee shop, running through issues such as whether Islam is the only solution to the growing poverty, whether being a "believer" means being a better person, whether religious activists do better in outreach, and whether people put their trust more in a "believer." Meanwhile, people began to gather outside the bread kiosk to participate in our conversation. Many shared stories about rising food prices, indigestible bread, contaminated meat, the absence of basic foodstuffs, and hunger. A father of three told me that life has been worsening since the revolution and said, "Jobs pay too little, and food costs too much. Where is the bread, dignity, and justice?" In Egypt's first democratic parliamentary elections in 2011, he voted for the Muslim Brotherhood because "they understand how Egyptians struggle. They are not terrorists like people think. They help for the love of God and give us some dignity back. And most of all they are not corrupt."

Not to lose their place in the queue, the people, mostly men, moved closer to the outlet. Karim and I moved away. "Our faith drives us to do and be good," Karim said. "Our efforts are done with respect and humility. The objective is to facilitate the distribution of food for every Egyptian who needs it, without discrimination between women or men, Muslim or Christian." Smiling, he stroked his beard and said, "Just because we have beards doesn't make us evil."

We saw large wooden trays of round earthy flat layers of bread arriving. The crowd got loud; people pushed and shoved, trying to reach the small window out of which bread is distributed. Desperate faces. It was a painful sight. A man with his hand on his young son's shoulder looked at my camera and implored, "Please don't take a picture. Let us keep some of our dignity." I put the camera away. Out of nowhere young men with trimmed beards walked over. One walked into the store; the others stood outside and graciously greeted the shopkeeper. The crowd calmed down. "Who are these young men?" I asked. "Muslim Brotherhood food vigilantes," laughed the father with the son. According to Karim, these are irregular visits carried out to neighborhoods that have suffered from clashes in bread queues. The Brothers, Karim said, are never involved in violence; "On the contrary, we come to calm down people." He described the visits as "food jihad." What he meant by that is worth reproducing at length:

> For us the Qur'an is the literal word of God, and it was revealed by the Prophet Muhammad and recorded by his companions as he recited it. This is our all-embracing approach to Islam and it is universal. We share it with all other Muslims. It unifies us in our day-to-day struggle. For us, like all Muslims, to have faith comes with commandments and recommendations, and it shapes the way our lives will be lived and end. The Qur'an is always in our mind. The "Book" is not only part of our culture, it is also gives us emotional support for our jihad—our struggle for justice. Jihad means effort and not terror. Jihad means the struggle for the love of God. What you see today is a struggle [for the Brotherhood] to keep away food traders who bribe storekeepers into selling subsidized bread, which is then later sold in the streets at a higher price.

This example began with me asking Karim if he would point me to Brotherhood activities in public food outlets and his decision to show me what he described as an example of state food corruption or, as he put it, "the immorality of state economics. Whether you trade in arms or wheat it's the same thing. The common people are the ones that feel most of the pain. We want to heal and give them hope." The totality of Islam, Karim explained, extends to all the concerns of everyday life. As I have studied their charity work for close to two decades, this is another example I have observed of how Brotherhood efforts burrow into the community by providing an array of faith and outreach. The statement of the father of three in the bread queue that "they [the Brotherhood] are not terrorists like people think" dispels fears of the Brotherhood's sectarianism by describing how they "watch over" communities. Davis and Robinson show how this "watching over" goes back to the vision of the founder, Hassan al-Banna: "It's the religious duty of every Muslim to work towards the transformation of society. Words alone were not enough to re-Islamize Egyptian society; action was needed" (2012: 59).

What I have noticed in the years I have followed their efforts, especially during the period when I was at Tahrir Square in 2011 and during the first hundred days of the country's Islamist regime, is that although the wish for community outreach continues, young members are critically questioning older members of the Society. Young Brothers are becoming more assertive and demanding a much younger and more dynamic profile in the Brotherhood and its decision-making channels. Young members of the Brotherhood are involved in civil society, and as in the above situation at the bread outlet, they are in poor neighborhoods and are able to represent themselves and the faith for "the best possible reasons," as Karim said. The Brothers' moral obligation, Karim explained, "is to show solidarity and to provide people with the possibility of a decent meal and try to prevent food corruption. Food, health, and education is the only way to heal the Egyptian sense of dignity and calm down society." "How easy is that?" I asked. "Easy, we mobilize or join other young people in their protests. The difference between us and the other protesters is that we do it through the route of Islam and the struggle for justice—jihad. True Islam is what you have seen today on your visit."

What my visit also did was draw attention to how, in the context of bread queues, Islamic activism in the field of struggle mobilizes and constructs collective piety that inspires solidarity with people's grievances. Actively engaging in the distribution of bread is a public demonstration of the Brotherhood's extension of "true Islam." The meaning and applicability of food jihad, for Karim, is a direct response to the political order, economic hardship, and social life.

Mikhail Bakhtin (1981) wrote something to the effect that hell is the absolute lack of being heard. Karim, like the other Brothers, said that they not only hear but see the faces of humiliated Egyptians standing in endless bread queues and "show solidarity." The difficulties of standing in bread queues are not confined to matters of grasping the struggles of those who live "ordinary sufferings" (Bourdieu, Accardo, Ferguson, et al. 1999). My interlocutors also address the ways in which the Brothers drive relentless food jihad in the midst of the field of struggle to reorder the world through actions that involve food, which I argue requires human anticipation and hope.

Hope as a key component in healing people's grievances featured strongly in my conversations with Karim and other young Brothers. Shortly after my visit with Karim to the bread outlet, I was interviewing a young Brother who complained about how corrupt economics destroys traditional Egyptian family values, and the subject of "broken human spirits" came up. I asked him about the causes of broken spirits, and he listed several items, including "a spiritually broken and offended body."

In its extreme version, incarnated in the rising prices of grain and the scarcity of bread, the people in the bread queues manifested the absolute and arbitrary nature of crude economics on the human body. The body is the primary site on which the imprint of economics can be noticed and the human spirit damaged. Whether it is set in the context of the order of eating or the disorder of bread queues, the body is invested, in the sense that it is the means by which the veracities of the food economy are expressed and demonstrated. Whenever the body is well nourished or hungry, it is the last resort that "bears witness" (Fassin 2012) to political power and food justice.

In response to my question on whether Islam—having sufficient faith, as it were—is enough to bring about change, one of my interlocutors, who regularly does volunteer work at a low-cost grocery store, responded by saying simply, "Of course." When I questioned him further, he replied, in a matter-of-fact way, "We are guided by conscience. It is not always easy to do the right thing. But with a pure conscience I am able to balance between the here and now and the hereafter when God will judge my deeds." Using religion and providing faith enacted the capacity and potentiality for compassion and the possibility to bring about change. Through their efforts for justice, the Brothers aim for feelings of moral solidarity that can reach out and enable community and individual agency. This form of activism and aspiration for change resides in a complex mix of being themselves, cultivating relationships with others, and imagining a new order. It is this idea of human agency as human potential that I expand on elsewhere (Naguib 2010) and to which I return in this chapter. It is interesting to note how the Brothers' aspirational food ideas begin to break toward new potentiality and hope. I would suggest that their attempts to reestablish links between Islamic values and society demonstrate how they see themselves in relation to society and how they make sense of their lives and the lives of those they provide for. This link between aspirations and agency serves as a way to reconstruct hopeful futures for themselves and society (Appadurai 2007).

Bread Value

Bread signals prosperity, distress, anxiety, and social and political mobilization. Bread is a remarkable commodity that represents both substance and symbol. It provides nourishment and serves as a key mode of communication with spiritual, cultural, social, political, and economic inflection. Bread is literally one of the key actors in Egyptian social, political, and economic life. This was powerfully displayed during the 2011 revolution when women held up pieces of bread and men made head helmets from bread. The slogan was "Bread, Dignity, and Social Justice." Bread has a significant influence on private and public relationships, bringing about positive memories of meals and equally strong emotions about deprivation. Bread forges the complicated links between people and faith, justice and injustice, hope and anguish, whole and part, producer and consumer, seller and buyer, and—most of all, as one of the bakers the Brotherhood took me to said—"loyalty and duty."

Eating bread is one of the more satisfying things involving human senses: the mouth-watering smell of freshly baked bread, its warmth in our hands, and its fulfilling taste. "Remember," Mustafa told me, "the word for bread in Egyptian Arabic is 'aish'—life." Mustafa is an engineer and food activist who goes to bakeries to ensure they are not mixing the coarse government flour with dirt and sawdust when producing the traditional dark flat bread that is sold at the set price. As a small schoolchild he learned that Egypt was the breadbasket of the Roman Empire. Mustafa referred to what he read in the papers: "Bread is strategic. Egypt is the world's largest importer of wheat, and Egyptians eat the most bread in the world." Also, a report by the International Food Policy Research Institute argues that because of bread's significance in the Egyptian diet, "wheat is considered a strategic commodity in the country" (2000: 1). Calculating his household expenses Mustafa told me that food prices have been rising: "17 percent in just one year. In a nation where one in five live on an income of less than $1, subsidized bread is for millions of Egyptians the only calorie intake."

Mustafa went on to explain, "The challenge is that the amount of money that [it] is possible to make from this inferior flour would make anybody accept a bribe." Government bakeries receive flour from the government to produce subsidized bread. Although bakers receive a salary from the government, the problem of corruption starts when "the baker puts aside the flour and sells it on the black market for a larger profit." Mustafa explained that there are government inspectors whose job is to prevent this. These inspectors receive a government salary of about $50 (U.S.) a month. If they certify after three months that the baker has faithfully used the flour to bake bread, the baker gets a refund of about $1 for every bag of flour he has purchased.

Mustafa said that a baker who goes through forty sacks of flour a day over the three-month period gets back a decent sum,

> He can easily share [the money] with the same underpaid inspector who confirms that the baker has not broken any rules. Poverty pushes people to compromise. The inspector is a man who gets 50 American dollars. Say he wants to feed his children three times a day, send them to the government school. Of course going to any government school they will need afternoon tutoring. And say this inspector wants to take his wife out for a simple meal of Egyptian street food. Perhaps even take the kids along. What if this man wants to surprise his wife with a half kilo of good meat for Friday lunch? Maybe he even desires to buy her a new dress, shoes, or anything to make her happy? He can't. But he wants to—very much.

When I asked Mustafa if food inspectors take bribes, he replied, "Yes, they do." Mustafa's account shows the gray zones of wheat and bread subsides. The case illustrates the divisive and repressive connection between politics and economy that the Brotherhood activists seek to eradicate.

Food and Practice

Osman Galal is a young, sophisticated, articulate, and French-speaking Brotherhood member. Osman is a member of the Brotherhood against his family's wishes. At his home in an upscale neighborhood, we talked about the possible reasons for the Brothers' popularity among Egyptian men of different social backgrounds.

Osman attributed the group's success to its "openness and respect for the diversity of Egyptian society." It is linked, he said, to the ways the Brotherhood negotiates first the sympathy and then the recruitment of individuals. Osman described how the Brotherhood creates a pool of new members who are invited "but never forced to join meetings or campaigns." Instead, the Brothers connect with people's ordinary lives, and "when people see that we care they join the Brotherhood. We move easily from our personal everyday life to activism." Their outreach infrastructure is based on networking in communities and building communal locations like mosques, clinics, schools, food outlets, women's vocational training centers, and soccer fields, where they fulfill their promises of social and economic assistance.

An active Brotherhood presence in people's everyday lives lends material legitimacy to its message that Islam is the true path to democratic development. Osman explained, "Our message is not just a set of empty ideas debated by leaders you only see on TV; our message of faith is linked to practical activities that attend to people's real concerns—like food on the table." Key to their success, Osman said, is that "our ideas are tied directly to action" in concrete and identifiable ways. "For example, when we say Islam is the solution we don't mean, Let's go kill people; we mean, Let's build a mosque, let's provide shelter for orphans, kindergartens, clinics, and let's make sure people get their bread and not grimy bread. We demand good bread for all."

As an Islamic food activist, Osman feels a particular sense of satisfaction that allows him to imagine a better future for himself and others. His reasoning shows how the relationship between ideas and the structure of the group is key to overcoming the universal problem of varying degrees of commitment and beliefs.

Unfinished Food Business

Despite the obvious, inevitable, and strong linkages between the young Brothers and Islamic guidelines, their food activism demonstrates the need to be analytically attentive to specific forms of religious and social entanglements. The Islamic food activists discussed in this chapter are not part of a fanatical opposition movement. Their tracts, efforts, and conversations reveal actions concerned with contemporary economic issues, such as the food supply and food corruption. Their food activism is linked with Islam in such a way that each movement is strengthened and made more resilient and attractive to Egyptians from different backgrounds. A Brother described his obligation to heal people's food grievances as "food for the soul." Their efforts and slogans, rooted in Islamic concepts and representations, are tied to everyday events and ordinary Egyptian household economies. Therefore, the group is easily accessible to those who rely on its support, which strengthens the potential for Brotherhood recruiting.

In writing out my material for this chapter, I wanted to do more than simply bring together conversations with Islamic activists and highlight their personal relationships with piety and food justice. The format of their efforts, told here with emphasis on bread and bread queues, promotes exploration of generational gaps within Islamic movements, particularly those emerging from young men demanding fresh forms of political, economic, and social engagement. The material experience of bread—its fundamentality to Egyptian households and its moral basis for piety and society—is a crucial part of the Brothers' driving force and activism. Their physical engagement with the supply of bread to the people, the regular nonviolent battles against the corruption of flour, and the spectacle of their peaceful actions are illustrations of how and why individuals modify, recreate, and aim for practices that may potentially lead to social changes.

Activism involves a shifting praxis in the realms of everyday religious life and social actions. While Islamic food activism involves giving recognition, hope, and significance to people's everyday misfortunes, my ethnographic material shows that religion as the principal driving force for activism is not totalizing, nor are its outcomes easily predictable. In this chapter I wanted to provide an interpretation of how young members of the Brotherhood drive institutional outreach and infuse community with Islam through their own brand of faith-based activism. It is an attempt to understand what particular actions involving Islam and food mean and how they link religion, pragmatism, and activism. For anthropology, faith-based food activism revives questions of piety and practice as analytical units and invites us to go beneath discourses on Islamists, veils, beards, and orthodoxy. As an ethnographic study of an Islamic outreach movement in a largely Muslim country, I hope this chapter can encourage more research about how the rhythm of faith-based activism intersects the pulse of daily life and engages with concrete contemporary concerns that are not only about religion but about religion through food.

Acknowledgements

Research for this chapter was supported by the "Muslim Devotional Practices, Aesthetics and Cultural Formation" project financed by the Norwegian Research Council. I wrote the chapter during my stay as a visiting scholar at the Institut d'Études de l'Islam et des Sociétés du Monde Musulman in Paris in the spring of 2012; I would like to express my gratitude to Bernard Heyberger for inviting me and for showing interest in my work. Thanks also to Nathalie Bernard-Maugiron, Rémy Madiner, and Hélène Dauchez for making my stay at the institute so agreeable.

Note

1. All the names of interviewees in this piece are pseudonyms chosen by the men.

References

Appadurai, A. (2007), "Hope and Democracy," *Public Culture*, 19/1: 29–34.

Bakhtin, M. M. (1981), *The Dialogic Imagination*, Austin: University of Texas Press.

Bourdieu, P., Accardo, A., Ferguson, P. P., et al. (1999), *The Weight of the World*, Cambridge, UK: Polity.

Burgat, F. (2002), *Face to Face with Political Islam*, Oxford: I. B. Tauris.

Davis, J. D., and Robinson, R. V. (2012), *Claiming Society for God: Religious Movements and Social Welfare*, Bloomington: Indiana University Press.

Fassin, D. (2012), *Humanitarian Reason: A Moral History of the Present*, Berkeley: University of California Press.

International Food Policy Research Institute. (2000), *Egypt Integrated Household Survey 1997–1999*, Washington, DC: International Food Policy Research Institute.

Jackson, M. (2011), *Life within Limits: Well-Being in a World of Want*, Durham, NC: Duke University Press.

Lia, B. (1998), *The Society of the Muslim Brothers in Egypt: The Rise of an Islamic Movement, 1928–1942*, Beirut: Ithaca Press.

Munson, Z. (2001), "Islamic Mobilization: Social Movement Theory and the Egyptian Muslim Brotherhood," *Sociological Quarterly*, 42/4: 487–510.

Naguib, N. (1996), *Med kall til ledelse* [Men of commitment], Oslo: Universitetsforlaget.

Naguib, N. (2010), "For the Love of God: Care-Giving in the Middle East," *Social Sciences and Missions*, 23/1: 124–145.

Singerman, D. (2004), "The Networked World of Islamist Social Movements," in Q. Wiktorowicz (ed.), *Islamic Activism: A Social Movement Theory Approach*. Bloomington: Indiana University Press, 143–163.

Tadros, M. (2012), *The Muslim Brotherhood in Contemporary Egypt*, Oxon, UK: Routledge.

Thompson, E. P. (1991), "The Moral Economy Reviewed," in E. P. Thompson (ed.), *Customs in Common*, London: Merlin, 259–351.

Wickham, C. R. (2004), "Interests, Ideas, and Islamist Outreach in Egypt," in Q. Wiktorowicz (ed.), *Islamic Activism: A Social Movement Theory Approach*, Bloomington: Indiana University Press, 231–249.

Zahid, M. (2012), *The Muslim Brotherhood and Egypt's Succession Crisis: The Politics of Liberalisation and Reform in the Middle East*, London: I. B. Tauris.

Part IV

Transnational Networks

–11–

Information and Democracy
in the Global Coffee Trade

Daniel Reichman

For over twenty years, the global coffee trade has been a focal point for food activism. From fair trade to organics to sustainability programs like shade-grown and bird-friendly certification, the coffee sector has been the locus of novel partnerships between consumers, producers, states, nongovernmental organizations (NGOs), and retailers. These partnerships have created new institutions of private governance, like the fair trade system, that are often on the leading edge of movements to reform international food systems.[1] Given the explosive growth of ethical-trade initiatives and the bewildering array of certification systems around coffee, it would not be too much of an exaggeration to say that the coffee industry has served as a laboratory for various forms of food activism since the late 1980s, particularly in Latin America.[2] Recently, the landscape of food activism around coffee has undergone a notable change. The fair trade system, which has always placed a strong moral emphasis on alleviating poverty and labor exploitation among coffee producers, has spawned alternative "systems of private regulation" (Neilson 2008) that create codes of compliance for food safety, environmental protection, and good agricultural practices (GAPs), but downplay the issues of economic and social justice that have long been important components of fair trade.

One of the hallmarks of the new systems of private regulation is their emphasis on transparency and "legibility" as a basis for food democracy. In contrast to movements like fair trade that have explicitly political or moral agendas, some of the newer certification systems attempt to provide detailed, transparent information about the provenance of food, without making any political claims. Transparent information is supposed to engender change by allowing consumers to make informed choices. These new attempts to create "transparent" food systems are of special interest to activists and scholars of food activism because they lead us to consider exactly what food activism is. Psyche Williams-Forson and Carole Counihan define food activism as "counter-hegemonic" political action, encompassing a variety of "individual and collective efforts to change the world by changing the way food is produced, distributed, and consumed" (2011: 5). While demands for transparent food systems may change the way food is produced, distributed, and consumed, they are not necessarily counterhegemonic projects and therefore blur the line between food activism and corporate-driven reform. This chapter poses a simple question: is food *transparency* food *activism?*

Within the coffee industry, the trend toward transparency is aptly illustrated by Utz Certified, a certification system founded in 1997 as a partnership between Guatemalan coffee producers and the European supermarket chain Ahold. Utz certifies coffee and other commodities that are produced in compliance with specific norms for GAPs, environmental sustainability, traceability, and workplace safety. While many corporations and NGOs have internal codes of conduct and standards for GAPs, what makes Utz unique in the world of traceability is its "track and trace" system, which allows consumers to use a dropdown menu on a website to learn the origins of the coffee they consume. This may seem like a minor innovation—after all, thousands of single-origin coffees can be easily traced back to a particular farm, and the stories of these farms are told ad nauseum in marketing and promotional literature, printed on bags of coffee or on signs in stores and coffee shops (West 2012). Utz's key innovation is that it applies the "farm-to-cup" narrative of traceability to mass-produced blended coffees, which can contain beans from literally dozens of different places of origin. For example, trace a bag of espresso from IKEA with an expiration date of July 10, 2010, and you will find that the bag contains coffee from Guatemala, Honduras, Indonesia, two sources in Brazil, and Colombia. Click on the names of any of the individual producers, and you will get information about a specific farm, which varies greatly in level of detail but usually includes images of smiling farmers, verdant coffee fields, and modern processing mills.

The Utz system takes the desire to know the biography of one's food and scales it up to the highest possible level, tracing one of the world's most traded commodities across complex global supply chains. Utz certification is an ambitious attempt to account for every single bean that is bought and sold by major coffee vendors, requiring a significant amount of accounting and auditing work to determine which beans from a particular farm end up in a particular bag of coffee. As of this writing, "track and trace" is operational for coffees sold by major European retailers like IKEA and Douwe Egberts, and Utz plans for all of its consumers to be able to trace their coffee back to its source in the near future.

In contrast to fair trade, traceability systems like Utz are not tied to a particular set of moral or political values beyond the value of transparency itself. As Utz states in its promotional literature:

Fairtrade and UTZ CERTIFIED are both leading coffee certification programs. However, we are not the same....

Fairtrade is a poverty reduction program that invites consumers to choose Fairtrade-labelled products and actively participate in social and environmental improvements by paying a premium price. The price paid by consumers for Fairtrade coffee goes to disadvantaged farmers to make them more prosperous.

...UTZ CERTIFIED believes people want to continue buying their favorite brand for its quality, taste and price, while knowing that it is being produced in a sustainable way. UTZ CERTIFIED is about professionalism in coffee growing and traceability to ensure this.[3]

By providing information online, Utz offers consumers a tool to monitor or verify the source of their coffee without making any effort to reform the political economy of coffee by promoting better conditions for producers. Utz aims to raise farmer incomes by certifying coffee that can fetch a premium price on the open market. Unlike fair trade, Utz does not prioritize small producers over large farms, nor does it offer social premiums to growers who support community projects. Utz certification promotes the production of high-quality, safe, traceable coffee that will allow farmers to sell their crop at an above-market premium (about 10 percent in 2008), no matter the size or politics of the participating farm or cooperative. Utz may transform the relationship between the consumer and the product by providing coffee buyers with new and interesting information about provenance, but it does not explicitly attempt to change the relationship between producers and consumers.

Given its relatively apolitical agenda, Utz might be seen as a corporate co-optation of food activism. Daniel Jaffee notes that in virtually every social movement that has arisen around food, a "third-party civil society initiative was eventually challenged by a newer, industry-sponsored" system (2012: 99). These new systems tend to water down the agendas of the original activist projects. When viewed alongside fair trade, the rise of the Utz system seems to follow this pattern. However, the debate over the political value of transparency points toward even broader questions about the meaning of food democracy: Are consumers' demands to know the source of their food political ends in themselves? Or do demands for transparent food systems obscure important political economic inequalities in the name of uncritical faith in the power of information? Does the impulse to know the source of food create a new form of monitoring and surveillance? Put simply: Is transparency an effective tool of food activism?

These questions have recently been taken up by scholars from a variety of disciplines (Guthman 2007; Kleiman 2009; Pachirat 2012; West 2012), largely in response to the position that legible or transparent food systems are more trustworthy and safe than industrial food systems.[4] A comparison of the visions of food democracy offered by fair trade and Utz certification illustrates the virtues and drawbacks of transparency as a strategy for food activism. While traceability systems like Utz certainly offer the potential for political change, they must be accompanied by other kinds of political initiatives to meaningfully reform the relationship between coffee producers and consumers across increasingly complex global supply chains.

The discussion that follows begins with a sketch of the historical conditions and political economic interests that led to the creation of the fair trade and Utz certification systems. Taking the history of each certification system into account, I will use the case of La Quebrada, a coffee-growing community of 5,000 people in central Honduras that I have studied ethnographically since 2001, to illustrate how and why the Utz and fair trade systems have (or have not) been adopted in one community.[5] I do not intend to definitively suggest that one system is better or worse for farmers. Instead, I will use the case of La Quebrada to make explicit the strategies of political participation that are implicit in both the fair trade and Utz systems and to highlight some aspects of the coffee economy that remain invisible within transparency regimes.

Fair Trade and Utz Certification: Two Visions of Food Democracy

Fair Trade

Many readers of this volume will no doubt be familiar with the basics of the fair trade certification and labeling system. For coffee, a fair trade label indicates that a guaranteed minimum price of $1.40 (U.S.) per pound has been paid to small-scale coffee growers, who must be organized into democratically run cooperatives that can access preharvest credit from coffee buyers. The buyers also provide a "social premium" of $0.10 per pound of coffee, which supports local social and environmental initiatives. While the actual dynamics of the fair trade relationship have been called into question in various ethnographic settings (Lyon 2011; Lyon and Moberg 2010; West 2012), at the very least the fair trade labeling system aspires to strengthen the relationship between coffee farmers, roasters/retailers, and consumers.

Since the 1980s fair trade has transformed from a tiny fringe movement with a strong political agenda to a sophisticated global bureaucracy that now generates over $1 billion in revenue. Some of the world's largest corporations, like Wal-Mart and Nestlé, now buy and sell fair trade coffee, and fair trade standards are regulated by an international organization, the Fairtrade Labeling Organization International. While scholars and other observers have found much room for improvement within the fair trade system, it is hard to disagree with Julia Smith, who writes, "If the goal of the fair trade movement was to alter the way in which coffee was bought and sold, then it has succeeded beyond anyone's wildest dreams, at least within the specialty coffee market. Almost all specialty coffee vendors brag about how well they pay producers, the personal relationships they have created with producers, and the support they have provided for producer communities" (2010: 38). Regardless of whether or not a particular coffee is fair trade certified, the lives of coffee producers are very much on the minds of coffee buyers, and the relationships formed between farmers and retailers have even become fodder for marketing campaigns.

It is therefore easy to forget the activist roots of the fair trade movement. The first fair trade consumer label, the Dutch Max Havelaar label, was created in 1988 through a partnership between a Mexican indigenous coffee cooperative and Solidaridad, a Dutch Christian aid network (Lyon 2011: 12). In the United States, the roots of the fair trade coffee movement can be traced to political movements in the 1980s, when the U.S. role in wars in El Salvador, Nicaragua, and Guatemala made Central America a focal point for North American activism, especially among students. Virtually all of the major fair trade coffee initiatives in North America grew out of activist projects. In 1985 Paul Katzeff of Thanksgiving Coffee began selling Nicaraguan "Coffee for Peace," which included a $0.50 donation to the Sandinista revolution for every pound of coffee sold (Pendergrast 1999: 353). After the Reagan government banned the import of Nicaraguan coffee, two American activists founded Equal Exchange, a small coffee roaster in Massachusetts that began selling "Café Nica" to "offset the Reagan administration's trade embargo against the Sandinista government" (Lyon and Moberg 2010: 5). After a trip to Guatemala in the 1980s, Dean Cycon and Bill Fishbein created the Coffee Kids charity to support impoverished coffee-growing families. Paul Rice, who went on to found Transfair USA, the largest fair trade certification organization in the United States, helped to establish PRODECOOP, one of the most successful fair trade coffee cooperatives, in northern Nicaragua.

Until the late 1990s, fair trade coffee was not widely available in the United States, but activism around globalization generated significant public interest in the plight of coffee farmers around the world, particularly in Central America. In the late 1990s, activist organizations like Global Exchange and the U.S. Labor Education in the Americas Project launched protests against Starbucks, highlighting the exploitation and suffering of coffee farmers and pickers in Guatemala. The negative publicity these campaigns generated led Starbucks to establish its internal code of conduct for coffee purchasing, and other companies followed suit. By the mid-2000s, the fair trade coffee movement had pressured large-scale coffee buyers from McDonalds to Procter and Gamble to Nestlé to purchase at least some fair trade coffee.[6] While in many cases huge corporations "reap public relations benefits by incorporating a single fair trade item within a much wider line of products" without altering their business practices (Lyon and Moberg 2010: 11), the fact that they do anything at all signals that fair trade coffee has entered the mainstream.

The "mainstreaming" of fair trade has generated a significant amount of criticism highlighting the unequal power dynamics that shape the relationship between grower co-ops, certification outfits, and buyers. Sarah Lyon's (2011) study of one of the most successful fair trade–certified coffee cooperatives, Guatemala's La Voz Que Clama en El Desierto, found that the definition of a democracy within the co-op is highly contested, and certain social groups, especially women, are marginalized within the fair trade system. Similar claims have been made by Sarah Besky (2010) and Smith (2010), who have shown how fair trade's democratic rhetoric often hides power imbalances or outright exclusion of hired workers among commodity producers. Other criticisms of fair trade have focused on the relatively low quality of fair trade coffee, particularly in its early years, compared to other specialty coffees. More recently, fair trade has been criticized for not adequately raising the minimum price it guarantees to producers in order to keep pace with the international market. World coffee prices have reached all-time highs (over $2.00 per pound in 2011), but the fair trade minimum has increased only slightly in the past decade (from $1.25 to $1.40 in 2011, with the $0.20 premium for organic coffee rising to $0.30). While most case studies of fair trade coffee cooperatives have reported significant increases in prices paid to growers, these increases have never been as large as growers expected, nor have they been close to the guaranteed price that is advertised to consumers (Lyon and Moberg 2010). Mark Moberg's conclusions about fair trade banana cooperatives can also apply to coffee: "The research reveals that fair trade in practice falls considerably short of the new world of mutuality and transparency in producer-consumer relationships promised by many of the movement's advocates.... Nonetheless, it also demonstrates that the fair trade market has offered unequivocal material and social advantages to Caribbean farmers" (2010: 48).

While fair trade has generated modest successes for farmers, it has been criticized at a more abstract level for reducing large-scale economic and social issues to matters of individual consumer choice (Doane 2010; Fridell 2007; Jaffee 2007; Reichman 2008; West 2012). Under fair trade, the social welfare function that was historically performed by states becomes the responsibility of concerned shoppers, and in this sense, fair trade is often seen as epitomizing a neoliberal response to socioeconomic inequality, using a private, market-driven system to promote and enforce norms of socioeconomic and environmental justice. The shift to privatized strategies for social justice is especially striking when one considers that the world's coffee trade was regulated by an international treaty, the International Coffee Agreement (ICA), which set and maintained price controls for coffee farmers all over the world from 1962 to 1989. The ICA ended in 1989, leading to the liberalization of the global coffee market. At almost the exact same historical moment, fair trade emerged as a private system of market regulation for coffee. As Molly Doane writes, "The fair trade social movement operates in an environment in which it is no longer legitimate to expect global regulation or price supports. Activists can agitate to strengthen state regimes, or they can find new foci of reform" (2010: 231).

Utz Certified

The Utz system is an excellent example of a private institution that performs the regulatory role of the state at a transnational level. In 2010 more than 300,000 metric tons of coffee were stamped with an "UTZ Good Inside" label, which indicates that the beans were produced in compliance with Utz standards for GAPs. Utz standards are listed in the "Good Inside Code of Conduct," which "is an internationally recognized set of criteria for economic, social and environmentally responsible coffee production…based on the international ILO Conventions and including the principles of good agricultural practices" (Utz Certified 2010: 3). Utz sets uniform international standards for labor practices, crop management, and bookkeeping, and "specific issues covered include soil management, appropriate use of fertilizers, hygienic procedures for harvesting, postharvest processing and storage, waste and pollution management, worker health safety and welfare, including worker rights and provisions for education and potable water, conservation policies in place, and energy use" (Courville 2008: 294). Looking at such an exhaustive list of criteria for certification, it is hard not to see the parallels between Utz and the bureaucratic apparatus of the state. The key question, of course, is whether Utz (or any private regulatory institution) can use the carrots and sticks of the market to effectively monitor and enforce such a huge set of regulations.

Utz was formed in 1997 by the Ahold supermarket chain and a consortium of Guatemalan coffee exporters (Renard 2005). It was originally based on the EurepGAP system, a set of standards developed by a consortium of the world's largest grocery chains to improve the safety of fresh produce in European supermarkets in the aftermath of several high-profile food scares in Europe. Whereas fair trade began as an activist movement that came to be adopted by corporations, Utz began as a corporate-driven project that has partnered with civil society organizations and coffee producers. The Utz protocol does not offer a guaranteed minimum price to producers, but certification does increase the price their coffee can command on the open market. The system assures corporate coffee traders and consumers that coffee has been produced according to transparent standards.

Utz is part of a growing system of private governance that Maki Hatanaka, Carmen Bain, and Lawrence Busch (2005) call "third party certification" (TPC). The rise of TPCs is the end result of large-scale transformations in the food system, as liberalized transnational markets made national-level regulatory systems obsolete. The consolidation of the retail foods sector gave a few large firms unprecedented power to make demands on food producers. If particular food producers wanted access to a given market, they had to play by the rules set by multinational retailers. In the early stages of their development, TPCs sought to create a transparent set of standards for food and workplace safety, as well as environmental impacts, across the European Union. This would give food producers a uniform set of standards for compliance, rather than forcing them to navigate between multiple sets of retailer-specific standards. EurepGAP created a system of traceability so that contaminated food could quickly be tracked back to its source and removed from the food supply. TPCs have moved beyond the European Union, and as Utz demonstrates, they now audit far more than food safety.

Although TPCs are technically voluntary, in practice food producers must comply with their codes to sell their products to many of the world's largest food retailers.

They are, therefore, playing an increasingly important regulatory role in creating standards that affect food producers all over the world. Some scholars (Bain 2010; Busch 2010) worry that these systems are top-down and nondemocratic. Although Utz has made an effort to involve various stakeholders in the creation of its standards, it is still perceived as a system in which coffee buyers set the rules that producers follow. There is a risk that TPCs are creating a new, nondemocratic "command economy" in which large corporations (or third-party certifiers acting in their interests) play the role once played by the centralized state, but "instead of a democratic state, it is a corporate and bureaucratic state that—often in the name of transparency— is increasingly opaque" (Busch 2010: 346).

Fair Trade and Utz in La Quebrada, Honduras

In 2001, when I first began to study coffee in La Quebrada, the world coffee market was in serious decline. The international coffee price, which is set at the New York Board of Trade, was $0.50, and farmers in town were getting less than $0.15 a pound for washed Arabica coffee. By 2003 the market had entered into a freefall, and farmers were being paid less than $0.10 per pound. This rapid decline made coffee farming an unsustainable enterprise for farmers who did not have secondary sources of income. Migration to the United States became the most common strategy for farmers to deal with the crisis (Reichman 2011).[7]

At that time, Honduran coffee was considered inferior to that of its Central American neighbors, Guatemala, Costa Rica, El Salvador, and Nicaragua. For a variety of historical reasons, including the dominance of mining and banana interests, Honduras did not develop a large, influential coffee-growing elite in the nineteenth century, and its coffee sector was perceived as a "sleeping giant" until very recently (see Euraque 1996; Williams 1994). Honduras exported less coffee than the other Central American countries, and its coffee was discounted by as much as 15 percent on the international market.

In 2001 the Honduran coffee sector was the recipient of a large amount of aid and technical assistance from the U.S. Agency for International Development (USAID), the U.S. Department of Agriculture, and other international donors that came to the country in the aftermath of Hurricane Mitch, which struck the country in late 1998 (Ensor 2009). The specialty coffee industry was designated by USAID and the Honduran government as an area of potential economic growth, and a great deal of resources were directed toward improving quality and helping coffee farmers enter the rapidly expanding specialty market. At this time, two local coffee farmers in La Quebrada began to investigate entrance into the fair trade market. They rented a *beneficio* (mill) with assistance from several international organizations with plans to establish the community's first certified organic cooperative. They hoped to enter the fair trade system after the transition to organic was complete.

The attempt to establish a cooperative in La Quebrada was unsuccessful for two reasons. First, in order to participate in fair trade, Honduran farmers needed to be classified as small-scale producers according to country-specific definitions. The leaders of the co-op, as well as the majority of interested growers, held over 35 acres of land on average, which made their farms too large to qualify for fair trade certification. These relatively large farmers (whose holdings were still very small by most Central American standards) were the people who were best equipped to take the financial and personal risks involved in starting a co-op. They had the capital necessary to absorb the costs of transitioning to organic farming and fair trade certification, and they had enough political influence to organize sympathetic farmers into a cooperative. They also had the skill and experience needed to deal with the bookkeeping and auditing work necessary to enter the fair trade and organic markets. While some smallholder families were interested in fair trade, their coffee plots were almost always supplemented by subsistence farming, temporary hired work, and remittances from relatives abroad. They were not willing or able to risk joining a risky, fledgling coffee cooperative in the midst of the worst downturn in coffee prices in the last century.

The international coffee crisis, which had nothing to do with the fair trade system itself, was the second reason that the cooperative in La Quebrada never really got off the ground. From 2001 to 2004, coffee prices were far below the cost of production. It would have taken between one and two crop years for farmers to transition to organic production and meet the criteria for fair trade certification. During that time, they would keep some of their fields "conventional" to generate income during the transition, which lowered crop yields in the organic plots by as much as 30 percent. They needed good returns in the conventional plots to make up for the decreases in yields in the transitional organic plots, but with prices so low, even the most efficient and productive farmers were having trouble making ends meet. There was simply no way that growers could survive the transitional phase and make the necessary changes to make certification possible. For that reason, the co-op ceased to exist after the 2003 crop year.

I spent much of 2003–2004 in La Quebrada and then did not return until late 2008, by which time world coffee prices had increased dramatically. The Honduran coffee industry had significantly expanded overall production, from 2.5 million bags in 2004 to 4.5 million bags in 2008, and prices had risen from $0.65 to $1.75 per pound (International Coffee Organization, ICO, Indicator Price). Investments in quality improvement made by USAID and Instituto Hondureño del Café (IHCAFE), the quasi-state agency responsible for managing the Honduran coffee sector, had begun to generate real benefits. The country's Cup of Excellence program, an online cupping competition and auction of the country's very best coffees, had improved the reputation of Honduran coffee. While low-grade coffees from Brazil and Vietnam continued to dominate the market in terms of volume, Honduras had become the world's sixth-largest coffee producer. The combination of increased quality, higher prices, and rising worldwide demand for coffee meant that coffee exporters were searching hard for reliable sources of quality Honduran coffee. It was a dramatic reversal of the conditions I had observed only a few years earlier, as coffee buyers were now desperate for high-quality beans.

In 2008 the first coffee farm in La Quebrada had only recently been certified by Utz. The farm of over 200 acres of high-quality coffee finca belonged to a farmer who had not been involved in the formation of the cooperative and who had agreed to sell his entire certified crop to Honducafé, the third-largest exporter of Honduran coffee. In conjunction with Utz, Honducafé provided the farmer with technical support and financial assistance to help bring the farm into compliance with Utz standards. Honducafé was able to secure a reliable, traceable, and high-volume source of coffee for its customers, at a time when such coffee was in extremely high demand. For his part, the farmer got free technical support that helped increase productivity and coffee quality and offered an above-market premium for certified coffee.

The changes needed on the farm were modest. They included accurately measuring the area of fields and demarcating borders; accurately measuring the altitude, which is an important determinant of coffee bean quality; constructing wooden sheds to keep fertilizers and other chemicals in locked, marked spaces; building outdoor latrines for hired farmworkers; installing first aid kits and posting instructions for how to administer first aid for workplace injuries, chemical accidents, or fires; separating refuse into "organic" and "inorganic" containers; posting instructions for workers on how to properly pick coffee and handle it postharvest; and installing barriers and fencing in fields to prevent erosion.

The changes were basically technical measures that would bring the farm into compliance with Utz codes. The leader of a local coffee growers' union described the changes as "basically aesthetic." He was not intending to be critical of Utz or to claim that it was not meeting its goals. He was simply observing that the changes stipulated by the Utz code of conduct were, in his opinion, relatively superficial. The entire system was designed to formalize practices to make them visible to a specific audience—the certification agencies that would visit on an annual basis. Whether the signs and regulations were actually heeded was less important than having a bureaucratic artifact to prove their existence.

Conclusion: Transparency, Communication, and Food Democracy

Trace a bag of Utz coffee online, and a small Google map will appear with markers indicating the countries from which the coffee within originated.[8] Click the marker on Honduras, and a list of producers will pop up on the screen. Some of these producers are local or regional coffee cooperatives; others are large-scale coffee exporters, including Honducafé. The pages that provide information about the coffee cooperatives tend to have testimonial quotations about the value of Utz certification. For example, one page reads, "By selling my UTZ CERTIFIED coffee the consumer gets to know that my family and I have produced the coffee in the package. With the premium he is willing to pay, I can recover some of the investments made to achieve the certification and I also can grant my children access to education and hence a brighter future and give my family a better life." The pages that describe the large coffee enterprises like Honducafé are far less detailed and often give a generic statement about the company's commitment to sustainability and high-quality coffee, while listing the total land area under Utz certification and the number of people employed by each company.

One potential problem with this information is that coffee buyers may have almost no context to evaluate the information presented online. Utz gives no indication that Honducafé, for example, is not a coffee producer but a huge coffee exporter that buys coffee from farmers all over the country. While none of the Utz information is untrue, it can easily give false impressions about the farmers "behind the bean." It is indeed fascinating to see just how many people from all over the world can play a part in the production of one small bag of coffee, but what do we do with this information? As the example of Honducafé suggests, one would need a tremendous amount of knowledge of the coffee industry in any given country to give any real meaning to this content. An individual—no matter how well versed in coffee—cannot be expected to put information about coffee farmers from Brazil to India into any meaningful context. There is, therefore, a risk that ostensibly transparent information becomes just another form of marketing, used strategically to transform the relationship between the consumer and the *product.* While this kind of detailed information about coffee is certainly interesting and appealing, it also exemplifies some of the limitations of transparent information as a platform for democratizing food systems: more information does not necessarily mean more democracy.

Julie Guthman, an incisive critic of the view that "transparency equals democracy" for food, argues that the desire to know more about the source of food products may be an obstacle to political reform (2007). Guthman is part of a growing number of critics who have questioned the faith in personal verification and monitoring that underlies much of the activism around food (Pachirat 2012; Stoll 2006). This perspective is most evident in Michael Pollan's *The Omnivore's Dilemma* (2006), which popularized the idea that "legibility" and "visibility" are the sine qua non of food democracy (Kleiman 2009). In his best-selling book, Pollan advanced the idea of the "glass abattoir," a transparent slaughterhouse that would shock meat eaters into political action by making visible the hidden practices of industrial meat production. The book contains a more general appeal to the value of "knowing" one's food, championing local food economies, farmers' markets, CSAs, and other institutions designed to make the relationship between producer and consumer more proximate.

As Guthman writes, "The local is paired against the distant, global, unknowable, and as the logic goes, untrustable. Pollan shares a growing sensibility that the only way to trust food is to see it for yourself. Conceding the rules of neoliberalism, transparency is the name of the game; various certification schemes are a second best choice to looking the farmer in the eye" (2007: 263). For Guthman and other critics of Pollan's localism, the emerging culture of the "personal audit" around food is a troubling symptom of the breakdown of state regulatory power under neoliberalism (Guthman 2007: 263; Kleiman 2009: 411; Reichman 2008). Governmental oversight of food, labor, and the environment has been either co-opted by large corporations or eclipsed by global supply chains that are beyond the scope of any public regulatory agency. Guthman sees "food biographies" as "neoliberal anti-politics" (2007: 264) that eschew a complex engagement with political economic analysis in favor of simplistic "farm-to-table" stories.

When it comes to coffee, Guthman is correct in many respects. Both fair trade and Utz have limited power as regulatory agencies, compared to international institutions like the ICA. Recall that the single biggest determinant of the well-being of coffee farmers in La Quebrada is the price for coffee on the international commodities market, something neither Utz nor fair trade can play any meaningful role in regulating. Coffee is the second most traded commodity in the world after oil, and prices are determined by global supply and demand for coffee as well as macrolevel economic conditions. In the recent past, for example, coffee prices have been driven up by investments in commodities as hedge fund investors fled the stock market. Additionally, rising demand for coffee in Korea, China, India, and Brazil has played a role in rising prices. These are the kind of issues that the price controls and production quotas maintained by the ICA were designed to address, but they are simply beyond the scope of any system of private regulation.

This is not to say that demands for transparency are misguided. As of now, it is too soon to say how the Utz system will actually be used by consumers, but it is possible that seeing the sheer number of producers involved in producing one simple bag of coffee will lead some to appreciate the complexity of the coffee trade and recognize the need for more powerful forms of regulation. However, for transparency to become a path to effective reform, the challenge will be turning information into communication. The interests of coffee producers must be communicated and incorporated into effective political institutions, or they risk being presented as mere marketing content, the desires of what Paige West calls "fantasy farmers" (2012: 234). Two decades of activism around coffee have led to novel experiments in transnational governance and regulation that have incorporated new interest groups into the coffee system. What began as the project of a small group of committed food activists has transformed into a billion-dollar industry that involves some of the world's largest corporations. The very existence of the "track and trace" system for mass-produced coffees illustrates that the desire to shorten the symbolic distance between coffee farmer and drinker is no longer just an attribute of a small niche market. Moving forward, we must make sure that new technologies of governance can effectively institutionalize communication between producers, consumers, and retailers to form a democratic political space. It is still unclear whether private regulatory systems are up to the task.

Notes

1. Fair trade standards, for example, are now applied to dozens of commodities, including tea, sugar, bananas, palm oil, and cacao.
2. The Specialty Coffee Association of America has published an eight-page chart that summarizes each of the major coffee-certification schemes: organic, fair trade, Rainforest Alliance, Smithsonian Bird Friendly, Utz Certified, and the 4C Common Code (a new transnational certification scheme).
3. Utz Certified [website], http://consumer.utzcertified.org/index.php?pageID= 211#, accessed November 11, 2009.
4. This view is most apparent in Michael Pollan's best-selling book *The Omnivore's Dilemma* (2006). See Kleiman 2009 for a trenchant analysis of Pollan and his critics.
5. This research is based on four periods of fieldwork conducted in La Quebrada, Honduras (a pseudonym), during 2001–2008 (see Reichman 2011). Fieldwork included participant observation with coffee farmers, processors, buyers, and laborers. Interviews with local representatives of Utz were conducted in December 2008.
6. Rick Peyser, the director of social advocacy at Green Mountain Coffee Roasters, who has been one of the most visible champions of fair trade coffee since the late 1990s, details the role of activists and their direct and effective impact on corporate coffee companies in his autobiography (Peyser and Mares 2012).
7. In her study of the Honduran community of La Campa, Lempira, Catherine Tucker (2008) found that emigration was not common among coffee farmers.
8. "Trade and Traceability," Utz Certified, http://utzcertified.org/aboututzcertified/traceandtraceability?lang=, accessed July 12, 2013.

References

Bain, C. (2010), "Structuring the Flexible and Feminized Labor Market: GlobalGAP Standards for Agricultural Labor in Chile," *Signs,* 35/2: 343–370.

Besky, S. (2010), "Colonial Pasts and Fair Trade Futures: Changing Modes of Production and Regulation in Darjeeling Tea Plantations," in S. Lyon and M. Moberg (eds.), *Fair Trade and Social Justice: Global Ethnographies,* New York: New York University Press, 97–122.

Busch, L. (2010), "Can Fairy Tales Come True? The Surprising Story of Neoliberalism and World Agriculture," *Sociologica Ruralis*, 50/4: 331–351.

Courville, S. (2008), "Organic and Social Certification: Recent Developments from the Global Regulators," in C. M. Bacon, V. E. Méndez, S. R. Gliessman, D. Goodman, J. A. Fox (eds.), *Confronting the Coffee Crisis: Fair Trade, Sustainable Livelihoods, and Ecosystems in Mexico and Central America*, Cambridge, MA: MIT Press, 288–310.

Doane, M. (2010), "Relationship Coffees: Structure and Agency in the Fair Trade System," in S. Lyon and M. Moberg (eds.), *Fair Trade and Social Justice: Global Ethnographies*, New York: New York University Press, 229–257.

Ensor, M. O. (ed.) (2009), *The Legacy of Hurricane Mitch: Lessons from Post-disaster Reconstruction in Honduras*, Tucson: University of Arizona Press.

Euraque, D. (1996), *Reinterpreting the Banana Republic: Region and State in Honduras, 1870–1972*, Chapel Hill: University of North Carolina Press.

Fridell, G. (2007), *Fair Trade Coffee: The Prospects and Pitfalls of Market-Driven Social Justice*, Buffalo, NY: University of Toronto Press.

Guthman, J. (2007), "Commentary on Teaching Food: Why I Am Fed Up with Michael Pollan, et. al.," *Agriculture and Human Values*, 24: 261–264.

Hatanaka, M., Bain, C., and Busch, L. (2005), "Third-Party Certification in the Global Agrifood System," *Food Policy*, 30: 354–369.

Jaffee, D. (2007), *Brewing Justice*, Berkeley: University of California Press.

Jaffee, D. (2012), "Weak Coffee: Certification and Co-optation in the Fair Trade Movement," *Social Problems*, 59: 94–116.

Kleiman, J. (2009), "Local Food and the Problem of Public Authority," *Technology and Culture*, 50: 399–417.

Lyon, S. (2011), *Coffee and Community: Maya Farmers and Fair Trade Markets*, Boulder: University Press of Colorado.

Lyon, S., and Moberg, M. (eds.) (2010), *Fair Trade and Social Justice: Global Ethnographies*, New York: New York University Press.

Moberg, M. (2010), "A New World? Neoliberalism and Fair Trade Farming in the Eastern Caribbean," in S. Lyon and M. Moberg (eds.), *Fair Trade and Social Justice: Global Ethnographies*, New York: New York University Press, 47–71.

Neilson, J. (2008), "Global Private Regulation and Value-Chain Restructuring in Indonesian Smallholder Coffee Systems," *World Development*, 36/9: 1607–1622.

Pachirat, T. (2012), *Every Twelve Seconds: Industrialized Slaughter and the Politics of Sight*, New Haven, CT: Yale University Press.

Pendergrast, M. (1999), *Uncommon Grounds: The History of Coffee and How It Transformed Our World*, New York: Basic Books.

Peyser, R., and Mares, B. (2012), *Brewing Change: Behind the Bean at Green Mountain Coffee Roasters*, Shelburne, VT: Wind Ridge.

Pollan, M. (2006), *The Omnivore's Dilemma: A Natural History of Four Meals*, New York: Penguin.

Reichman, D. (2008), "Justice at a Price: Regulation and Alienation in the Global Economy," *PoLAR: Political and Legal Anthropology Review,* 31/1: 134–149.

Reichman, D. (2011), *The Broken Village: Coffee, Migration, and Globalization in Honduras,* Ithaca, NY: Cornell University Press.

Renard, M. (2005), "Quality Certification, Regulation, and Power in Fair Trade," *Journal of Rural Studies,* 21/1: 419–431.

Smith, J. (2010), "Fair Trade and the Specialty Coffee Market: Growing Alliances, Shifting Realities," in S. Lyon and M. Moberg (eds.), *Fair Trade and Social Justice: Global Ethnographies,* New York: New York University Press, 28–46.

Stoll, S. (2006), "The Smallholder's Dilemma," *Technology and Culture,* 47/4: 808–813.

Tucker, C. (2008), *Changing Forests: Collective Action, Common Property, and Coffee in Honduras,* New York: Springer Academic.

Utz Certified (2010), "UTZ Certified Good inside Code of Conduct for Coffee" [report], Amsterdam: Utz Certified.

West, P. (2012), *From Modern Production to Imagined Primitive: The Social World of Coffee from Papua New Guinea,* Durham, NC: Duke University Press.

Williams, R. (1994), *States and Social Evolution: Coffee and the Rise of National Governments in Central America,* Chapel Hill: University of North Carolina.

Williams-Forson, P., and Counihan, C. (eds.) (2011), *Taking Food Public: Redefining Foodways in a Changing World,* New York: Routledge, 1–7.

–12–

Cultures of Corn and Anti-GMO Activism in Mexico and Colombia

Elizabeth Fitting

Without corn there is no country. (Sin maíz, no hay país.)

—Slogan from Mexican anti-GMO network In Defense of Maize

We [the Zenú] are maize seeds, we are people of corn. We have more than thirty native varieties that are the legacy of our ancestors who for hundreds of years conserved them for us, their children.

—Statement posted on website of the Red Agroecologica del Caribe (RECAR), Colombia (November 4, 2009)

In Colombia activists have organized a campaign against transgenic or genetically modified (GM) seeds and crops. Much like their counterparts in Mexico, activists use maize (or corn) as a symbol of national sovereignty, as well as campesino (peasant) and indigenous cultures, which they believe are undermined by transgenic varieties of corn. Genetically modified organisms (GMOs) are "global objects of contention" (Müller 2006) that take on specific characteristics and meanings in particular times and places. In Latin America, activists see transgenic maize as an embodiment of contemporary imperialism or neoliberal capitalism—a foreign threat to political autonomy, native varieties and genetic resources, national and regional cultures, and economic independence.

This chapter argues that when activists mobilize narratives about the cultural importance of traditional corn varieties (*criollos*),[1] they highlight the specificity of place on the one hand and participate in transnational activist networks to share information and strategies on the other. Among the Colombian anti-GMO activists and indigenous leaders I spoke to, maize represents indigenous culture. In Mexico maize is a symbol of indigeneity but also of the nation, with its complex history of cultural and racial mixing (*mestizaje*).[2] Activist slogans and statements such as "We are a people of corn" and "Without corn there is no country" emphasize maize as a *place-specific* way of life, food, agricultural crop, biological resource, and cultural practice.

This sense of place and culture is multiscalar. In other words, maize invokes, at times, elements of shared culture across different scales of place, from the small rural community or region to the nation-state to indigenous and rural Mesoamerica.

By looking at narratives about maize we also see how activist groups *share* strategies and information. During my interviews I learned that maize became a strategic focus of the anti-GMO campaign in Colombia based, in part, on lessons learned from the 2001 controversy in Mexico over gene flow between transgenic and native varieties of maize, which was seen by activists as the world's first case of "genetic pollution" in a crop's center of biological diversity and origin. Narratives about maize as culture threatened by transgenic varieties resonate differently in these two countries, however. Part of the reason why the public response to GMOs in Mexico and Colombia differs so greatly, I suggest, has to do with the degree to which maize is an effective symbol of home or cultural identity for people beyond activist circles.

I explore agency in three related ways. First, Mexican and Colombian campesinos and indigenous maize farmers are not simply the victims of globalization, as they are sometimes portrayed. The farmers discussed here have collectively organized and teamed up with professional activists in an effort to raise awareness about how agricultural biotechnology affects them, to save and use criollos and to bring about policy changes at the community, government, and even international levels. I should also point out that in a previous phase of research among a community of indigenous campesinos and migrants in the Tehuacán Valley of Mexico, I found that even though residents were not involved in antiglobalization or anti-GMO activism, they had adapted to and strategized around the effects of neoliberal globalization on their lives and livelihoods, and that this too is a form of agency (Fitting 2011).

Second, I illustrate that agency is enacted through "globalization from below" as it is built *horizontally,* initiated between groups from the Global South, rather than just from Global North to South. Globalization from below refers to the transnational "linking of knowledge and political action in hundreds of civic initiatives" (Falk 1997: 19) that challenge what is sometimes referred to as "globalization from above," or the neoliberal policies of international institutions and national governments and the influence of transnational corporations. These activists are agents of change in sharing information and building networks horizontally.

Third, I suggest that as a powerful symbol of place (albeit to differing degrees), maize has catalyzed anti-GMO activism and forged or deepened links between nongovernmental organizations (NGOs), activist organizations, and individuals. Activists in Mexico and Colombia voice not only the concerns about GMOs that are heard in other parts of the world but also ones that are specific to their region. By framing transgenic maize as a cultural issue (in addition to the environmental concerns and often scientific discussion about gene flow and biological diversity) activists generate solidarity among different types of groups and individuals. They connect and enroll actors and political struggles *beyond* the question of agricultural biotechnology and thus express a third form of agency.

This chapter is based on interviews with activists and indigenous leaders in Colombia (from the fall of 2011 to the spring of 2012); ethnographic research in Mexico with maize producers; interviews with participants in the GM corn debates, such as activists, biologists, and regulators (2000–2002, with extended visits over the next six years); and analysis of national media coverage on GMOs in both countries (particularly newspapers, activist Listservs, and websites). I begin by providing a brief discussion of the importance of maize in the two countries, some background information about the regulation of GMOs, and the reasons for activists' concerns about them. I then turn to how Mexican activism and the controversy over transgenic corn influenced anti-GMO activism in Colombia.

Cultures of Corn

Maize is such a powerful symbol because of its multifaceted economic, cultural, and political importance. Corn continues to be grown among campesinos because it is a traditional crop and a mainstay of the rural diet in various corn-based foods and beverages, such as *tortillas, tamales,* and *atole* in Mexico and *arepas, tamales,* and *mazamorra* or *peto* in Colombia. These maize-based foods are regularly consumed in cities, but in the countryside every part of the corn plant is put to use. The shelled cobs are burned as fuel for fires, the leftover stalks are given to animals as feed, and in Mexico the dried husks are used to wrap tamales. When cash is needed in emergencies, the grain can be sold in small amounts (although often at a loss). Additionally, because traditional varieties of corn tend to be well adapted to local conditions and environments, corn is considered hardier than other cash crops.

In Mexico, maize is cultivated on nearly 20 million acres (8 million hectares), most of which is rain fed and involves nonindustrial farming (Turrent Fernández, Wise, and Garvey 2012: 7). The farming, milling, and cooking of maize are a key part of everyday life in the countryside. The crop is so central to the rural diet that a meal is considered incomplete without tortillas. In many indigenous regions of the Americas, maize seed retains a strong spiritual significance and is the focus of a variety of rituals involving the blessing of seed, celebrating of the harvest, and so on. For many indigenous peoples, like the Zapotecs of Oaxaca, maize has a soul (González 2001).

In rural Colombia, while maize is also regularly eaten in both rural and urban areas, generally speaking it is not required to complete a meal. It is grown on approximately 460,000 hectares (in 2010), largely along the Atlantic Coast in the department of Córdoba, followed by Sucre and Cesar, but also in the interior departments of Tolima, Meta, Valle, and Huila (Federación Nacional de Cultivadores de Cereales y Leguminosas [Fenalce] 2011). While maize represents a way of life for indigenous groups like the Zenú who grow the crop, it is not as central to the idea of the nation as a whole—what it means to be Colombian—as it is in Mexico.

Transgenic Crops: Transgressing Nature, Trespassing Territory

Transgenic or GM plants contain DNA material inserted from other plants or species. They are products of biotechnology, a set of recombinant DNA techniques first developed in the 1970s that use organisms, their parts or processes, to modify or create living organisms with particular traits. Conventional plant breeding and farming practices also produce new gene characteristics in plants, but unlike genetic engineering, they work at the level of the whole plant. While biotech corporations portray biotechnology as the latest accomplishment in a long history of human intervention and improvement of nature (Levidow 1991), anti-GMO activists often suggest that such technology transgresses or defiles nature because it moves genetic material across species.

The "most intense, sustained, and effective" campaigns against agricultural biotechnology have taken place in western Europe, where anti-GMO activism has successfully mobilized consumers around issues of food safety, ideas about preserving rural society, and ethical concerns about genetic engineering as "playing God" or the defilement of the natural boundaries between species (Schurman 2003: 9–10). In the Global South, resistance to this technology tends to focus on a different set of issues: property rights and the effects of GMOs on the environment and small-scale farmers' livelihoods (11).

Anthropologists have shown that foods that blur distinct cultural categories are often seen as impure or dangerous (Douglas 1966). GM foods and crops carry this sense of danger because they are undetectable by appearance; they are indistinguishable from nontransgenic varieties in the field and from traditional foods at the grocery store. With the expansion of the industrial food system and the related rise in food scares from the 1990s on (such as salmonella, *E. coli,* and bovine spongiform encephalopathy), consumers are increasingly worried that they do not know where their food comes from nor what they are eating. The portrayal of GMOs as "Frankenfoods"—a term used by activists around the world—reflects this consumer anxiety about foods made from a technology that can transfer genes from one species to another (Whatmore 2002). Activist campaigns employ the image of Frankenfoods in very different places, such as Europe and across the Americas.

Anthropologists have also found that in places like Mexico, France, and Costa Rica GMOs have come to represent neoliberal globalization or U.S. economic and political dominance that threatens regional or national sovereignty (Fitting 2006a,b, 2011; Heller 2002; Pearson 2009). Among Mexican and Colombian activists, transgenic corn in particular is seen as a foreign threat. In my interview with a Pijao community leader from Tolima, Colombia, he explained what he saw as the problem with transgenic corn: his community wants to protect native varieties from seed that both "come[s] from outside our culture" and "runs counter" to it (February 2012, Bogotá).

Controversy erupted in 2001 when Ignacio Chapela and David Quist published the results of their study that three different transgenic DNA sequences were found in traditional corn from the highlands of Oaxaca, Mexico.[3] The likely source of such corn was imports from the United States, where at the time 25 percent of the crop was transgenic and unlabeled as such. Today 88 percent of U.S. maize is transgenic (U.S. Department of Agriculture, Economic Research Service 2012). Scientists and activists found similar evidence in other parts of the country, including the government's corn supply (Ezcurra, Ortiz, and Soberón 2002; INE-CONABIO 2002).

The finding of transgenic maize in Mexico garnered considerable media and activist attention around the world as the world's first case of "genetic pollution" in a crop's center of biodiversity and origin. It became a cause célèbre for international environmental NGOs like Greenpeace, seed and food groups such as the small international nonprofit GRAIN, and the transnational peasant and farmer group Via Campesina. The controversy was debated at activist-organized events like press conferences, rallies, and seed exchanges and in academic and scientific research papers, government debates before Congress, government and activist working groups and conferences, and the national and international media.[4]

The unintentional gene flow between transgenic corn and native varieties in Mexico was discussed by activists as contamination, a kind of genetic pollution or trespassing of unwanted living material that has, or could have, negative environmental impacts (Cleveland, Soleri, and Aragon 2003; Soleri et al. 2005). Such impacts include increased herbicide tolerance and pest resistance, unforeseen negative consequences for nontarget organisms, and the loss of traditional seed varieties.[5]

In addition to the environmental impact of transgenic seeds and crops, activists in both Mexico and Colombia tend to raise concerns about the effect of GMOs on cultural autonomy and practices related to food and agriculture (particularly in the case of maize) and the commodification of the seed, which have economic and political ramifications for farmers' livelihoods. Not only are small-scale producers and peasants facing more expensive inputs or costs (at a time when state financial and technical support for such farmers has been cut), but they have been largely excluded from regulatory decisions and frameworks for GMOs.[6]

The Neoliberal Food Regime: Biotechnology and Biocapital

The commercial planting of biotech crops around the globe went from 1.7 million hectares in 1996 to 160 million hectares in 2011 (International Service for the Acquisition of Agri-Biotech Applications 2011). Food scholars have suggested that genetic engineering and its regulation are central to an emergent neoliberal food regime—the institutional structures, norms, and practices of food trade, governance, and political economy (Pechlaner and Otero 2008). This new food regime and phase of capitalism (what some have called biocapitalism) involves the harnessing and management of biological processes and resources in order to generate profit. Transgenic seed is often accompanied by intellectual property rights (IPRs) that require users to pay a licensing fee in addition to the initial cost of purchasing seed. IPRs run counter to peasants' and farmers' widespread practice of saving and exchanging seed for replanting and provide another way to overcome the free reproduction of seed, or seed's "biological barrier to commodification" (Kloppenburg 1988). The commercialization of seed, including IPRs, contributes to "accumulation by dispossession," or the accumulation of capital by undermining a group's access to and control over the resources it needs to maintain its livelihood (Harvey 2003: 147–148).

One of the striking features of this food regime is that countries from the Global South now import staple foods that they themselves produce. Both Mexico and Colombia have seen rising corn imports in recent years for animal feed, food, and industrial purposes. In Mexico imports have reached 8 to 9 million metric tons per year (or higher in years of production shortfalls).[7] In Colombia imports have increased since the 1990s, reaching 3.3 million metric tons in 2010, although a new government program hopes to reduce imports (Fenalce 2011: 4). Trade agreements and the World Trade Organization tend to protect farm subsidies in the Global North, "while Southern states have been forced to reduce agricultural protections and import staple, and export high-value, foods" (McMichael 2009: 148). However, as Gabriela Pechlaner and Gerardo Otero importantly point out, "despite prevailing trends, sufficient local resistance to the technology could modify, or even derail, the technology's role in individual nations, and accordingly, in the unfolding food regime as a whole" (2008: 352). Indeed, many anti-GMO activists act as policy watchdogs, and in places like Mexico have been quite successful in raising public concern around the import, testing, and commercial production of transgenic maize.

Scientists and government regulators began to debate the risks and benefits of transgenic maize in Mexico during the mid-1990s with the impending commercial release of GM corn in the United States. The Mexican Ministry of Agriculture started to grant permits in 1988 for scientific field trials of GM crops, advised by an ad hoc committee consisting of scientists from various disciplines and government agencies, which became the National Agricultural Biosafety Committee (Comité Nacional de Bioseguridad Agrícola, CNBA) in 1992. In a period of ten years, Mexico approved the commercial release of over thirty-one agricultural GMOs for human consumption, including alfalfa, canola, cotton, tomatoes, soybeans, potatoes, and maize (Pechlaner and Otero 2008). In late 1998 the National Agricultural Biosafety Committee—now the Specialized Agricultural Subcommittee of the Inter-Ministerial Commission on Biosafety (Comisión Intersecretarial de Bioseguridad de los Organismos Genéticamente Modificados, CIBIOGEM)—imposed a de facto moratorium on GM corn trials because the traits most commonly tested were not of any particular benefit to Mexico (Alvarez-Morales 1999: 91) and the committee had concerns about the possibility of transgenic corn hybridizing with or displacing native varieties and *teosinte,* a wild relative of maize (Serratos 1999).

In Colombia the regulation of GMOs began in the late 1990s, under Decree 4525, which was modified in 2005, establishing three technical committees (on health, agriculture, and the environment) to evaluate GMOs. The National Agricultural Institute (Instituto Colombiano Agropecuario, ICA), a branch of the Ministry of Agriculture and Development, is responsible for "ensuring the quality of agricultural inputs and seeds used in Colombia, while regulating and controlling the use of living modified organisms by genetic engineering to agriculture."[8] Colombia's first GMO approved for commercial production was the blue carnation in 2000, followed by cotton in 2003, transgenic corn in 2007, and soybeans in late 2010. As in Mexico, approval is given on a case-by-case basis. The cultivation of maize requires a buffer zone between the plot and any other crops, which is monitored by the ICA.

In Defense of Maize: Mexican Anti-GMO Activism

The anti-GMO campaign and network In Defense of Maize was established in 2002 in response to the scandal over transgenic corn. The network consists of over 300 environmental, food activist, peasant, and indigenous rights organizations, most of which are Mexican.[9] Two transnational organizations with offices in Mexico City, Greenpeace Mexico and the Action Group on the Environment, Technology and Concentration (ETC Group), are important participants and founding members of the network. Mexican members of Via Campesina have also been active in the network, as are numerous academics, researchers, and scientists unaffiliated with activist organizations or NGOs. Members are involved in an enormous variety of projects that include running media campaigns, promoting criollo seed exchanges and fairs, establishing seed banks, hosting workshops for campesinos on seed saving, organizing a network of GMO-free tortillas, testing for transgenes in fields, participating in government consultations on biodiversity and biosafety (for example, in the making of the Biosafety Law of 2005), and conducting various types of research (environmental, legal, sociocultural, etc.) on the impacts of transgenic varieties.

Activists from In Defense of Maize argue that the regulation of agricultural biotechnology needs to be politically transparent and socially inclusive and that transgenic corn should not be cultivated, imported, or tested in the crop's center of biodiversity. Furthermore, as one maize scientist explained during the height of the controversy, "Promoters of biotech say how wonderful it is that Bt corn was found in Oaxaca because it's going to help peasants. But this is incorrect because in Mexico we don't have the pests that Bt was designed to attack" (Dr. José Antonio Serratos, interview, January 28, 2002). In my interviews, scientists who were involved in the network emphasized that they were not against agricultural biotechnology per se but rather against the testing and cultivation of transgenic corn *in Mexico*, where it is unsuitable and even a risk.

Corn continues to dominate the debates over biotechnology in Mexico because of its importance. Other transgenic crops like cotton have been grown in the country without the same level of public attention or concern. Mexico is the crop's center of origin and biological diversity. Maize is a key element of the Mexican diet and culinary traditions, the main crop grown throughout the country, the cornerstone of rural livelihoods, and, as suggested by the slogan "Without corn there is no country," a powerful and longtime symbol of the Mexican nation.

At the various workshops and forums organized by In Defense of Maize groups in Mexico City that I attended over the years, I heard campesinos and indigenous farmers speak about the importance of maize in their lives and communities. An activist from the National Support Center for Indigenous Missions (Centro Nacional de Ayuda a las Misiones Indígenas, CENAMI)[10] got up to the microphone to explain how the government views small-scale corn producers: "[the government perspective is that] we don't need peasants, nor do we need indigenous communities. We need people that can work in the *maquiladoras* [factories]. This is the solution that the neoliberal government wants to propose to us." The ways policies displace rural farmers were discussed at length. Participants in the network frame the import and regulation of transgenic maize as part of a broader critique on the effects of neoliberal policies and global capitalism in rural Mexico, a critique that forges and deepens connections between environmentalists, anti-neoliberal activists, peasant and indigenous groups, and concerned scientists and academics both within and across national borders (Fitting 2006b, 2011). With this broadening of focus, activists suggest that the appropriate experts for evaluating potential harm are *not only* biotechnologists and other scientists but also consumers and Mexico's large number of small-scale corn producers or campesinos. As a symbol of place, maize represents numerous struggles that Mexico—particularly rural Mexico—faces under neoliberal reforms and the expansion of agribusiness. Notably, however, this shift from a focus on the risks of gene flow to a broader debate still uses scientific studies about gene flow to advance the cause, and some of the most public figures in the anti-GMO network are scientists, such as members of the Union of Concerned Scientists Committed to Society.

Ana de Ita, from the Center for Studies of Rural Change (Centro de Estudios para el Cambio en el Campo Mexicano, CECCAM),[11] is an activist based in Mexico City who was involved in the network from its origins. In an interview she explained what she saw as the successes of the anti-GMO campaign:

> We [CECCAM] were involved in organizing workshops, making links between different groups, testing corn for evidence of transgenes, outreach to rural communities. I think one of the successes of [the] In Defense of Maize campaign [and network] is the level of indigenous involvement. Communities wanted to know how to protect their seed. Another success is the pressure we put on DICONSA [a government agency that distributes food to rural communities] to stop buying corn imports that included transgenic corn....Another success is the level of public awareness on the issue. Not to the extent that we wanted, but still the issue is out there. (July 24, 2006)

Despite the efforts of anti-GMO activists, the moratorium on field trials of trans-genic corn ended in 2009. Since the end of the moratorium, six permits have been granted to corporations to grow pilot plots of transgenic corn in northern Mexico (two in Sinaloa, four in Tamaulipas). Corporations and research institutes are required to take a phased approach. First they plant experimental plots on less than one hectare and destroy all the corn produced. If these plots did not harm the envi-ronment or contaminate native varieties, they then grow pilot plots of ten hectares, and after that, they submit applications to commence commercial planting.

As of early 2013, the commercial cultivation of transgenic maize is still pro-hibited. However, there have been reports of farmers growing transgenic maize illegally in the north for several years (Center for Latin American and Border Stud-ies 2009). And Monsanto, Dow Chemical, and DuPont's Pioneer seed units have all applied to enlarge their small experimental plots of transgenic corn, with the goal of planting the first commercial plots in northern Mexico shortly (Reuters 2011). Monsanto and Pioneer have filed applications to plant 1.4 million hectares in Sinaloa and over 1 million hectares in Tamaulipus (GRAIN 2012: 3). Mexican activists and their international supporters have been intensifying their efforts to pressure the new government of Peña Nieto to reject these corporate applications to grow transgenic corn. The National Union of Autonomous Peasant Organizations (Unión Nacional de Organizaciones Regionales Campesinas Autónomas, UNORCA), which has been involved in the anti-GMO network for years, held a sit-in and hunger strike against transgenic corn at Mexico City's Angel of Independence monument in early 2013. Farmers' organizations in Oaxaca have named 2013 "the year of resistance to trans-genic maize."

While Mexican activists organize protests and press conferences and write letters of protest calling for the rejection of commercial production of transgenic maize, Colombia had a record year for the planting of transgenic corn, reaching close to 50,000 hectares during the first half of 2012 (Birkett 2012).

Semillas de Identidad: Anti-GMO Activism in Colombia

The first indigenous *resguardo*[12] in Colombia to declare itself a transgenic-free terri-tory (TFT) was San Andrés de Sotavento of the northern departments of Córdoba and Sucre in 2005. This Zenú territory is also home to the Caribbean Agroecology Net-work (Red Agroecologíca del Caribe, or RECAR), which has been the driving force behind the national Seeds of Identity campaign to promote the conservation and exchange of criollo varieties of seed in Colombia. Initiated in 2002, the campaign is the work of RECAR, the Bogotá office of SwissAid, and the Colombian NGO Grupo Semillas (the Seed Group), the most active groups to challenge the cultiva-tion of GMOs and the privatization and commercialization of seed, and to promote the saving and exchange of criollo varieties. In their declaration, the Zenú point to

Colombia as a center of biological diversity of maize and to its cultural, alimentary, and socioeconomic importance for the Zenú. They also contend that the import of transgenic maize and other products from the United States generates "negative impacts on our seeds, our agriculture and our food sovereignty." Since the declaration, at least five other TFTs have been declared: in the resguardo of Cañamomo y Lomaprieta in Caldas; the Municipio de Natagaima in the Resguardo Indígena de Palma Alta, Tolima; in a resguardo of la Guajira; and two in Huila (Mauricio García A., interview, April 12, 2012; Orlando Pamo, interview, February 11, 2012).

The Zenú began the process of declaring their resguardo—a territory of approximately 20,000 hectares[13]—"free of transgenics" more than a decade ago when they started an initiative to recuperate criollos, particularly maize. They also worked on developing the Seeds of Identity campaign with the Bogotá office of SwissAid. In this campaign, criollo varieties of maize are a marker of place—indigenous, rural Colombia. Representatives of the Zenú see corn as embodying the essence of their culture. The 2005 TFT Declaration states, "We conserve and cultivate twenty-five criollo varieties of corn, and possess an ample culinary culture based on this sacred food; for these reasons, we consider ourselves 'children of corn.'" Activist publications similarly discuss maize as the heart of indigenous Colombia, representative of indigenous culture, peoples, and biological/productive resources.[14]

Food sovereignty, mentioned in the Zenú declaration, is a term that was coined by the transnational peasants' rights group Via Campesina in the mid-1990s and denotes a level of control, autonomy, and self-determination. It calls for food "security" in the sense of sufficient access to food but also for producers' control over their productive resources, such as land, water, seeds, and so on (Wittman, Desmarais, and Wiebe 2010: 3)—precisely those resources that face, on a global level, increasing levels of commodification and usurpation by corporate interests. Food activists employ the term to refer to various scales of experience and analysis, from the household to the national and even transnational. In both Mexico and Colombia, where maize is representative of the "nation"—be it the nation-state or an indigenous people and territory—the import and cultivation of transgenic corn are seen as undermining political, economic, cultural, and food sovereignty.

By speaking at regional and national indigenous congresses about their experiences and strategies in declaring their territory transgenic free, the Zenú have provided an example to other indigenous communities in Colombia. For example, when I asked Efren, who was involved in declaring his resguardo in Caldas a TFT, why it was important to make this declaration, he explained:

Because of the loss of our seed, the introduction of technical packages [of improved seed], and the lack of respect for our traditions and regulations we decided to shut the door to this seed. In 2007 or so, the mayor's office received a proposal for technical extension work [from a seed company] to establish some parcels of land with transgenic soybeans. This was taking advantage of indigenous peoples' need. The packet included everything for the producer [initially at no charge . . .]. The first TFT was in Córdoba [and Sucre] and we talked to the Zenú about their experience. We had heard about their dec-laration through the indigenous network and congress. The campaign Seeds of Identity also helped us a lot. It was a difficult process [because our mayor was initially against the idea]. It generated a discussion in the community about what is a gene, what is improved seed. And when it understood, the community helped with the process [of declaring a TFT]. We started to promote seed exchanges, and at all of our meetings we started to put aside an hour to exchange seed. According to our internal norm of 2009, the use of improved seed [including GM varieties] is now prohibited. (interview, February 2012)

In addition to mentioning how his community heard about the first TFT in Cór-doba, among the Zenú, Efren points to concerns about the displacement of traditional seed, and the attempts of seed companies to "take advantage of indigenous neces-sity" by offering technical packages of transgenic soy at no or low cost. Although producers from Efren's home in Caldas first learned about GMOs through offers of transgenic soy, anti-GMO activists from indigenous resguardos like his, and in Bogotá, have focused on corn as the key crop in their campaigns. For indigenous groups, maize is traditionally a much more meaningful crop than soy, and as I dis-cuss, several pivotal activists in the anti-GMO campaign in Colombia looked to the Mexican campaign for information and strategy.

The Zenú TFT declaration in 2005 had an impact beyond setting an example for other indigenous groups. Because their declaration preceded any government approval of transgenic corn, when the ICA did decide to approve "controlled plots" of Monsanto and DuPont varieties of transgenic corn in 2007, they took the decla-ration into consideration: The ICA approved GM maize under the condition that it would not be grown in indigenous territories and must be grown at a minimum dis-tance of 328 yards (300 meters) from any resguardo. Activists are concerned about the growth in area of these controlled plots: from less than 15,000 acres (6,000 hect-ares) in 2007 to more than 123,000 acres (50,000 hectares) in the first half of 2012 (Germán Vélez, interview, December 15, 2011; Birkett 2012).

Corn as Culture: A Transnational Activist Strategy

Corn is cultivated by indigenous peoples, and in reality by most rural peoples. . . . It is the most traditional crop. . . . Corn is, let's say, because of its reproductive cycle, its cultural importance, for the foods made from it, for all of these factors plus the threat of trans-genic seeds, *it became a strategic crop.*

—Mauricio García A., SwissAid, Bogotá, April 27, 2012[15]

As Mauricio from SwissAid Colombia explains above, maize "became a strategic crop" in the Colombian campaign against transgenic agriculture because of its cultural importance as a key food and crop. Following the height of the controversy over transgenic corn in Mexico, Mauricio, along with Edenia Montaño, a leader from RECAR, and indigenous leaders from the Zenú territory, traveled to Mexico to learn about the experience of indigenous peoples with the issue. The "contamination" of corn and the anti-GMO campaign in Mexico struck a chord with activists and indigenous leaders in Colombia, where maize is also central to rural livelihoods. Mexican activists tell a compelling story about why transgenic corn is inappropriate technology and too great a risk for Mexico. Their focus on corn as a symbol of sovereignty and the difficulties faced by rural producers resonate with activists and indigenous producers in Colombia.

Transnational advocacy and activist networks exchange information and strategies in an effort to influence policy at the international level as well as in specific countries, and to try and "transform the terms and nature of the debate" (Keck and Sikkink 1999: 93). Often these connections are made between groups from the Global South and North. While anti-GMO organizing in Mexico, and to a lesser extent Colombia, has involved organizations from the Global North (such as the ETC Group, Greenpeace, and SwissAid, who have Mexican or Colombian offices and staff), the case of transgenic corn raises the issue of how information is shared *between* activists from the Global South. Colombian and Mexican activists discussed and shared perspectives and studies on the perceived risks associated with transgenic crops, details about their regulation in the two countries and internationally, and strategies for raising awareness and organizing campaigns. The Mexican focus on maize as a symbol of place—its people, culture, and biological resources—clearly resonated with activists in Colombia. In turn, the Zenú declaration of a TFT provided an example to other Colombian indigenous groups.

Following Margaret E. Keck and Kathryn Sikkink's terms, there are two kinds of politics relevant to understanding the debates over transgenic maize in both the countries under discussion. The first is "information politics," or when activist groups try and influence public debate in the media both at home and abroad by moving "politically usable information quickly and credibly to where it will have the most impact." The other is "symbolic politics," or the "ability to call upon symbols, actions or stories that make sense of the situation or claim for an audience that is frequently far away" (1999: 95).

The cultural and symbolic significance of maize in parts of Colombia, much like in Mexico, is deeply connected to the everyday experience and livelihood struggles of rural peoples. Activists point out that Colombia is home to a considerable diversity of criollo varieties (although not a center of origin like Mexico) and that these varieties are put at risk by policies that undermine small-scale agricultural production and the free exchange of seed and foster dependency on imports. Colombia went from being self-sufficient in maize in the 1990s to importing some 85 percent of corn for domestic consumption in 2010 (Germán Vélez, interview, December 15, 2011), much of which is transgenic. Mexican activists had also highlighted this connection between GMOs, trade liberalization, and increasing corn imports in their country based on their experience with the North American Free Trade Agreement.

The Colombian anti-GMO campaign has had an impact on regulation, as the ICA qualified its approval of transgenic corn with the stipulation that its cultivation must be accompanied by a buffer zone, and it is prohibited in resguardos. In interviews, however, activists and a representative from the biotechnology advocacy group (the Colombian office of AgroBIO) confirmed my observation that the issue of GMOs is not discussed or debated much in public forums. Media coverage on agricultural biotechnology in Colombia is sparse and often positive (with the exception of activist publications and websites).

In comparison to the effects of armed conflict in rural Colombia, the issue of GMO cultivation can seem minor in media coverage and public debate; it is a challenge for anti-GMO activists to generate support for their cause outside of activist circles or indigenous resguardos. A form of "biohegemony" may also be at work in which "the benefits and value of agricultural biotechnology acquire the status of common sense and go largely unquestioned" (Newell 2009: 38). In contrast, GMOs have generated more critical press coverage and mobilizations in Mexico than in Colombia, where images of Mexico as a people and culture of corn resonate beyond activist networks and Mexican activists regularly publish research and opinion pieces in national newspapers (notably in, but not restricted to, the leftist *La Jornada*).

Conclusion

Resistance to agricultural biotechnology (as well as support for it) is found in many different countries around the world, but *why* and *how* it is resisted (or supported) may differ. In Mexico and Colombia, activists oppose transgenic seeds, particularly transgenic maize, because of its potentially harmful effects on criollos and campesino and indigenous livelihoods. I have argued that these campaigns against transgenic corn illustrate how indigenous maize farmers and campesinos help shape "globalization from below" by sharing information and strategies *horizontally* through networks between regions and countries of the Global South. I have also suggested that while they share concerns and strategies with anti-GMO activists internationally, their campaigns highlight the cultural meaning of maize at various scales of place from the local village to the transnational region. Maize is a symbol of cultural uniqueness or difference, threatened by neoliberal globalization.

Activists strategically focused on maize as a powerful symbol of *their* region, its peoples, and its cultures. Although this focus has different degrees of success and resonance in Mexico and Colombia, I hope the comparison serves as a reminder to look for influences and connections horizontally between activists of the Global South and to ask whether activists engage symbols and narratives that have histories, broader meanings, and a wider audience than their own activist circles.

Acknowledgments

Over the years I have relied on the insights of countless individuals in Mexico, for which I am very grateful. In Colombia, I would like to thank my interviewees, particularly Mauricio García Alvarez and Germán Alonso Vélez. I would also like to thank the editors of this collection for their thoughtful comments and Lindsay DuBois and María Mercedes Gómez for offering feedback along the way. All errors are, of course, my own.

Notes

1. *Criollo* is commonly used in Spanish to refer to "traditional" varieties, which are landraces and creolized varieties.
2. Maize has a long history as a symbol of indigenous and rural Mexico, and a more recent history as a symbol of mestizo (or racially/culturally mixed) Mexico, particularly in the twentieth century. Associations with the rural and indigenous have been positive and celebratory at times (among environmentalists and anti-GMO activists today, for instance), while at other moments corn production has been portrayed by government officials and rural experts as a backward, traditional, noncompetitive crop. See *The Struggle for Maize* (Fitting 2011), *¡Que vivan los tamales!* (Pilcher 1998), and *Corn and Capitalism* (Warman 2003 [1988]).
3. The *Bacillus thuringiensis* (Bt) toxin gene, the cauliflower mosaic virus (CaMV) gene promoter, and the nopaline synthase (NOS) terminator sequence (Chapela and Quist 2001; Quist and Chapela 2002).
4. See the Mexican In Defense of Maize (http://redendefensadelmaiz.net/) and the Argentina-based Biodiversity in Latin America (http://www.biodiversidadla.org) for lists of key activist websites. For posts in support of agricultural biotechnology see AgroBio Mexico (http://www.agrobiomexico.org.mx) or the international site AgroBio World (http://www.agrobioworld.org).
5. Non-GMO seed that is improved through plant breeding can also contribute to the loss of traditional varieties.
6. Other issues raised are food safety and a call to adhere to the precautionary principle in biosafety assessment, which states that the absence of scientific knowledge about a risk should not hinder actions to reduce a risk (National Research Council of the National Academies 2002: 64). This principle has been employed in various international treaties and declarations like the Cartagena Protocol on Biosafety.
7. This rose in 2011 to 12 million tons due to production shortfalls in Mexico. Most imports are used for animal feed or industrial uses. Recent figures are from Rodríguez 2011. Mexico imported corn in years previous to the neoliberal period

of austerity measures in the 1980s and trade liberalization in the 1990s but not at the current levels.

8. From the ICA website, http://www.ica.gov.co/El-ICA.aspx (accessed August 15, 2012).

9. These include the Environmental Studies Group (Grupo de Estudios Ambientales, GEA), the National Association of Rural Commercialization Enterprises (Asociación Nacional de Empresas Comercializadoras de Productores del Campo, ANEC), National Support Center for Indigenous Missions (Centro Nacional de Ayuda a las Misiones Indígenas, CENAMI), the Union of Concerned Scientists Committed to Society (Unión de Científicos Comprometidos con la Sociedad, UCCS), and Seeds of Life (Fundación Semillas de Vida).

10. CENAMI is a nonprofit based in Mexico City that works to support indigenous pastors and churches in various regions of the country. Beyond this, their mission includes supporting indigenous projects to defend and promote indigenous culture, territory, and rights. See http://www.cenami.org.

11. CECCAM is a Mexican nonprofit founded in 1992. It is a link (*punto de enlace*) for exchanging information and research. It services campesinos and indigenous groups from distinct backgrounds in sharing experiences and challenges in confronting rural modernization. See http://www.ceccam.org.

12. *Resguardos* are indigenous territories based on communal landholdings. Under the Colombian Constitution of 1991, indigenous peoples were given the right to manage the political and administrative affairs of their territories. There are currently 710 legally recognized *resguardos* located in 27 departments and 228 municipalities (ABColombia 2010: 16).

13. The Zenú have colonial title to approximately 165,560 acres (67,000 hectares) of land, but they have recuperated only 49,421 acres (20,000 hectares) of noncontiguous parcels, located in municipalities such as Córdoba and Sucre.

14. See RECAR's website and Grupo Semillas's magazine *Semillas* (no. 22/23) from November 2004.

15. Translation and emphasis mine.

References

ABColombia (Christian Aid, CAFOD, Oxfam GB, SCIAF, Trócaire) (2010), "Caught in the Crossfire: Colombia's Indigenous Peoples," report, October. London: ABColombia, http://www.abcolombia.org.uk/downloads/Caught_in_the_Crossfire .pdf, accessed January 31, 2013.

Alvarez-Morales, A. (1999), "Mexico: Ensuring Environmental Safety while Benefiting from Biotechnology," in G. J. Persley and M. M. Lantin (eds.), *Agricultural Biotechnology and the Poor*, Washington, DC: Consultative Group on International

Agricultural Research, http://www.cgiar.org/biotech/rep0100/Morales.pdf, accessed January 31, 2013.

Birkett, R. (2012), "Colombia Plants Record GM Maize Area," *Agrow*, August 29, https://www.agra-net.net/agra/agrow/markets-regulatory/south-america/colombia-plants-record-gm-maize-area-57939.htm, accessed July 12, 2013.

Center for Latin American and Border Studies (2009), "NAFTA Commission Gets GM Corn Complaint," *Frontera NorteSur* [online news], January 29, http://fnsnews.nmsu.edu/nafta-commission-gets-gm-corn-complaint/, accessed January 31, 2013.

Chapela, I., and Quist, D. (2001), "Transgenic DNA Introgressed into Traditional Maize Landraces in Oaxaca, Mexico," *Nature*, 414/6863: 541–543.

Cleveland, D., Soleri, D., and Aragon, F. (2003), "Transgenes on the Move," American Anthropology Association Meetings, Chicago, November 21.

Douglas, M. (1966), *Purity and Danger: An Analysis of Concepts of Pollution and Taboo*, London: Routledge and Kegan Paul.

Ezcurra, E., Ortiz, S., and Soberón, J. (2002), "Evidence of Gene Flow from Transgenic Maize to Local Varieties in Mexico," in C. R. Roseland (ed.), *LMOs and the Environment: Proceedings of an International Conference*, OECD, Raleigh-Durham, North Carolina, November 27–30, 2001: 289–295, http://www.oecd.org/science/biotrack/31526579.pdf, accessed July 12, 2013.

Falk, R. (1997), "Resisting 'Globalisation-from-Above' through 'Globalisation-from-Below,'" *New Political Economy*, 2/1: 17–24.

Federación Nacional de Cultivadores de Cereales y Leguminosas (Fenalce) (2011), "Plan Maíz-País," *El Cerealista*, 96: 4–7, http://www.fenalce.org/pagina.php?p_a=25, accessed December 12, 2012.

Fitting, E. (2006a), "Importing Corn, Exporting Labor: The Neoliberal Corn Regime, GMOs, and the Erosion of Biodiversity in Mexico," *Agriculture and Human Values*, 23: 15–26.

Fitting, E. (2006b), "The Political Uses of Culture: Maize Production and the GM Corn Debates in Mexico," *Focaal: European Journal of Anthropology*, 2006/48: 17–34.

Fitting, E. (2011), *The Struggle for Maize: Campesinos, Workers and Transgenic Corn in the Mexican Countryside*, Durham, NC: Duke University Press.

González, R. (2001), *Zapotec Science: Farming and Food in the Northern Sierra of Oaxaca*, Austin: University of Texas Press.

GRAIN (2012), "Red Alert! GMO Avalanche in Mexico," report, November, http://www.grain.org/article/entries/4621-red-alert-gmo-avalanche-in-mexico, accessed January 30, 2013.

Harvey, D. (2003), *The New Imperialism*, Oxford: Oxford University Press.

Heller, C. (2002), "From Scientific Risk to *Paysan* Savoir-Faire: Peasant Expertise in the French and Global Debate over GM Crops," *Science as Culture*, 11/1: 5–37.

INE-CONABIO (2002), "Evidencias de flujo genético desde fuentes de maíz trans-génico hacia variedades criollas," presented by E. Huerta, En Defensa del Maíz Conference, Mexico City, January 23.

International Service for the Acquisition of Agri-Biotech Applications (2011), "Global Status of Commercialized Biotech/GM Crops: 2011," Brief 43-2011, http://www.isaaa.org/resources/publications/briefs/43/executivesummary/default.asp, accessed April 9, 2012.

Keck, M., and Sikkink, K. (1999), "Transnational Advocacy Networks in International and Regional Politics," *International Social Science Journal*, 51/159: 89–101.

Kloppenburg, J. (1988), *First the Seed: The Political Economy of Plant Biotechnology, 1492–2000*, Cambridge: Cambridge University Press.

Levidow, L. (1991), "Cleaning Up on the Farm," *Science as Culture*, 2/4: 538–568.

McMichael, P. (2009), "A food regime genealogy," *Journal of Peasant Studies*, 36: 139–169.

Müller, B. (2006), "Introduction: GMOs—Global Objects of Contention," *Focaal: European Journal of Anthropology*, 2006/48: 3–16.

National Research Council of the National Academies (2002), *Environmental Effects of Transgenic Plants: The Scope and Adequacy of Regulation*, Washington, DC: National Academies Press.

Newell, P. (2009), "Bio-Hegemony: The Political Economy of Agricultural Biotechnology in Argentina," *Journal of Latin American Studies*, 41: 27–57.

Pearson, T. (2009), "On the Trail of Genetically Modified Organisms: Environmentalism Within and Against the Neoliberal Order," *Cultural Anthropology*, 24/4: 712–745.

Pechlaner, G., and Otero, G. (2008), "The Third Food Regime: Neoliberal Globalism and Agricultural Biotechnology in North America," *Sociologia Ruralis*, 48/4: 351–371.

Pilcher, J. (1998), *¡Que vivan los tamales! Food and the Making of Mexican Identity*, Albuquerque: University of New Mexico Press.

Quist, D., and Chapela, I. H. (2002), "Biodiversity (Communications Arising (Reply)): Suspect Evidence of Transgenic Contamination/Maize Transgene Results in Mexico Are Artefacts," *Nature*, 416/6881: 602.

Resguardo indígena Zenú Córdoba y Sucre, Colombia (2005), "Declaración del resguardo indígena Zenú, Córdoba y Sucre, como Territorio Libre de Trasngénicos," San Andrés de Sotavento, October 7.

Reuters (2011), "More than 10 Permits Sought Again for Pilot Projects," September 19.

Rodriguez, C. M. (2011), "Mexico Corn Imports to Surge to Record as Output Outlook Cut," *Bloomberg News*, August 12, http://www.bloomberg.com/news/2011-08-12/mexico-corn-imports-to-surge-to-record-as-output-outlook-cut-2-.html, accessed January 30, 2013.

Schurman, R. (2003), "Introduction: Biotechnology in the New Millennium," in R. Schurman and D. Doyle Takahashi Kelso (eds.), *Engineering Trouble: Biotechnology and Its Discontents*, Berkeley: University of California Press.

Serratos, J. A. (1999), "Evaluation of Novel Crop Varieties in Their Center of Origin and Diversity: The Case of Maize in Mexico," in J. Komen, C. Falconi, and H. Hernández (eds.), *Turning Priorities into Feasible Programs, Proceedings of a Policy Seminar on Agricultural Biotechnology for Latin America*, Agricultural Biotechnology Policy Seminars no. 4, Lima, Peru, October 6–10, 1996, 68–73.

Soleri, D., Cleveland, D. A., Aragón, F., Fuentes, M. R., Ríos, H., and Sweeney, S. H. (2005), "Understanding the Potential Impact of Transgenic Crops in Traditional Agriculture: Maize Farmers' Perspectives in Cuba, Guatemala, and Mexico," *Environmental Biosafety Research*, 4/3: 141–166.

Turrent Fernández, A., Wise, T. A., and Garvey, E. (2012), *Achieving Mexico's Maize Potential*, Global Development and Environment Institute Working Paper no. 12-03, Medford, MA: Tufts University.

U.S. Department of Agriculture, Economic Research Service (2012), "Genetically Engineered (GE) Corn Varieties by State and United States, 2000–2012," http://www.ers.usda.gov/data-products/adoption-of-genetically-engineered-crops-in-the-us.aspx, accessed August 14, 2012.

Warman, A. (2003 [1988]), *Corn and Capitalism: How a Botanical Bastard Grew to Global Dominance*, trans. Nancy Westrate, Chapel Hill: University of North Carolina Press.

Whatmore, S. (2002), *Hybrid Geographies: Natures, Cultures, Spaces*, Oxford: Oxford University Press.

Wittman, H., Desmarais, A. A., and Wiebe, N. (2010), *Food Sovereignty: Reconnecting Food, Nature and Community*, Halifax, NS: Fernwood.

−13−

Peasants' Transnational Mobilization for Food Sovereignty in La Vía Campesina

Delphine Thivet

The concept of "food sovereignty" was introduced for the first time in a public arena in 1996:

> Food is a basic human right. This right can only be realized in a system where food sovereignty is guaranteed. Food sovereignty is the right of each nation to maintain and develop its own capacity to produce its basic foods respecting cultural and productive diversity. We have the right to produce our own food in our own territory. Food sovereignty is a precondition to genuine food security. (La Vía Campesina 1996)

From that time forward, the concept of food sovereignty has been identified as the key motto of La Vía Campesina.[1] This transnational social movement was born in May 1993 in Mons (Belgium) to oppose the negative social impacts of the neoliberal economic globalization of agriculture. Since then it has continued to grow, attracting more and more organizations from all over the world. Organized into nine regional secretariats, a rotating International Operative Secretariat,[2] an International Coordination Committee (ICC), and various commissions or working committees, La Vía Campesina has a rather heterogeneous membership (Borras 2008: 274). It is now comprised of 163 rural organizations made up of peasants, small- and medium-scale farmers, organic farmers, rural women, rural workers, and indigenous and landless people from the Americas, Asia, Europe, and Africa; it represents about 200 million members from seventy countries. The term *food sovereignty* was originally coined by farmer and landless activists during the Second International Conference of La Vía Campesina, held in Tlaxcala, Mexico, in 1996. The term offered an alternate concept to *food security,* which was advocated and promoted by the United Nations Food and Agriculture Organization (FAO) and the World Bank. Since 1996 food sovereignty—broadly defined as the right of each nation or people to define their own agricultural and food policies—has been adopted by various nongovernmental organizations (NGOs), development advocates, environmental groups, academics, and even certain nation-states and governments, such as Venezuela, Bolivia, Ecuador, Mali,[3] and Nepal, as a strategic goal to promote change in the current food system.

194 · *Food Activism*

The present chapter explores how, under the banner of food sovereignty, small farmers and landless rural workers have contributed to reframing the debate on world hunger and asserted the democratization of the food system by developing a new mode of agrifood activism at the transnational level. Drawing theoretically on the frame analysis developed by David Snow, Robert Benford, and their collaborators (1986) and on the available literature on social movements, I will show how the concept of food sovereignty provides men and women engaged in small-scale agriculture with possibilities to resist the process of intensified marginalization and impoverishment they have been undergoing since the 1980s and 1990s as a result of structural adjustment programs and bilateral/regional free trade agreements. The chapter will also show how the concept serves as a catalyst to bring them together and sustain their collective action across borders.

Since its creation the concept of food sovereignty has been undergoing continual reformulations, which sometimes result in conflicting interpretations in the course of its circulation across different geographic and sociocultural contexts.[4] In spite of its potentially unstable meaning, it has nonetheless fostered among smallholder farmers in both the Global South and the Global North a shared understanding of the impacts of the implementation of neoliberal policies in agriculture and an urgency to act in concert with other social agents to bring about a change in the global food system. The participants in La Vía Campesina have indeed experienced a common deepening sense of dispossession from their means of production since the Uruguay Round of the General Agreement on Tariffs and Trade in the early 1990s. It was precisely to challenge the increasing global concentration and integration in the food chain and in agriculture that they decided to converge transnationally toward what can be qualified as a radical agrifood activism. As I will show, this activism combines discursive practices and direct-action protests, along with alternative agro-ecological initiatives and emancipatory politics.

The chapter begins by describing how La Vía Campesina activists originally framed the concept of food sovereignty. I will show that through the reshaping of existing human rights language and food security discourse, they gave rise to an interpretative frame that challenged and drew new meanings in the hegemonic discourse of institutions on world hunger and put forward a more comprehensive understanding of the production and distribution of food. In the second section, my analysis focuses on how they challenged the invisibility of small peasants in the international arena by asserting their status as "food producers" but also by undertaking direct protest actions against corporate control of the global food system. The third and last section moves to La Vía Campesina's commitment to social change. Here I examine in particular how the movement promotes self-reliant farming based on "seed sovereignty" and agro-ecological practices and how it challenges inequalities of power in the food system through a feminist orientation.

The ethnographic fieldwork that informs my chapter was carried out between 2009 and 2012 as a part of my PhD project on the transnationalization of solidarities and farmers' movements. It consisted of about sixty semistructured interviews conducted with international delegates of La Vía Campesina from the ICC, international and regional technical support staff, national farmer and landless leaders, and local activists in organizations taking part in La Vía Campesina, most in France, Brazil, and India.[5] My study also includes participant observation of rallies and public meetings at the national and international levels and extensive archival research on the sociogenesis of La Vía Campesina since the early 1990s.

Reframing the World Hunger Problem

Following Benford and Scott Hunt's (2003) constructionist analysis of public problems, one approach to understand the food sovereignty mobilization by La Vía Campesina may be linking it to the social construction of the world hunger problem. Indeed, while the latter is now recognized as a major issue on the global public agenda,[6] the definition and interpretation of its specific causes and potential remedies themselves still constitute a "contested terrain" (Benford and Hunt 2003: 154). To understand the key role the concept of food sovereignty plays in the politicization of food politics and the world hunger problem, I refer to "framing" as the signifying work or construction of meanings by social movement activists, that is to say, "the struggle over the production of mobilizing and counter mobilizing ideas and meanings" (Benford and Snow 2000: 614).

As a concept naming the problem of world hunger and malnutrition, food security has occupied a prominent place on the international agenda since the 1970s. It is difficult to trace a consensual definition of food security, as its conceptualization has shifted over time. One of the first significant occurrences of the term was during the FAO World Food Conference in 1974, following the world oil crisis and related food crisis of the previous two years. This conference offered a conceptualization of hunger, focusing mainly on inadequate food supplies at the national and international levels. This "flat keying of the hunger frame"[7] became consolidated under the influence of transnational corporations, the World Bank, the International Monetary Fund, the FAO, and the U.S. State Department, defining world hunger as a "global food supply" problem to be solved mainly by increased trade liberalization. In fact, the 1996 First World Food Summit declared that "Trade is the key element in achieving food security. We agree to pursue food trade and overall trade policies that will encourage our producers and consumers to utilize available resources in an economically sound and sustainable manner" (FAO 1996: 1).

Despite this statement, the liberalization of the agricultural economic sector—under regional free trade agreements and the World Trade Organization's (WTO) Agreement on Agriculture, signed in 1994—has far from improved access to food and eradicated hunger. On the contrary, this neoliberal economic orientation has led, in particular in the Global South, to a shift from agricultural production for domestic consumption to production for international external markets, throwing a country like India, for instance, into unprecedented and severe agrarian distress (see Vasavi 2012). Among the numerous signs of the latter, the most dramatic is the epidemic of farmers' suicides across the country.[8] Based on a strategy of export-led growth, the opening up of Indian agriculture to the world market led to the displacement of local food staples by the production of export crops in the name of the Ricardian theory of comparative advantages. The removal of trade barriers and quantitative restrictions to imports, moreover, placed millions of food-grain producers under the threat of increased competition from foreign countries, which most often heavily subsidize their own farm products and thereby enable the export of vast quantities of low-priced grain (Patnaik 2003: 41). Consequently, many developing countries that used to be self-sufficient in basic food commodities are now witnessing a new food dependency on the world economy, exposing small-scale farmers to the adverse fluctuations and volatility of international prices (Wise 2009: 867–868).

It is precisely to contest, as Philipp McMichael puts it, this "shift in the 'site' of food security from the nation-state to the world market engineered during the Uruguay Round" (2005: 281) that the concept of food sovereignty was introduced by La Vía Campesina. It is noteworthy, however, that the above-mentioned definition occurred on the sidelines of the 1996 First World Food Summit. Indeed, as part of a social movement, La Vía Campesina's delegates were not granted accreditation to attend the official summit. Isabel Cruz Hernández, a Mexican delegate of La Vía Campesina, precisely stresses the paradox of this exclusion:

We are the point of view closest to production and although our point of view isn't the only one, it is the missing element here [at the World Food Summit]. Communities of farmers and small producers see the globalization of food production from below. And from our point of view, this globalization of production is also producing a globalization of hunger. (quoted in Bacon 1997)

The emergence of the food sovereignty concept "from below" exemplifies well the constraints within which a framing process takes place. It is indeed important to keep in mind that framing activity does not "occur in a structural or cultural vacuum" (Benford and Snow 2000: 628).[9] From this perspective, it is interesting to note that La Vía Campesina's declaration refers dialogically to the "hegemonic discourse," that is, to the predominant discursive repertoires shaping the international debate on the world hunger problem. It indeed invokes the "right to food," a human right recognized by the Universal Declaration of Human Rights, Article 25, and by the International Covenant on Economic, Social and Cultural Rights (1966), Article 11. Moreover, food sovereignty is defined as a right in itself. Over the past two decades, the language of rights—in particular, the transnational discourse of human rights—has emerged as a common language of ethical obligations. As part of a "universalization project," the "language of rights" indeed provides the social agents with "a flexible vehicle for formulating interests and demands" as well as a means to "restate the interests of the group as characteristics of all people" (Kennedy 2002: 188). However, La Vía Campesina's activists did not comply passively with the human rights discourse. As a contentious process, the generation of interpretative frames imports new meanings into the hegemonic discourse by seeking "to stretch, reshape, or even invert the meanings implied" in dominant languages (Li 2001: 653). Indeed, through the notion of food sovereignty, they invite their audience to take into consideration the conditions under which fundamental rights such as the "right to food" can be implemented so as to achieve "genuine food security." What is a right to food without the right of peoples to exercise sovereignty over their territory, which means sovereignty over their land, water, seeds, and other natural resources as well? While adopting the language of rights, La Vía Campesina activists demonstrated skills in going beyond conventional human rights talk. By expanding and exploiting the "multivalent character of rights" (Polletta 2000: 392), they departed from a narrow individualistic, depoliticized, and state-dependent bias reflected in international standards. Advocating a "peoples' right" they insisted on self-determination and on the socioeconomic and political prerequisites essential to the realization and enjoyment of human rights.

Bringing the Small Food Producers Back In

The introduction of the food sovereignty frame allowed small farmers, traditionally marginalized in the public arena, to assert themselves as an independent voice in international debates on food and agricultural policies.[10] La Vía Campesina's activists regularly express a demand for autonomy from political parties, churches, and NGOs. A delegate of the ICC for Europe, who was also a farmer in the southwest of France and a member of the Confédération paysanne, asserted that La Vía Campesina was precisely born "to release small farmers from the yoke of NGOs' paternalism" and to "allow peasants' organizations to speak autonomously."[11] The founding meeting of the movement in 1993 resulted in fact in a radical clash with the Dutch NGO Paulo Freire Stichting, which initially brought together farmer leaders in Mons (Belgium). The divergence in agendas between the peasant leaders and the NGO staff person—that is to say, between a militant stance and a perspective more oriented toward research and policy development—has heavily marked to this day the ambivalent relationship between La Vía Campesina and NGOs (Borras, Edelman, and Kay 2008: 28).[12] For instance, as one of my interviewees who took part in the La Vía Campesina's delegation in Rome explained, NGOs attending the 1996 World Food Summit failed to envision a social change and a political struggle beyond institutional and legal reform;[13] consequently, the delegates of the farmers' movement refused to sign the NGO Forum Statement and made a separate statement:[14]

The right to food was on the NGOs' agenda, not on ours. Because we thought that this legal dimension was too narrow. Law is only an instrument; it may be useful, but from our viewpoint, the struggle primarily must be political. What we aim at is creating a people's initiative. The concept of food sovereignty was very much broader [than the right to food]. . . . So even if NGOs tried to pressure us during the parallel summit, we refused this concept because it sounded too restrictive. . . . Besides, for a long time, only NGOs were speaking on behalf of small farmers. The right to food was their concept, not ours. On the contrary, food sovereignty was a concept coined by us. So finally we did not sign the final statement made up by the NGOs. They got very angry because of that. (Dutch male, international staff of La Vía Campesina, personal phone interview, July 2010; my emphasis and my translation from French)

The limitations of the right-to-food and food security approach also lie in the incapacity of these concepts to counter the increasing sway of agro-industries and transnational chemical corporations over the world's agricultural production and the global food system. On behalf of the right to food, Cargill, for instance, has pointed out the possibility of financing food programs but with the intention of leaving "the power structures [of the system of production] intact and more profitable than ever" (Kneen 1999: 165). Through the concept of food sovereignty, La Vía Campesina thus aims to bring back to the forefront of the public debate on world hunger the social basis of food production and the need to address some fundamental issues within the existing global food system: *Where* does food come from? *How* is it grown? And, above all, *by whom* is it produced? As Jan Douwe Van Der Ploeg underlines, a prominent feature of the globalization of agriculture is precisely the creation of "invisibility . . . since production is moved to 'non-places' where the origin of food (or its many ingredients) is hidden behind the façade of lookalike products, and primary producers are made anonymous and interchangeable. They tend to be converted into 'non-persons' whose identities and skills do not matter" (2008: 269). The construct of food sovereignty was coined by the activists of La Vía Campesina to challenge the widespread blindness regarding how food is produced and to expose the silence[15] about the "social control of the food system" (Patel 2009: 665).

What is at stake in the globalization process is thus the recognition that small farmers and peasant agriculture are the "key part of the solution" (La Vía Campesina 2008) to eradicate world hunger and to democratize the agrifood system. From this perspective, the current international coordinator of La Vía Campesina, Henry Saragih, called for a shift in the commonly held right-to-food perspective, claiming that "the right *to produce* food is much more fundamental to fulfilling the rights to food" (2005: 7; my emphasis). For small farmers' "right to produce" is more and more in jeopardy when faced with the growth of corporate power in agriculture. Paradoxically, while rural peasants make up almost half of the world population and grow at least 70 percent of the world's food, "hunger is mainly rural: peasants, small

landholders, landless workers, fisher folk, hunters and gatherers suffer dispropor-
tionately.... Some 50 percent of the world's hungry are small holder farmers who
depend mainly or partly on agriculture for their livelihoods, but lack sufficient access
to productive resources" (Saragih 2010).

Refusing to let smallholders be doomed to extinction, La Vía Campesina's
activists reclaim the small farmers' status as food producers, laying emphasis more
particularly on their "food producing vocation" for the nation (La Vía Campesina
2010: 5). Contradicting Cargill's and Monsanto's claim that transnational corporations "feed the world" (Kneen 1999: 162), they underline, for instance—relying on
data from Brazil—that most of the food consumed within the country is produced
largely by peasants and family farmers:

> In country after country, small farmers control less than half of the farm land, yet produce
> the majority of the food that is consumed....A typical example comes from the most
> recent agricultural census in Brazil....Peasants have less than 25% of farm land, yet they
> generate 40% of all agricultural value....It is still Brazilian peasants and family farmers
> that feed the Brazilian people, a pattern repeated around the world....Brazilian agribusi-
> ness is more likely to feed cattle in Europe or produce ethanol for automobiles than it is
> to feed a hungry child in Brazil. (La Vía Campesina 2010: 4–5)

In my fieldwork in Brazil with organizational members of La Vía Campesina-
Brasil,[16] interviewees always attached importance to showing me the productive
capacity of their farm or the *assentamento*[17] where they were living. They would
show me around the farm or the plot of land, walk me through the fields, display
seeds from different crop varieties, explain the making of biodynamic liquid manure,
or take me to visit the new small agro-industrial factory. These actions affirmed the
centrality of their identity as producers.

La Vía Campesina's self-assertion as a movement of food producers, resisting and
confronting the global corporate food system, also comprises a dramaturgical and
public dimension in Erving Goffman's sense. Constituting themselves as "*dramatis
personae*," as "a We opposed to a They in a cast of characters" (Cefaï 1998: 146),
activists from the movement assert their right to grow food and to feed themselves
by making themselves *visible* at public meetings and global civil society gatherings. At the People's Climate Summit parallel to the United Nations Climate Change
Conference held in Copenhagen (Denmark) in December 2009, about forty delegates of La Vía Campesina from Europe, Asia, Africa, and the Americas performed
what the movement calls *mística* (or "mystique"). They denounced the international
food regime based on cheap genetically modified (GM) soy exports from Brazil for
the large-scale and intensive European meat industry. Standing in a circle in front
of the Danish Agriculture and Food Council, some, with La Vía Campesina green
scarves around their necks, held baskets full of vegetables and flowers and arm-
fuls of wheat ears as symbols of abundance and plenty. Others, dressed up like pigs

and representing the agro-meat industry, were covered with posters displaying the names of the transnational corporations. Miming a fight between the two camps, the activists embodied the dialectic between their struggle and their hope,[18] their present condition and the future as they envision it, that is, the final victory of small farmers over global corporate power. The *mística*—a cultural and political practice that La Vía Campesina borrowed from the Movimento dos Trabalhadores Rurais Sem Terra (MST; Landless Rural Workers Movement) and that derives from liberation theology—plays a significant role in the movement. Present in many opening and closing meetings, it usually consists of a playlet, songs, poetry, or dance, intended to represent symbols[19] of the social change activists yearn to create.[20] By enhancing among them the feeling of being part of a common struggle but also by allowing them to recharge collectively their "emotional batteries," it thus operates as a powerful consolidating element of the movement and sustains further commitment from its participants.

La Vía Campesina regularly engages in other symbolic rituals expressing their resistance to the corporate agrifood system. Of particular importance is the exchange or distribution of seeds originating from their respective countries. Annette Aurélie Desmarais, for instance, explains that at the 1996 World Food Summit, the movement "distributed its declaration accompanied with a package of seeds to all delegates attending the official summit.... It also brought truckloads of earth into the city [Rome] to form a plot of land and representatives engaged in a symbolic act of planting seeds" (2008: 141). La Vía Campesina's critical stance toward the corporate domination of the current agrifood system is also made visible through direct actions. Framed as the main "enemy" of the movement, transnational agrifood, agrichemical, and seed corporations (such as Monsanto, Syngenta, DuPont, Bayer, Cargill, BASF, Dow, Limagrain, etc.) are indeed the major target of activists' disruptive strategies. Apart from more or less routine repertoires of action, such as marches and demonstrations, activists engage in actions outside legality, which are likely to seize the attention of the media. Two examples of such illegal actions may be highlighted. On January 26, 2001, at the sidelines of the first World Social Forum held in Porto Alegre (Rio Grande do Sul), about 1,200 activists from the MST, Vía Campesina-Brasil, and La Vía Campesina-International[21] occupied a Monsanto experimental biotech farm and research center in the heart of the soy-growing region (Não-me-Toque). Newspaper reports indicate "The protestors uprooted soy and corn crops, burned soy stored in warehouses and held a burial ceremony for a coffin marked 'Monsanto' and covered with a U.S. flag."[22] Three years earlier, in India, on the symbolic date August 9, 1998,[23] the Karnataka Rajya Ryota Sangha (KRRS; Karnataka State Farmers' Association) and a coalition of Indian NGOs launched a campaign, "Quit India Monsanto." They opposed the "re-colonization of India" by transnational corporations through the WTO agreements. KRRS activists undertook several occupations of Monsanto's field trials and burned Bt cotton crops grown there ("Operation Cremate Monsanto") (Kingsnorth 1999).

Food Sovereignty and Social Transformation

La Vía Campesina's food sovereignty framing catalyzed small farmers' mobilization across borders and allowed them to become a voice of resistance increasingly heard in international and domestic policies. However, the movement is concerned with not limiting itself to transnational advocacy work. Far from focusing only on small-scale farmers' and rural workers' rights against transnational corporations and the WTO, the movement has much broader aspirations: "Our objective is always social change. We really define ourselves as a movement that wants to transform society."[24] According to most activists I met, struggling for food sovereignty principles requires consistency both in their farming practices and in the shaping of their social relationships. This process goes through a reversal of the values and priorities of the dominant corporate food system (Schanbacher 2010: 99). Stating that "food is first and foremost a source of nutrition and only secondarily an item of trade" (La Vía Campesina 1996), the movement aims at reorienting agriculture from an exclusive focus on commodification so as to give priority to its broader cultural, social, and environmental function.

The new global agriculture regime resting on industrialization and the promotion of exogenous methods, such as agrichemical inputs and GM seeds, amounts to a process of "abstraction" (McMichael 2005: 286), namely, the disembedding of the social but also of the ecological and cultural basis of agriculture. Agriculture is increasingly "systematized," homogenized, and decontextualized, disregarding the plurality and diversity of local contexts (for instance, local variations of the soil and climatic conditions). As A. R. Vasavi underlines, "It largely displaces the local knowledge and autonomy of agriculturists and substitutes the uniform and market-oriented prescriptions of the bureaucracy" (1994: 294). While agriculture is becoming increasingly globalized and centralized, "eliminating . . . self-reliance, self-provisioning, and autonomy" (Kneen 1999: 163), the sense of the political struggle lies also "at the farm level," as a member of the South Indian Coordination Committee of Farmers Movements[25] highlights it:

> It is not only a political fight against corporates. . . . It is also on the ground, at the farm level. For example, I am telling you, I'm working for the farmers' movement, but my father is not really listening to me. . . . For example, I asked him, "Who has given you these seeds?"—"I do not know the company!" Then I discovered it is from Syngenta. So multinational corporations are there even in my field! So it has to be the change from the farm-level resistance. Every farm should become self-reliant. This is another way we can have the chemical and seed companies out. . . . So the fight . . . the struggle should be from farm level to political level. Both levels, the fight should go on, hand in hand. Otherwise farmers who are taking part in the struggle against multinational companies would continue to use multinational seeds, chemicals, everything . . . on their farms. So it should be a people's movement in the countries where the people should be able to keep the companies off of their farms. (Indian male, personal interview, Bangalore, November 2011)

From this perspective, La Vía Campesina engages in modeling alternative agrifood systems by promoting "seed sovereignty" (that is to say, farmers' rights to save, use, exchange, sell, and protect farm-saved seeds)[26] and agro-ecological practices at the global, regional, national, and local levels. Native seed conservation projects have been established in several peasant farm communities in Brazil, among them Bionature Agroecological Seeds, founded in 1997 in the south of Rio Grande do Sul. Furthermore, activists from the MST receive training courses in sustainable agriculture at the Chico Mendes Center for Agroecology (Ponta Grossa, Paraná) as well as in the Latin American School of Agroecology (in Varinas, Venezuela) since 2005— thanks to a partnership between the federal government of Venezuela, the Federal University of Paraná, and La Vía Campesina. Small Brazilian delegations are also involved in "international brigades" so as to promote and disseminate a self-reliant and largely input-free agriculture among peasants in other countries, such as in Haiti since 2009 ("Dessaline Brigade"). Likewise, the KRRS promotes agro-ecology by organizing training and exchange programs about the methods of "Zero Budget Natural Farming": for instance, on November 1–6, 2011, an international delegation of about forty representatives of Asian farmers' organizations that are part of La Vía Campesina shared their experiences and visited farmers practicing "natural farming" in the surroundings of Mysore (Karnataka, India). Peter Rosset, a Mexican American who provides technical support for the Sustainable Peasant Agriculture Commission of La Vía Campesina, outlined the social transformation issue at stake at the closing conference of the Mysore workshop:

> As a social movement promoting agro-ecology, we are not just talking about farming techniques, we are really talking about something much larger: we are talking of agro-ecology as part of a much larger transformation of society, as one piece of an overall struggle for another kind of society.... We see agro-ecology as a tool for the transformation of our rural reality, by collective action, by working together and sharing knowledge, and we see agro-ecology is very exciting to many farmers, it is socially activating, it gets people working together and cooperating with each other and this is the first step for transforming a larger reality. (public meeting at B. N. Bahadur Institute of Management, Mysore University, November 6, 2011; my transcription)

In addition to transforming the farming system, the movement aims to eliminate the social inequalities of power relationships within the existing international food system, notably through a global campaign for agrarian reform and claims to fair prices for farmers. But La Vía Campesina also addresses the need for a deeper social change and understanding of power and control in society. The movement indeed points out the "equality-distorting effects of sexism, patriarchy, racism, and class power" (Patel 2009: 670). This association of food sovereignty with emancipatory politics includes in particular a feminist perspective that emphasizes the critical roles and rights of women and indigenous peoples in food production.

To ensure women's increased participation and representation in food and agricultural policy, the movement committed—only one year after its foundation—to fighting against patriarchalism and achieving gender equality within it. The ICC emphasized gender parity,[27] and an International Commission of Gender was established to promote feminist and leadership training courses for peasant women.[28] In addition, since 2000, an International Women's Assembly precedes the international conferences of the movement. Desmarais outlines the specific contribution that women taking part in La Vía Campesina made in defining food sovereignty in 1996 (2007b: 143), notably by adding a human health dimension to the right to food. "Food is a basic human right. Everyone must have access to safe, nutritious and culturally appropriate food in sufficient quantity and quality to sustain a *healthy* life with full human dignity" (La Vía Campesina 1996; my emphasis). This is precisely the health dimension that the woman in charge of the MST national sector of food production stresses, describing a direct action undertaken on International Women's Day (March 8, 2007) in Fortaleza (Ceará):

> Until recently, the sector of food production in the MST was very male-dominated. But the *companheiras* [women comrades] organized themselves. For instance they organized a mobilization against a McDonald's. They put in huge outside street kitchens, along five meters of the sidewalk, just in front of the fast-food restaurant. Then they cooked traditional meals such as *feijadas,* based upon recipes they inherited from their grandmothers who were European migrants or African slaves.... You know, they cooked meals that are very nutritious, that really give energy and health and also that highlight the great cultural diversity of Brazil. So we shouted out in the street to passers-by: "Which would you prefer? Diversity, health, quality of life or limitation in the breadth and choices of food?" *Companheiras* are not against the "right to food", this is very good, but we must specify: the right to healthy food, not just food for food! Not only *arroz e feijão* [rice and beans stew], not chemicalized and pesticized food! (Brazilian woman, headquarters of the MST, São Paulo, personal interview, October 2010; my translation from Portuguese)

Finally, the movement engages in exploring the inequalities in power that characterize the agrifood system, from the domestic to the global level. While women often bear the brunt of the rural work, they have less secure access to land and to productive resources than men. Chukki Nanjundaswamy, a female delegate of La Vía Campesina for Asia from 2004 to 2008 and general secretary of the KRRS, indeed notes "Socially, Indian peasant women have almost no rights and are considered an addition to men. Peasant women are the most untouchable of the untouchables within the social caste system" (La Vía Campesina 2006: 16; my translation). They also suffer from underpaid agricultural employment. At the fifth international conference, in Maputo (Mozambique) in October 2008, La Vía Campesina officially endorsed the idea that democratizing the food system requires challenging this situation. The assembly therefore approved the launch of a campaign targeting all forms of violence (physical, sexual, social, cultural, economic, etc.) faced by women in rural areas as well as in the broader society, stating, "Food sovereignty is about an end to violence against women."

Conclusion

This chapter has explored how rural social agents from the Global South and North, marginalized by the current trends of economic globalization, have engaged since the 1990s with a specific mode of agrifood activism organized across borders. Facing worldwide destruction of local agricultural production through corporate monopolization of agriculture and the increasing concentration in the food chain, smallholder farmers and landless rural workers taking part in La Vía Campesina point out the contradictions of the current food system, as it engenders hunger amid abundance. Desiring to bring back to the forefront of the public arena the social basis of production, they resist the disempowering aspects of economic globalization by making themselves more visible as food producers in the international arena. They confronted the hegemonic concept of food security by elaborating an alternate frame, food sovereignty, that is to say, the right of peoples to define their agricultural and food policies. By actively appropriating the language of rights and coining a more political concept, the activists of La Vía Campesina offer a powerful tool for reorienting the global politics of food away from an exclusive focus on commodification and rethinking it in terms of self-determination, social justice, public health, cultural appropriateness, and sustainability. This chapter also provides insights into the way La Vía Campesina's agrifood activism has aimed, over the last twenty years, at fostering a broader social change through the promotion of self-reliant agro-ecological farming practices and the shaping of new social relationships based on gender equality. While small farmers and landless rural workers taking part in La Vía Campesina have undoubtedly succeeded in redefining their areas of action and resistance by transcending local and regional boundaries, strengthening the links with urban struggles for "food justice" remains one of the challenges facing them in the coming years.

Notes

1. La Vía Campesina translates into English as the "Peasant Way" or the "Peasant Road." I have used the Spanish spelling Vía with the accent. The English spelling has no accent on Via. Both spellings are used and accepted by La Vía Campesina.
2. The International Operative Secretariat was established in 1996, even though it previously existed informally from 1993 to 1996; at that time the position was held by Paul Nicholson, member of the Basque Farmers' Union (Euskal Herriko Nezakarien

Elkartasuna) and was located in Europe (Brussels). Then it moved to Honduras, in Central America, and was held by Rafael Alegría, member of the Honduran Coordinating Council of Peasant Organizations (Consejo Coordinador de Organizaciones Campesinas de Honduras). Since 2004 it has been based in Jakarta (Indonesia) and held by Henry Saragih, secretary-general of the Federation of Indonesian Peasant Unions (Federasi Serikat Petani Indonesia). In 2013 the International Operative Secretariat moved to Africa, in Zimbabwe, and is now hosted by the Zimbabwe Small Organic Farmers Forum (ZIMSOFF). For more insights into La Vía Campesina's organizational structure and decision-making process using consultation and consensus, see Desmarais 2007a: 28–30 and Martínez-Torres and Rosset 2010: 164–166.

3. Even if food sovereignty was included in Mali's Agricultural Orientation Law in 2006 (Title I, Article 3; III, Article 51), many ambiguities surround current agricultural policies in Mali, in particular large-scale land acquisitions by foreign investors such as Malibya in June 2008 (Libyan lease of 250,000 acres [100,000 hectares] of farmland). Marie Hrabanski (2011) also shows how food sovereignty in the case of Senegal has been exploited by President Abdoulaye Wade for petty political ends.

4. On the importance of the sociocultural circumstances in which the framing process takes place and the dynamic instabilities in the very process of discourse ("multivocality"), see, for instance, Steinberg 1999.

5. To deepen the understanding of the transnationalization of farmers' movements, my PhD project takes a comparative and multisited approach in focusing on three organizations of La Vía Campesina (the Confédération paysanne from France, the Movimento dos Trabalhadores Rurais Sem Terra from Brazil, and the Karnataka Rajya Ryota Sangha from India) and examines how they are building solidarities beyond and across national borders.

6. According to the statistics of the FAO, over one billion people—that is, one in six human beings—are hungry in the world.

7. Drawing on Erving Goffman's (1974) metaphor of "keying," Patrick Money and Scott Hunt refer to a "flat keying" of a frame as a process that "reinforce[s] extant dominant interpretations and practices, usually advanced by power holders" (2009: 471).

8. According to the National Crime Records Bureau of the Indian Ministry of Home Affairs, 150,000 farmers committed suicide between 1997 and 2005.

9. Myria Marx Ferree reminds us of the "relation of power to framing" (2003: 308); that is to say, the deep power asymmetries between social agents determine their ability to reshape an existing discursive field.

10. The emergence of La Vía Campesina also signified a break with the influence of the International Federation of Agricultural Producers, led mainly by large-scale commercial farmers and officially representing farmers' interests at international and intergovernmental institutions since 1946. Since November 2010 the federation has, however, been dissolved due to bankruptcy.

11. Transcript of speeches held during a training workshop on food sovereignty organized by the Confédération paysanne (Bagnolet, France, February 19, 2009; my translation from French).

12. As Saturnino Borras Jr., Marc Edelman, and Cristóbal Kay underline, "For *Vía Campesina*, it is not the NGOs *per se* that are problematic. Rather it is the term of the relationship that matters" (2008: 29), that is to say, the relations of power stemming from great disparities in resources and goals. In this sense, the movement seeks to build alliances with a few progressive NGOs sharing a similar vision and concerned with the establishment of an equal partnership (Food First Information and Action Network, Land and Research Action Network, Association pour la Taxation des Transactions pour l'Aide aux Citoyens [ATTAC], Oxfam, GRAIN, etc.).

13. This strategy to "keep resonance" (Ferree 2003) with international conventional food security discourse through the adoption of a "reformist" stance may be related to NGOs' dependence on governmental and international donors to get funds.

14. "Statement by the NGO Forum to the World Food Summit" (Rome, November 17, 1996).

15. Marc Steinberg points out that "an essential part of the power produced through discourse, and a cornerstone of hegemony, is the capacity to construct silences within common sense" (1998: 855).

16. Movimento dos Trabalhadores Rurais Sem Terra, Movimento das Mulheres Camponesas, Movimento dos Pequenos Agricultores, and Movimento dos Atingidos por Barragens.

17. *Assentamento* refers to a permanent settlement established once the landless families win the land they occupied. It is divided into family or common lots.

18. La Vía Campesina's slogan is "Globalize the Struggle—Globalize the Hope!"

19. Daniela Issa emphasizes the importance of the use of symbols in the practice of *mística* because of the peasant culture's oral tradition (2007: 133).

20. According to Ademar Bogo, a former Catholic seminarian, the objective of the *mística* is "to reduce the distance between the present and the future, helping us to anticipate with certainty the objectives we want to reach" (Bogo 1991: 3; my translation from Portuguese).

21. The French José Bové and François Dufour from the Confédération paysanne and the Honduran Rafael Alegría, second international coordinator of La Vía Campesina, also took part in the action.

22. *Agencia Latinoamericana de Información, La Jornada*, and *Financial Times*, January 27, 2001. See also "Somente lutando outro mundo é possível," 2001.

23. At midnight on August 8–9, 1942, the "*Quit India*" movement, a civil disobedience movement, was launched in response to Gandhi's call for immediate independence.

24. Paul Nicholson, personal interview, Irún, Spain, April 2010; my translation from French.

25. The South Indian Coordination Committee of Farmers Movements is a coalition of South Indian farmers' unions taking part in La Vía Campesina that was founded in 2009.
26. From 2003 on, La Vía Campesina launched a global campaign "Seeds: Heritage of Rural Peoples in the Service of Humanity," coordinated by women activists.
27. The ICC includes one woman and one man from each of La Vía Campesina's regions.
28. A World Congress of Women of La Vía Campesina was, for instance, organized at Santiago de Compostela, Spain, from October 18 to 21, 2006.

References

Bacon, D. (1997), "Still Hungry," January, *Z Net: The Spirit of Resistance Lives*, http://www.zcommunications.org/still-hungry-by-david-bacon, accessed July 13, 2013.

Benford, R., and Hunt, S. A. (2003), "Interactional Dynamics in Public Problems Marketplaces: Movements and the Counterframing and Reframing of Public Problems," in J. A. Holstein and G. Miller (eds.), *Challenges and Choices: Constructionist Perspectives on Social Problems*, New York: De Gruyter, 153–186.

Benford, R., and Snow, D. (2000), "Framing Processes and Social Movements: An Overview and Assessment," *Annual Review of Sociology*, 26: 611–639.

Bogo, A. (1991), "A mística nos núcleos," *Jornal dos Sem Terra*, 103: 3.

Borras, S. M., Jr. (2008), "La Vía Campesina and Its Global Campaign for Agrarian Reform," *Journal of Agrarian Change*, 8/2–3: 258–289.

Borras, S. M., Jr., Edelman, M., and Kay, C. (2008), "Transnational Agrarian Movements: Origins and Politics, Campaigns and Impact," in S. M. Borras Jr., M. Edelman, and C. Kay (eds.), *Transnational Agrarian Movements: Confronting Globalization*, Malden, MA: Wiley-Blackwell, 1–36.

Cefaï, D. (1998), "Making Sense of Politics in Public Spaces: Phenomenology of Political Experiences and Activities," in L. Embree (ed.), *Schutzian Social Science*, The Hague: Kluwer, 135–158.

Desmarais, A. (2007a), *La Vía Campesina: Globalization and the Power of Peasants*, Halifax, NS: Fernwood; London: Pluto.

Desmarais, A. (2007b), "The Vía Campesina: Peasant Women on the Frontiers of Food Sovereignty," *Canadian Woman Studies/Cahiers de la femme*, 23/1: 140–145.

Desmarais, A. (2008), "The Power of Peasants: Reflections on the Meanings of La Vía Campesina," *Journal of Rural Studies*, 24: 138–149.

Ferree, M. M. (2003), "Resonance and Radicalism: Feminist Framing in the Abortion Debates of the US and Germany," *American Journal of Sociology*, 209/2: 304–344.

Food and Agriculture Organization (FAO) (1996), "Rome Declaration on World Food Security," Rome: FAO.

Goffman, E. (1974), *Frame Analysis: An Essay on the Organization of Experience*, New York: Harper & Row.

Hrabanski, M. (2011), "Souveraineté alimentaire: Mobilisations collectives agricoles et instrumentalisations multiples d'un concept transnational," *Revue Tiers Monde*, 3/207: 151–168.

Issa, D. (2007), "Praxis of Empowerment: *Mística* and Mobilization in Brazil's Landless Rural Workers' Movement," *Latin American Perspectives*, 34/2: 124–138.

Kennedy, D. (2002), "The Critique of Rights in Critical Legal Studies," in W. Brown and J. Halley (eds.), *Left Legalism/Left Critique*, Durham, NC: Duke University Press, 178–228.

Kingsnorth, P. (1999), "India Cheers While Monsanto Burns," *The Ecologist*, 28/1: 9–10.

Kneen, B. (1999), "Restructuring Food for Corporate Profit: The Corporate Genetics of Cargill and Monsanto," *Agriculture and Human Values*, 16: 161–167.

Li, T. Murray (2001), "Masyarakat Adat, Difference and the Limits of Recognition in Indonesia's Forest Zone," *Modern Asia Studies*, 35/3: 645–676.

Martínez-Torres, M. E., and Rosset, P. M. (2010), "La Vía Campesina: The Birth and Evolution of a Transnational Social Movement," *Journal of Peasant Studies*, 37/1: 149–175.

McMichael, P. (2005), "Global Development and the Corporate Food Regime," in F. Buttel and P. McMichael (eds.), *Research in Rural Sociology and Development*, New Directions in the Sociology of Global Development 11, Amsterdam: Elsevier, 269–303.

Money, P. H., and Hunt, S. A. (2009), "Food Security: The Elaboration of Contested Claims to a Consensus Frame," *Rural Sociology*, 74/4: 469–497.

Patel, R. (2009), "What Does Food Sovereignty Look Like?" *Journal of Peasant Studies*, 36/3: 663–673.

Patnaik, U. (2003), "Global Capitalism, Deflation and Agrarian Crisis in Developing Countries," *Journal of Agrarian Change*, 13/1–2: 33–66.

Polletta, F. (2000), "The Structural Context of Novel Rights Claims: Southern Civil Rights Organizing, 1961–1966," *Law & Society Review*, 34/2: 367–406.

Saragih, H. (2005), "The World Peasant Farmers Need a Peasant Farmers Rights Convention: The Way for the United Nations to End the Oppression and the Extinction of Peasant Farmers," Geneva: Centre Europe-Tiers Monde, http://www.cetim.ch/en/documents/05-onu2-saraghi.pdf, accessed July 13, 2013.

Saragih, H. (2010), "Rights of Peasants: Ending the Discrimination against Peasants," speech, Fourth Session of the Advisory Committee of UN Human Rights Council, Geneva, responding to the report of the Advisory Committee "Discrimination in the Context of Right to Food" (A/HRC/AC/4/2), January 27.

Schanbacher, W. (2010), *The Politics of Food: The Global Conflict between Food Security and Food Sovereignty*, Santa Barbara, CA: Praeger.

Snow, D., Benford, R., Rochford, E. B., Jr., and Worden, S. K. (1986), "Frame Alignment Processes, Micromobilization, and Movement Participation," *American Sociological Review*, 51: 464–481.

"Somente lutando outro mundo é possível" (2001), *Jornal dos Sem Terra*, 207: 11.

Steinberg, M. (1998), "Tilting the Frame: Considerations on Collective Action Framing from a Discursive Turn," *Theory and Society*, 27/6: 845–872.

Steinberg, M. (1999), "The Talk and Back of Collective Action: A Dialogic Analysis of Repertoires of Discourse among Nineteenth Century English Cotton Spinners," *American Journal of Sociology*, 105/3: 736–780.

United Nations General Assembly (1948), "Universal Declaration of Human Rights," Paris.

United Nations General Assembly (1966), "International Covenant on Economic, Social and Cultural Rights," New York.

Van Der Ploeg, J. D. (2008), *The New Peasantries: Struggles for Autonomy and Sustainability in an Era of Empire and Globalization*, London: Earthscan.

Vasavi, A. R. (1994), "*Hybrid Times, Hybrid People*: Culture and Agriculture in South India," *Man*, new ser., 29/2: 283–300.

Vasavi, A. R. (2012), *Shadow Space: Suicides and the Predicament of Rural India*, Gurgaon, Haryana, India: Three Essays Collective.

La Vía Campesina (1996), "The Right to Produce and Access to Land," World Food Summit, Rome, November 11–17, http://www.voiceoftheturtle.org/library/1996%20Declaration%20of%20Food%20Sovereignty.pdf, accessed July 13, 2013.

La Vía Campesina (2006), "Labregas sementando igualdade," Congreso Mundial de Las Mujeres de La Vía Campesina, Santiago de Compostela, Spain, October 18–21.

La Vía Campesina (2008), "Vía Campesina Proposal to Solve Food Crisis: Strengthening Peasant and Farmer-Based Food Production," open letter to Jacques Diouf, secretary-general of the Food and Agriculture Organization of the United Nations, Jakarta, April 28.

La Vía Campesina (2010), "Sustainable Peasant and Family Farm Agriculture Can Feed the World," Jakarta: La Vía Campesina.

Wise, T. A. (2009), "Promise or Pitfall? The Limited Gains from Agricultural Trade Liberalisation for Developing Countries," *Journal of Peasant Studies*, 36/4: 855–870.

–14–

Oscillating between Village and Globe: Articulating Food in Sri Lankan Activism

Wim Van Daele

Food constitutes human life as a whole and each of its biological, social, cultural, economic, political, and psychological aspects.[1] Hence, food spurs intense emotions and reactions when affected by multifarious changes, such as technological innovations (e.g., the green revolution, genetic modification), trade policies (e.g., liberalization, privatization), and environmental calamities (e.g., climate change). Food activism is but one possible expression of the deep insecurities and reactions that arise when food is affected. Food fears (e.g., Rozin 1999) and food-revitalization practices (e.g., the rise of "authentic" cuisine) are some of the less political expressions. In what follows, I tease out the specificity of the activist articulation of food and related concerns by adopting a contrastive, contextual, and relational perspective. Instead of exploring food activism as a phenomenon in and of itself, as many studies on activism tend to do (e.g., Keck and Sikkink 1998; Tarrow 2006), I pose the question of what is specific in food activism *in contrast to and in relation to* the wider environment in which it operates and articulates itself. More specifically, I explore the ways that Sri Lankan activists relate to and subsequently translate and articulate some of the widespread food concerns that are negotiated differently in rituals performed by the farming villagers whom the activists claim to represent. In this way, their *shared* concerns and *differentiated* articulations come to the fore, enabling analysis of the hallmarks of the activists' expressions of food and related anxieties.

Here, I utilize the term *articulation* to specify that food is an assemblage composed of interconnecting heterogeneous components including environmental factors, cultural practices, bodily efforts, biological processes, existential concerns, political relations, and economic laws that all mutually affect each other and the food assemblage.[2] When food enters a new context, it acquires different components and changes, as in the transformation of food from a physical substance and commodity in the economic market into a chopped, cooked, and convivial substance that has an altered form and expression on the domestic plate. Hence, food constantly changes (in both meaning and matter) as it continually enters into such new relationships and contexts. I later discuss the differences between food in ritual and in activist contexts where variation emerges in the expressions and actualizations of food in these respective contexts. More specifically, I will show, as I have discussed in greater depth elsewhere (Van Daele 2013a,b), that in Sri Lankan ritual, food becomes an assemblage of cooking processes, materials, and fire but also of existential concerns, desires, and myths. Hence, in rituals these heterogeneous components are connected in specific ways that create a distinct context-related articulation of food that entails the translation, remaking, and forging of new connections between heterogeneous aspects, whether physical or symbolic (Latour 2005: 108). When activists attempt to articulate villagers' concerns about the precariousness of life as condensed and materialized in food rituals, they connect food to other contexts (often political and economic) and different issues. Hence, they create a specific activist articulation of food. Whether an item is articulated as a "ritual food" or an "activist food" thus becomes clear only in its relationships established in particular contexts.

Food not only results from but also produces change in the contexts in which it appears. For instance, in ritual offerings and preparations, food connects and condenses various concerns and becomes a ritual agent that collaborates with human beings in transforming a situation of anxiety into one of well-being, fertility, and prosperity (Van Daele 2013a,b). In popular Sinhalese practical epistemologies according to which plants and animals act from a "thinking and (dis)liking" capacity, agency is not an exclusive human faculty but instead is distributed unevenly across human and nonhuman entities, which exhibit different degrees of agency. These entities have the capacity to aspire and to act with some intentional purpose, which is always being modified as various things, beings, or events interfere with the aspired course of life, complicate the journey, and contribute to existential insecurities or new possibilities.

In what follows, I will first briefly introduce a few core existential themes that food affects by its participation in ritual practices. Second, I will indicate how these rather implicit concerns with desire, precariousness, and regeneration are shared between Colombo-based activists and Sri Lankan villagers (Van Daele 2013b). I will then focus on the differing expressions of these shared concerns by exploring the ways in which activists translate, articulate, and alter the food assemblage. I subsequently turn toward the activists themselves to situate their specific articulation of food in the context of their personal lives and histories. Finally, I conclude by summarizing the activists' differentiated articulation through food of the deeper concerns they share with villagers.

I draw on more than ten months of ethnographic fieldwork in a village in the Kurunegala district in northwestern Sri Lanka during 2008–2009, three months of field research in another village nearby, and my intermittent collaboration with the Movement of National Land and Agricultural Reform (MONLAR). For eight months during the years 2004–2010 I interacted with the MONLAR activists on the green revolution and post-tsunami reconstruction over the Internet and at the office in Colombo, the capital of Sri Lanka. I collected information both in the village and at the MONLAR office through participant observation, collection of life stories, and extended open-ended interviews, always exploring food's "collaboration" with human beings in the crafting of their lives (Janeja 2010). During my work at MON-LAR, analysis of their documents and discourses was important, as activist engagement with food was more abstract and analytical than the villagers' more practical engagements. In village life, food plays a pivotal and yet not explicitly articulated role in mitigating at a very material level the precariousness of life in everyday and ritual events. The powerful and ambiguous capacity of food to regenerate and destroy life enables it to become a crucial agent in ritual events that deal with life transitions. It also hints at why activists passionately select it as a "*matter* of concern" (Latour 2005: 114–120; my italics) around which they mobilize to grapple with wider issues of well-being and economic and political justice insofar as these are connected to food. The shared fundamental concern with food and related situations of precariousness is what *indirectly* connects ritual and activist articulations and utilizations of food, yet at the explicit level there is a clear gap between them. The next section addresses existential themes articulated with food in ritual action.

Existential Concerns as Articulated in Ritual

The ritual boiling of milk rice, or *kiribath,* demonstrates the core existential concerns that are negotiated in ritual action transforming situations of precariousness into ones of well-being. First, villagers heat up coconut milk in an earthen pot on a log fire until it physically overflows in the four cardinal directions, to symbolically encompass the world and cosmos. It is important to balance all components correctly (the amount of fire, coconut milk, heat, human effort, etc.) to ensure a successful overflowing and ritual transformation toward prosperity and regeneration of the cosmos and life. When the overflowing of milk (*kiriutereme*) eases down, villagers add raw rice and cook it slowly to make a thick paste of milk rice, which is sometimes cut in diamond shapes to further articulate prosperity. Indeed, people prepare kiribath at occasions that are associated with hopes and aspirations for prosperity, fertility, and well-being, thereby linking the actual foodstuff to these concerns. Events such as births, birthdays, weddings, the New Year, and harvest rituals all involve the preparation and consumption of this mixture of rice and coconut milk. As this epitomic ritual food articulates the desire for a good life, it simultaneously acknowledges the possibility that things can go wrong, as any transition opens up the possibility for a transformation for the worse, the waning instead of the waxing of life, a core existential insecurity (Jackson 2005). Moreover, the rite not only expresses these existential concerns and hopes but actually seeks to bring about and materialize the related aspiration that all will go well in the next phase. For instance, in the harvest ritual, the kiriutereme and sharing of kiribath with deities serve to express the farmer's gratitude toward them and to solicit their goodwill to mitigate possible adverse events that may jeopardize a good harvest in the next year. Hence, in addition to acknowledging the precariousness and insecurity of cultivation and life sustenance, the offering of milk rice seeks to bring about positive outcomes by ensuring a prosperous harvest. The recurring connection with happiness and well-being stabilizes milk rice as an articulator of prosperity and a collaborator in materializing the good life, as the deities are pleased by this white, pure, and sweet substance and thus act to protect the next cultivation cycle and ensure prosperity.

Milk rice can never be used at funerals, as these are not about a transition in life but rather about death—a transition to otherworldly spheres that hopefully extinguishes attachment to this worldly life. Funerals require different foods to help achieve a "good" death and afterlife, engaging core concerns about attachment, craving, and desire and their annihilation. A person who possesses a craving at the moment of death can get stuck between death and rebirth and become a *preta*, a being defined by insatiable hunger and excessive desire or greed. Villagers fear that they or their relatives might become hungry ghosts in such a "bad" death and so perform a ritual at the funeral to prevent this possibility. Immediately after the burial, the relatives of the deceased cook his or her favorite meal in one pot and carry it outside the domestic compound to capture the deceased's spirit in the seductive food and guide it away from the home so that he or she can let go of attachments and depart to the next life. Hence, food's powerful agency—in this case its absorptive capacity—is utilized to ensure a good transition during funerary rites.

If, after a while, some pretas or hungry ghosts remain present, these invisible beings can attach themselves to people, causing disruptions in their capacity to achieve aspired outcomes. Such afflicted people are bound by the influence of the hungry ghost (*preta bandana*) and thereby lose control of their own desires and lives. They become unable to exert their agency and often suffer from ill health. In those cases, spirit mediums attempt to cut the bonds with these pretas, and here again, foods play an important collaborative role. The participants in the restorative ritual prepare seductive food offerings for the pretas and place these outside of the homestead. By way of their insatiable hunger and greed, the pretas remain tied to the offerings, while the affected people observe certain food practices (e.g., no red meat) to avoid attracting the spirits back. Hence, ritual participants collaborate with the capacity of food to incite desire during this restorative rite, which aims to rebalance desire among the afflicted and to regenerate their health, well-being, and ability to live a "good," fulfilling life again. These three rituals (kiriutereme, funerals, and liberation from pretas) embody the wish to lead a prosperous life without a detrimental excess of desire or greed.

To sum up, throughout various rituals, different food preparations and offerings articulate precariousness, existential uncertainty, and excessive desire and enable various modes of remedying these states to achieve prosperity and well-being. A central concern that emerges from this brief discussion is expressing the hope and desire for a good life while not falling into the trap (e.g., through preta bandana) of excessive and unbalanced desire, which can lead to ill health and loss of agency. I suggest, in line with Jean Comaroff (personal communication) and Michael Taussig (2010 [1980]: 5), that the pretas are fetishized formations of desire disembedded from social relations that form a phantom objectification and animation that exerts control over social relations. This particular fetishization of desire engages similar dynamics as the abstract laws of the economic market and consumerism, where it drives economic growth and the accumulation of capital. Here, too, people get bound by laws that inhibit free agency through their preta-like excessive desire, and, similarly, such unbalanced forms tend to be detrimental to other human and nonhuman beings. It is this deeper existential concern to limit excessive formations of desire and to restore its balanced forms to achieve prosperity and a good life that connects the villagers with the activists in Colombo. From a ritual perspective, it becomes clear why food would *matter* in the work of activists. Food is a powerful agent in shaping life and dealing with concerns of desire, precariousness, and the regeneration of the good life.

MONLAR's Articulation of Concerns

In this section I focus on how MONLAR articulates these shared concerns differently in food activism and explore the particular dynamics that underpin the differentiation between the ritual and activist articulations of food-related insecurities. MONLAR is a network organization that has about thirty people working in the office in Colombo and brings together about 100 member organizations around matters of land, agriculture, and food. MONLAR has evolved from an organization engaged in mobilizations, actions, and demonstrations into an organization that engages in advocacy and works predominantly "behind the scenes" in coordinating member organizations to influence policy at regional, national, and international levels. I have analyzed written statements, vision papers, and policy documents in researching MONLAR's approach to food. MONLAR sensitizes farmers by educating them on organic methods of farming. Even though they are no longer "on the barricades," I still count the people working at MONLAR as activists, as their advocacy and actions purposefully aim at achieving equitable well-being for all, including nonhuman entities such as the environment and animals, through public and political debates and mobilization.

MONLAR proclaims on its website in English: "Efforts made in integrating Sri Lanka's economy into the globalization process resulted in an unprecedented increase in rural poverty, breakdown in rural small farmer agriculture, malnutrition among children, high rate of anemia among mothers, low birth weight babies, large increase in income disparities, and loss of livelihoods."[3] Sarath Fernando, the moderator and "ideologist" of MONLAR, writes, "The plans pushed by global capital to capture, take control over world's natural resources and enslave the whole of human kind for the purpose of unceasing and limitless accumulation of capital obviously threaten the very survival of both" (n.d.: 1). He singles out the endless drive for profit, linked to excessive desire, as a core concern. The logic of accumulation and extraction of profit, labor, and resources expresses itself in an industrialized and commercialized agriculture that is, according to Sarath, epitomized by the green revolution. During the 1960s and 1970s, in the push for self-sufficiency with regard to rice, the postcolonial governments of Sri Lanka initiated World Bank (WB)-funded, large-scale irrigation and resettlement schemes to increase paddy production by introducing new rice varieties dependent on chemical inputs, which increased harvests but also the costs of production. Farmers initially benefited from subsidized seeds and fertilizers, minimum prices, centralized means of marketing (e.g., the Paddy Marketing Board), and buffer stocks (Moore 1985). MONLAR argues that this support from the state was dismantled under pressure from the International Monetary Fund (IMF) and WB to increase the scope for profit making and capital accumulation for transnational corporations. For MONLAR, the green revolution came to represent an industrial agriculture based on the logic of profit. Food became linked with additional economic components, such as input and output prices, market relations, trade, and neoliberal policies. MONLAR suggests that agribusiness destroys "traditional" farming, as farmers become increasingly indebted by having to obtain herbicides, fertilizers, and seeds. Agribusiness is driven by excessive desire that is fetishized into the "natural" need of the *Homo economicus* to accumulate capital, just as excessive desire is fetishized into hungry ghosts. The economic fetish of desire is detrimental to small-scale farming and pushes people out of agriculture as it is no longer viable. MONLAR criticizes the green revolution as it embodies the transformations in the Sri Lankan economy that were driven by international financial institutions (IFIs), the profit motive that uses up resources (natural, human, social), and by extension the whole capitalist system and the destructive, excessive desire it stands for.

MONLAR proposes a shift toward nonchemical traditional agriculture, which restores the capacity of the soil and nature to regenerate itself. When the soil is provided with organic manure or compost, it can recover its capacity to become an "eternal spring of gifts," in Sarath Fernando's words. He introduced "regenerative agriculture," based on reciprocity with nature, into MONLAR in opposition to the unsustainable parasitic extraction of resources in agribusiness.

Fernando attempts to justify regenerative agriculture by grounding his argument in the science of agroforestry and by referring to his own multilayered home garden in which various plants, ranging from vines to trees, provide both compost and food "at no cost." He argues that regenerative agriculture restores ecological relations, making farming viable again and accessible for anyone. This shift to no-input and organic farming also promotes better health, respects the Buddhist precept of non-killing, and liberates people from being preta extractors of resources and capital that destroy balances vital to life. Indeed, Fernando explicitly states, "Religious attitudes and beliefs provided a useful background for sustaining the regenerative potential. For example, greed and accumulation were seen as negative values" (n.d.: 3) He alludes to the Buddhist requirement of nonattachment that also informs everyday preoccupations with pretas among villagers. Indeed, nonattachment refers to extinguishing the flame of desire, a state important for reaching nirvana and thus also for avoiding becoming a preta.

MONLAR seeks to negotiate the detrimental consequences of excessive desire in its economic form by proposing more balanced relations of give and take as materialized in regenerative agriculture. An analogy exists between the work of MONLAR and the restorative ritual that appeases the effects of pretas mentioned earlier. The activists likewise collaborate with food, in its powerful capacity to act and bring about transformations in various situations, to achieve changes in society away from the logic of greed, extraction, and accumulation. Whereas ritual deals with issues of insecurity, desire, and restoration (or regeneration) on a very material and bodily level, MONLAR works on a wider geographic and more conceptual level, as well as on the level of political argumentation and justification. Its activists expand food to a wider national and international scale, on the one hand, and to a more abstract and general level of principles, on the other.

Abstraction as Scale Making, Generalization, and Reductionism

In what follows, I will explore the particular activist expression and articulation of food in more depth by looking at the dynamics that underpin this articulation. I draw on Luc Boltanski and Laurent Thévenot (2006) and their theory on the use of justifications in reaching agreements in political debates and arguments. They argue that to reach agreement negotiating parties need to share a common ground and principles from which to argue and justify different positions. In the political field this shared ground entails the common principle that humanity is endowed with the unique faculty of critical reasoning and rational thinking that can bring forth different and even opposing ideas. Someone who justifies his or her argument by referring to a divine source will not greatly impact the discussion in contexts where this inspirational source is not seen as a credible argument in the "rational" political game. Hence, in critiquing the organization of the current food system and in seeking access to the political field, MONLAR draws on rational arguments concerning increased market access for farmers or food subsidies for poor people, in which they also appeal to other common principles, such as the dignity of human beings and their human rights. In this way, MONLAR connects food to these rational, higher, and more abstract principles expressed in political and economic terms, and thus food acquires its specific activist articulation. The ritual articulation, materialization, and condensation of food in the practical ritual engagements with existential concerns then alters into the activist articulation of food at larger national and international scales, hence abstracting food from its intimate, practical, and experiential ritual connections. This abstraction is required if MONLAR wishes to enter the political field and to engage in dialogue and influence the policies of powerful political actors. The overall abstraction involves three related subdynamics that I discuss in more detail in the following: scale making, generalization, and reductionism. Thereafter, I look more closely at the reasons *why* MONLAR engages in these dynamics.

To make the contrast between this overall abstraction and the ritual articulation more tangible, I will give an example of how MONLAR approaches food. On its website, MONLAR blames the post-1977 policies of liberalization in agriculture and industry, under the guidance of the WB and IMF, for the breakdown of domestic agriculture and the loss of livelihoods of farmers, who make up about half the population.[4] MONLAR argues "The farmers became heavily indebted as cost of production became very high (increasing more than ten times within about a decade) and the cost of living too increased in a similar manner. . . . The prices obtained by the domestic producers dropped to very low levels, particularly during the harvest times, although the consumers continued to pay very high and increasing prices" (MONLAR 2005: 4). Here food is linked to poverty, markets, and segments of the national population and is no longer about the body, domestic relations of intimacy, and practical ritual negotiations of anxieties. MONLAR is then able to enter the political field, where it seeks to bring about transformations.

The first subdynamic of abstraction is evident: the making of a broader scale by articulating food in national market and policy terms and by referring to global political economic bodies, such as IFIs, as they affect national politics and span wider geographic areas. MONLAR reacts against national and global policies by proposing food sovereignty, which is based on the political notion of territorial integrity and is applied to countries and peoples to include their political right to "define their own food and agriculture; to restrict the dumping of products in their markets" (Windfuhr and Jonsén 2005: 2). By articulating food in these broad political economic terms in relation to larger geographic areas, MONLAR's formulation focuses on a broad scale that is abstract for many villagers.

Second, articulating food with larger-scale political and economic phenomena involves an increasing generalization as well. In its analysis and critiques, MON-LAR bundles the various aspects of food experiences into three general categories of land, labor, and capital that make up a political economic approach to agriculture (e.g., Bernstein 2010). MONLAR specifically singles out the component of capital in its Marxist analysis. It does so by critiquing transnational agribusinesses that accumulate capital by destroying natural resources through excessive extraction and by exploiting smallholders' labor and capital as much as possible. Hence, MONLAR focuses on the abstract and general notion of capital that thrives on excessive greed and accumulation, like a preta that craves endlessly. In some cases, MONLAR does connect topics of extraction and abstraction with higher principles of human rights and human dignity to come to an agreement with more moderate actors that are open to such higher common principles. It does so, moreover, by connecting the notion of capital to wide trends and concepts that mean different things to different people (as is often the case with high-level generality), such as "globalization," an "oppressive system," "development," and so forth, and that thus allows people from different backgrounds to share a common context and to mobilize.

A third aspect of abstraction entails the reduction of the multiplicity of particular experiences and situations to a degree that is manageable for discussion, with the aim of reaching an agreement to change policies. For instance, the multiplicity of experiences and social consequences of poverty and hunger cannot be dealt with in their full complexity at a national or global scale, hence the creation of poverty indexes and nutritional standards. Such standardization enables communication over large groups and across large distances but loses touch with grounded realities and local-level variations that may be important. Most often, MONLAR's reductionism favors political and/or economic figures, epistemologies, and principles, such as the land, labor, and capital tripod to which the multiplicity of food is reduced. That is related to the nature of MONLAR, its raison d'être as a mobilizing organization, its motivations, and the power of the political field it seeks to influence.

MONLAR's Political Economy

There are two main reasons why MONLAR performs this abstraction of food. On the one hand, MONLAR attempts to "bring about policy changes at [a] macro/national level,"[5] and on the other hand, MONLAR seeks to build awareness among the people affected by those policies. By formulating food-related insecurities and anxieties in more abstract and thus general, reductionist, and large-scale terms, people with varied experiences can identify themselves with such an articulation and connect with it. As such, the abstraction enables the mobilization of a larger and more diversified constituency, and of wider alliances with other organizations. It helps to retranslate wider economic processes to the farmer audiences at local meetings and campaigns where activists explain how national and international policies cause the problems that farmers are experiencing. Hence, the activists try to reconnect the abstract expression of food back to the personal experiences of farmers, but this is not easy. For instance, after a two-hour talk about economic structures and IFIs, the first question from a woman in the audience inquired whether MONLAR could help her in obtaining a well. This example shows that the abstraction can forge connections between phenomena and actors at higher levels and across larger distances while potentially alienating activists from the people they claim to represent.

Beyond the aims of sensitizing and mobilizing its constituency, MONLAR also builds alliances to galvanize support in bringing about policy changes at the national and international levels. MONLAR's work entails the dynamics of Margaret Keck and Kathryn Sikkink's (1998) "boomerang model," in which the organization moves vertically upward to forge links with other organizations operating at an international level to gain leverage to change international policies (e.g., the IMF and WB) and to achieve subsequent modifications at the lower national scale in Sri Lanka as well.

Hence, MONLAR has become a member of the globalized farmer's movement Via Campesina and has become related to (and funded by) organizations such as War on Want, Christian Aid, and Bread for the World in order to gain influence at both the national and international levels. This forging of alliances at international and cross-cultural levels requires a more generalized formulation of analyses and goals in order to build a common ground where commensurate principles of agreement can be crafted. Moreover, to obtain funding, MONLAR has to adapt to the aesthetics of the network and partnership into which it enters, including specialized language and logical frameworks.[6]

MONLAR oscillates between local-level farmers, where it seeks to build awareness and mobilize its constituency, and the international level of global campaigns and alliances. However, to successfully oscillate, MONLAR needs to translate concerns according to the contexts and scales to which communication is oriented, such as policymakers, IFIs, local constituencies, and international activist networks. The challenge remains to navigate between multiple levels and to not lose touch with the ground level that the activists wish to represent, while funding and political power are concentrated at higher levels.

The abstract articulation of food and related concerns into political economic terms is related not only to the scale at which MONLAR operates and forges alliances but also to the nature of its work and raison d'être. It seeks to influence policies and as such becomes a predominantly political organization that seeks to translate its concerns into the principles of how the political field functions. MONLAR cannot enter the political stage and perform rituals to alleviate the effects of hungry ghosts that thrive in an economic climate based on greed and desire. Instead, the organization must use sources of justifications commensurable with those of politicians and economists in order to advance its point. It must do so according to the practice of "argumentative reasoning" (Povinelli 2002: 8–15), in which rational arguments take precedence over ethical, spiritual, and emotional ones. These "rational" argumentations and justifications include their grounding in valorized scientific knowledge (e.g., agroforestry), in the reputation of international bodies (e.g., the United Nations Declaration of Human Rights and the right to food), and economic laws. In the different context of Sinhalese Buddhist nationalism, however, MONLAR invokes Buddhist values to make a case for regenerative agriculture that avoids any killing of life. In short, MONLAR has to adapt to the rules of the game set by the powerful field of politics that its activists seek to influence and also to the existential ground of the experiences of activists and their personal life worlds.

Activists' Personal Life Worlds

In this section, I suggest that MONLAR also performs this abstract articulation of food because the life world of the activists is at least partially different from that of farming villagers. Looking at the activists themselves, one can first distinguish between an old guard (to which Sarath Fernando belongs) and a young guard. Several members of the old guard participated in the first Marxist-oriented youth uprising in the early 1970s. These members grew up in larger towns and were either studying or teaching during that time. For instance, Sarath came from Moratuwa, a southwestern coastal town just south of Colombo, and quit his university study to follow his activist calling. Most members of the old guard have more experience in education and activist politics than in the practice of subsistence farming, even though some do have some experimental experience or possess some agroscientific knowledge through their higher education.

The young guard, some of whom are the children of the old guard, are not trained in the art of farming either, as most of its members have grown up and received education in urban centers. These members are drawn to MONLAR by their political passion and the appeal of a job at its office, which provides an income. Moreover, the work enables the younger people to combine their political passion with their fascination with computers, electronic devices, and the Internet, vital in maintaining MONLAR's global communication lines.

Common to the old and new guard is that many oscillate between a Christian and a Buddhist inspiration, taking the activist calling and vocation (important in advocacy) from their Christian sources, while deriving the shape of their discourses and passionate religious justification from Buddhist sources. Many had a Christian education and upbringing, and most have now converted to Buddhism, probably because of the wider Sinhalese nationalist trend. The way this religious oscillation impinges on the motivation to become a Marxist activist in Sri Lanka entails an interesting tension and in-betweenness that requires more research.

The location of the office in the capital further immerses the activists in an urban food environment where other components enter the food chain and assemblage. During the week, most activists, who come from places a few hours away, tend to sleep at the office and get their food from markets, shops, and food stalls, in contrast to subsistence farmers, who buy only some foodstuffs at local shops. I suggest that the activists' intensified experience of food as a commodity further enhances their political economic articulation of food. Indeed, their experiential ground of knowledge is already in part differentiated from those they claim to represent; hence, their focus is on food in the market.

However, the fact that many activists live and prepare their food in the office does produce a lively domestic atmosphere at times. This domestic office life partially resonates with life in rural and urban households and links MONLAR activists to general food habits and practices. After office hours, some members change into casual clothing and sit down in a convivial mood, sometimes drinking and singing or watching cricket on television. Later, some of the men prepare food, whereas others wash the dishes. Hence, the domestic office sphere entails a range of activities that link the activists at a personal level with practices in the wider society, except that the residing members at the office are all men who are performing cooking-related tasks. In regular settings, women generally perform most of these domestic tasks.

In their after-hours domestic being, in contrast to their civic MONLAR activist being, their relation to food is personal, intimate, and affective as it is in the wider domestic sphere in Sri Lanka. Food there exercises in its materiality its full capacity to forge and strengthen relationships. Moreover, in their personal lives, activists perform similar rituals to villagers and engage in similar forms of ritual cooking to deal with existential insecurities in life, such as the making of kiribath in life-transition rituals to bring about prosperity and fertility. Hence, the reasons for the activists' abstraction of food lie only partly in their different life world but more in the nature of their organization and political work.

Conclusion

Food is a powerful agent that makes or breaks life and spurs people to move into ritual action to achieve well-being or to become activists in a sociopolitical movement fighting economic precariousness. In the activist context, the food assemblage is transformed into an entity that actualizes as an abstract, large-scale, general, and reductionist expression. This abstract articulation of food occurs not only among Sri Lankan activists but also among transnational activists with whom the former link up, as well as among the global and national players they critique. This "activist food" becomes articulated with politics and economics that thrive on abstract concepts on large scales, and as such this food entails a very different expression compared to the condensed materialization of existential concerns in "ritual food." Both are powerful articulations of food, and both engage existential concerns, albeit in different ways. In order to make food activism more democratic, food should be diversified and rearticulated with local expressions and anxieties so as not to alienate the activists' constituency and to gain more credence and representative power. This requires a contextual and wider understanding of food concerns. If one focuses only on the large scale, as food activists tend to do too easily, there is the danger of obfuscating the rich and multifarious ways in which people negotiate their basic concerns through food. An anthropology of food activism can bring this multiplicity of food back into the picture by researching food activism, not as an isolated phenomenon, but in its connections and disconnections with the world that the activists aim to change.

Notes

1. See the diversity of food-related issues in Counihan and Van Esterik 2008.
2. The notion of assemblages as developed here draws on the works of Gilles Deleuze and Félix Guattari (1987), Manuel DeLanda (2006), Jane Bennett (2010), Karen Barad (2007), and Bruno Latour (2005).

3. MONLAR (2006), "About Us," http://www.oocities.org/monlarslk/about_us.htm, accessed February 13, 2013.
4. A new liberal government came into power in 1977 under the leadership of Junius Richard Jayawardene and his United National Party.
5. MONLAR, "About Us."
6. See Riles (2001) for an extended discussion on the way the aesthetics of networks shape information flows, gaps, and articulations.

References

Barad, K. (2007), *Meeting the Universe Halfway: Quantum Physics and the Entanglement of Matter and Meaning*, Durham, NC: Duke University Press.

Bennett, J. (2010), *Vibrant Matter: A Political Ecology of Things*, Durham, NC: Duke University Press.

Bernstein, H. (2010), *Class Dynamics of Agrarian Change*, Halifax, NS: Fernwood; Sterling, VA: Kumarian.

Boltanski, L., and Thévenot, L. (2006), *On Justification: Economies of Worth*, trans. C. Porter, Princeton, NJ: Princeton University Press.

Counihan, C., and Van Esterik, P. (eds.) (2008), *Food and Culture: A Reader* (2nd edn.), New York: Routledge.

DeLanda, M. (2006), *A New Philosophy of Society: Assemblage Theory and Social Complexity*, London: Continuum.

Deleuze, G., and Guattari, F. (1987), *A Thousand Plateaus: Capitalism and Schizophrenia*, trans. B. Massumi, Minneapolis: University of Minnesota Press.

Fernando, S. (n.d.), "A View on Sustainable Development in Agriculture: The Experience of the Peasant Movements in Sri Lanka," Colombo, Sri Lanka: MONLAR, http://www.oocities.org/monlarslk/publications/Agriculture/View_on_Sustainable_Development_in_Agriculture_2006.pdf, accessed February 17, 2013.

Jackson, M. (2005), *Existential Anthropology: Events, Exigencies and Effects*, New York: Berghahn.

Janeja, M. P. (2010), *Transactions in Taste: The Collaborative Lives of Everyday Bengali Food*, New Delhi: Routledge.

Keck, M. E., and Sikkink, K. (1998), *Activists beyond Borders: Advocacy Networks in International Politics*, Ithaca, NY: Cornell University Press.

Latour, B. (2005), *Reassembling the Social: An Introduction to Actor-Network-Theory*, Oxford: Oxford University Press.

MONLAR (2005), "Struggle for the Peasants' Rights in Sri Lanka: Lessons of the Farmers' Hunger Strike in Polonnaruwa, Sri Lanka August 2000," Colombo, Sri Lanka: MONLAR, http://www.oocities.org/monlarslk/publications/Agriculture/Struggle_for_Peasant_Rights.pdf, accessed February 18, 2013.

Moore, M. (1985), *The State and Peasant Politics in Sri Lanka*, Cambridge: Cambridge University Press.

Povinelli, E. A. (2002), *The Cunning of Recognition: Indigenous Alterities and the Making of Australian Multiculturalism,* Durham, NC: Duke University Press.

Riles, A. (2001), *The Network Inside Out,* Ann Arbor: University of Michigan Press.

Rozin, P. (1999), "Food Is Fundamental, Fun, Frightening, and Far-Reaching," *Social Research,* 66/1: 9–30.

Tarrow, S. (2006), *The New Transnational Activism,* Cambridge: Cambridge University Press.

Taussig, M. T. (2010 [1980]), *The Devil and Commodity Fetishism in South America* (anniversary edn.), Chapel Hill: University of North Carolina Press.

Van Daele, W. (2013a), "Igniting Food Assemblages in Sri Lanka: Ritual Cooking to Regenerate the World and Interrelations," *Contributions to Indian Sociology,* 47/1: 33–60.

Van Daele, W. (2013b), "The Political Economy of Desire in Ritual and Activism in Sri Lanka," *International Development Policy,* 4: 159–173.

Windfuhr, M., and Jonsén, J. (2005), *Food Sovereignty: Towards Democracy in Localized Food Systems,* Bourton-on-Dunsmore, Rugby, Warwickshire: ITDG.

–15–

Slow Food Activism between Politics and Economy

Valeria Siniscalchi

In an article that appeared in *La Repubblica,* one of the Italian newspapers, on August 18, 2010, Carlo Petrini, the president of the Slow Food International, denounced the industrial Sardinian cheese. He wrote:

> This cheese is bad (*cattivo*). Yes, you've read it right. Bad. And it isn't a matter of an organoleptic viewpoint. Nor one concerning health. It is a question of a bad cheese because it behaves badly. Badly with its territory, badly with the people who take care of this territory, day after day, season after season. . . . Badly with those Sardinian shepherds who created the reputation of this cheese, which is today produced without their knowledge, though under their name, and under the price they knew how to negotiate on the market. (Petrini 2010)

According to Petrini, using the Sardinian regional label, this cheese, made with milk coming from elsewhere, violates the pact that binds the territory and the local small producers. This excerpt contains a good many of the themes around which Slow Food's philosophy and actions are organized today: the small producers, the transmission of knowledge, the narrow ties with the territory but also the relation with the market, the opposition to agro-industry, the moral economy, and the political commitment. Behind Slow Food's critical approach to the system of food production and distribution lies an attention to the economic dimension. This has formed a key element of its ideals and its functioning since its emergence.

"Saying and Doing" the Economy

My analysis here addresses the articulation between the Slow Food movement's political dimension and the various discourses and practices of the economy expressed within it. We may conceive of these as economic registers. Taking into account the moral economy of food, the economy "of the producers," the economy of the salons, and the economy of budgets, enables me to look into the movement's more abstract, ideal, and "revolutionary" dimension as well as its more concrete and "classic" functioning and its modes of financing. Indeed, the "real" economy of the producers, of the salons, and of the association's budgets cohabit with the imagining of a new economic order that is "good, clean, and fair." These diverse registers allow us to pay attention to what is sometimes considered distinct in the approach to social and political movements: their philosophy and political commitment, and the real functioning and ways of approaching economic aspects that guarantee the movement's existence.[1]

In food activism, economic notions are used in the social arena with diverse signification and must be situated in specific times and places. The analysis of discourses and actions around the economy is a rich entry point to understand changing paradigms that are taking place through different forms of food activism and the frictions that they determine.

Politics and Economy

From the beginning of my research on Slow Food, at the end of 2006, I approached Slow Food as a political and economic object.[2] I started with participant observation and interviews in the Salone del Gusto and Terra Madre, two of the many international events organized by the movement. I then pursued my research in France, where I followed the evolution of Slow Food's French National Association and the activities of some of its local chapters (*convivia*). From 2009 to 2012, I spent about three years doing fieldwork in the city of Bra, where the movement's headquarters are located (the international and Italian associations as well as the Slow Food Foundation for Biodiversity). In Italy I studied the association's functioning and its economic and political challenges and issues, and I followed Slow Food's activities and international connections, particularly with France. During this time, I conducted repeated interviews with the personnel working or holding political responsibilities in the association (around 160 employees in Bra itself) as well as in other Italian regions and in some other European countries. I met people close to the association (including the producers) and others who had distanced themselves from the movement. Still, this was only one aspect of my fieldwork. A more substantial part consisted of long-term participant observation: of political bodies, of informal meetings, of the leaders' missions in Italy and abroad, and of international events and meetings. Examining the historical hub of the movement and its decision-making sites enabled me to follow the daily life of its employees and its leaders, as well as the genesis of certain projects, and to observe the internal dynamics as well as the contradictions and ways in which they are lived and integrated.

In these pages, through the analysis of different economic registers and their connection to the political level, some of these tensions within the movement can be sketched and understood. The analysis proposed here is situated within the recent current of economic anthropology that analyzes the forms of production, exchange, and circulation of material and symbolic goods as part of abstract economic logics as well as values and logics of specific social contexts. A simultaneous consideration of the economic and political dimension permits us to reflect on the articulations between abstract "market" logics and moral and social interests (always dense and "situated"), not from the point of view of economic systems, but from the perspective of individuals and groups (Gudeman 2005, 2008; Wilk 1996). From my point of view, not only is it not possible to separate the political from the economic dimension (cf. Wolf 2001), but market logics, morality, and political aims are always present together in the economic registers that I shall discuss in these pages, sometimes in more evident and sometimes in less visible ways.

Economy and politics appear closely linked since the early years of Slow Food. Slow Food was founded in 1986 at Bra, in the winegrowing region of Langhe, in the northwest of Italy. In the 1980s this region was hard hit by the scandal of methanol wines that had killed about twenty people in Italy. Slow Food's founders then took a position against the adulteration of wine, which was at the root of the human tragedy and of its economic outcomes, especially the collapse of the wine market. Slow Food leaders affirmed that it was necessary to aim at quality in order to get out of the crisis that was engulfing the world of enology. Today we can refer back to this position taken by Slow Food, and the actions that followed, as eminently political as well as economic.

But politics was also present at another level. Slow Food's founders came from Italian left-wing circles. They included militants and intellectuals involved in local politics or in the trade union movement. Some came from the ranks of the Communist Party or other non-parliamentary left parties. "We were the 'remnants' of 1968...bringing an experience of the '68 movement or hailing from the galaxy of the left.... We carried a load of disenchantment and exhaustion with the traditional manner of doing politics," one of Slow Food's "historical" leaders told me (A. F., September 21, 2010). Above all, they were looking for new ways and new spaces of engagement. Their initiatives are rooted in this period of "disenchantment" that characterized the 1980s in Italy, when the ideals and causes that had led large numbers to mobilize seemed to have vanished. The founders of Slow Food reintroduced terms like *pleasure* that had been set aside in the years of political and social tension and made them pillars of their philosophy. But the pleasure of drinking and eating well also has a collective value in Slow Food philosophy. It is linked with the idea of *conviviality* and is not lacking in political significance. The Slow Food Manifesto—"Manifesto dello Slow Food. Movimento per il diritto al piacere" (Portinari 1987), first published in the pages of the Italian left-wing newspaper *Il Manifesto* in 1987—clearly expresses the association's political positions. The term *Slow Food* opposes industrial food, the standardization of food, and the frenzy of modern life incarnated by fast food.[3]

Today, in the vast field of food activism, Slow Food is a difficult object to grasp even if it shares some of the characteristic features of other movements.[4] Its specificity probably resides in the multiple, sometimes contradictory facets found within it. Slow Food is an international association that dialogues and interacts with a certain number of national associations that are its emanations. It is an association with dues-paying members and statutes that regulate its functioning and its political positions. At the same time, Slow Food is a social and political movement supported by thousands all over the world. This is how Slow Food presents itself on the political scene and also partly corresponds to its development and means of diffusion of its actions and ideas. In some regards, if we consider some of its components, it is a private enterprise, particularly the department that organizes events and fairs or its publishing house. Since 2004, Slow Food has founded a private university where students, mainly from the United States, Latin America, Asia, and Europe, study the gastronomic sciences. At the same time, it is similar to a non-governmental organization if we consider its projects in the southern countries of the world. Its functioning is militant in some respects, and its modes of action are based largely on voluntary work. Its employees and directors have relatively modest salaries in comparison to the private sector, although inequalities of an economic kind as well as inequalities in access to power characterize its functioning.

Slow Food has become not only an actor in the political field of decisions concerning food but a legitimate actor in spaces of political and social contestation. The fights against intensive production, homogenization of taste and food, genetically modified organisms (GMOs), nuclear power and nonrenewable energy, nontraceability of products, and the privatization of water are the new battles of the movement. All these dimensions coexist in Slow Food, and they must be considered together in order to understand the functioning of this particular "militant" machine from the inside.

The Moral Economy of Food

In the space of three decades, Slow Food's fields of intervention have broadened, and new philosophies have been elaborated, integrating and reformulating new elements.[5] The article cited above, published in the daily newspaper *La Repubblica*, signals this evolution that sees Slow Food present in public platforms, giving its opinion and taking positions for or against a vast range of subjects with a common denominator of food: cultivate biodiversity, fight for the right to food sovereignty for everyone and against waste, protect the landscape and agricultural land, and work for education for the future. The intervention on industrial cheeses sold on the market as "Sardinian" cheese, which are in reality not produced from milk from the island's sheep, stands in this field and in the straight line of other initiatives and interventions that have marked the movement. These affirmations need to be taken together with the movement's key triad, "good, clean, and fair" (since the publication of the book *Buono, pulito e giusto* [2005] by its leader Carlo Petrini). "Good" refers to the taste and quality of food products. "Clean" shifts attention to the place and manner of production and hence to the environment. "Clean" also indicates products that respect the environment or use manners of production and forms of distribution that reduce or eliminate chemicals and environmental damage. Finally, the notion "fair" refers to social justice for producers. Production, distribution, and consumption are fair when they respect the rights and dignity of producers and defend fair wages and working conditions.

For Slow Food, "good, clean, and fair" are parameters of a moral economy, that is to say, in part an alternative to liberalism and in part a reform of it. The three terms "good, clean, and fair" demarcate new political spaces of action that must include not only consumers but also producers and the environment. In this framework, the notion of "good" is opposed to "bad" in the same semantic field. "Good" does not refer only to the organoleptic quality, to the goodness or nongoodness perceived in the mouth; "good" also has a moral value. The author of the article not only defends this link between knowledge and territory, between small producers and the quality of the products, which seem to be betrayed by industrial "usurpers." He also calls for a revolt against the infringement of moral rules, symbolized by this "bad" cheese. "The moral economy is one which creates value by respecting the environment and men," declares Petrini. The economic value of cheese, like that of any other food production, lies—from this point of view—in its respect for links with the social space of a given production, in its respect for fair working conditions for producers who must earn their living from their work. Social justice is first of all a justice from the perspective of producers' economic conditions.

Even if the more utopian and conceptual dimension of Slow Food's message that aims at bringing the poles of the food chain closer is not automatically translated into reality, it still traces the contours of a new moral economy. Indeed, in recent years, the movement's philosophy has evolved in the direction of a (re)definition of the limits of human action and the morality of the economy. Fair working conditions must be guaranteed to all producers, but, equally, good food must be accessible to all. This is accompanied by an increasing attention to the world of small production, to peasants but also to all the other minorities (particularly women, native populations, etc.) who are marginal and losing in the face of agro-industry: "Natives, peasants, women... We have left these categories behind us as they were the last part of the planet.... They will signal the right road, the right path" (C. P., October 21, 2010). Peasants and small producers of the Southern and Northern hemispheres are considered as a lever for a slow but possible transformation of the world. These peasants and minorities, who are thought to be working with respect for the environment and human beings, are conceived as actors of a new humanism as well as motors of change for economic (im)balances that govern food production and distribution. The Slow Food "food communities" are all those people who take part in the production and distribution of a food in a defined geographic area and are conceived as "communities" of goals woven around productive activities and "imagined" economies

(Anderson 1983). Food communities are conceived as being directly linked to an ideal past that ignored the damages of a present, caused by the anomalies of capitalism, of industrial production, and of the irresponsible exploitation of resources.

The term *food community* carries a perfomative value. Peasants and artisans of food appear every two years in Turin, during the Terra Madre meeting, to manifest the extension of networks and themes covered by Slow Food, while contributing to legitimizing it. Terra Madre is a huge intercultural meeting, which its organizers consider one of Slow Food's most important political platforms. "Terra Madre gathers all the actors of the agro-alimentary network who together defend agriculture, fishing and sustainable livestock and protect taste and food biodiversity."[6] In the opening event, the delegations parade in hundreds, with their flags and traditional costumes, in a big ceremony of human diversity and a display of languages, music, and folklore that above all welcomes people from the Southern Hemisphere of the world, representing small producers from Asian countries, Africa, the Pacific Ocean, and the Americas but also European countries where Slow Food is active. Around 4,000 small producers—mostly from poor countries—join researchers in dozens of workshops. For four days they discuss sustainable agriculture, local economies, and food problems and politics, and they exchange their experiences and know-how. Terra Madre could be seen as a big performance of mutuality, otherness, and connection among a network of small producers (cf. Siniscalchi 2013b).

"Slow Food is what we are and Terra Madre is what we do. Terra Madre is our project," say many Slow Food members, repeating the message that comes from their leaders. If this ritual creates a large imaginary community, an extended family that needs to be regularly reactivated, "staging Terra Madre" implies recreating this communitary dimension and this imaginary communitarian economy. Through exotic figures, Terra Madre illustrates and legitimizes Slow Food's discourses on the future of the economy and food production; more than good products, Terra Madre defends "good" economies, which are "moral" economies. As ritual, the economy declared and performed here presents an ideal and moral order.

This register of moral economy expresses itself through actions and discourses addressed not only to the movement's members but also to political representatives, and aims to redefine the spaces of production and distribution and reformulate economic balances. The notion of moral economy is increasingly present in scientific debates: The "moral economy" used by Slow Food is not so far removed from the meaning scholars have given this notion.[7]

This register of moral economy expresses itself through the defense of legality, a stand against fraud, corruption, and mafias. At the Italian Slow Food's seventh congress, in 2010, a Slow Food councilor from Lombardy drew members' attention to the links between legality and prices: "What does food have to do with legality? When we speak of food we are speaking of the mafia. In this field, our choices mark the beginning of the antimafia struggle. I should know that the lowest price is too high, because it has already been paid for by others.... If I buy tomatoes and I know that they carry the taste of the blood of Senegalese workers killed in Calabria Region. I no longer want them.... Eating local is eliminating illegality from the field. We can do it" (D. R., May 15, 2010).[8] The Sicilian region's Slow Food councilor took up the idea, declaring, "I like this portrait of saving the planet joyfully.... But I wish to speak here of the pleasure of legality.... Dealing with legality and the antimafia struggle is part of our approach.... We are antimafia and we are gourmets at the same time" (C. M., May 16, 2010). The struggle for legality is also a struggle to protect producers from rackets and to prevent the exploitation of workers. And it is part of the same register of the moral economy.

The Producers' Economy

This moral economy is also established through concrete actions in the fields of production where Slow Food is directly involved, which introduces another register, that of the producers' economy. One dimension consists of labeling products. Indeed, it is the field where contact with the world of production is probably the closest, and the dialogue between Slow Food and producers really takes place, at least in some phases of the work of labeling *Presidia*. Presidia are small, endangered, high-quality products.[9]

Presidia are not simply the result of labeling processes; they constitute an economic and political project. Today, more than in Slow Food's early years, they are conceived as a tool that encourages certain producers to legalize their sometimes "undeclared," "hidden" activities, since the production processes in question are frequently very small. Presidia projects embody Slow Food battles against the industrialization of food and are instruments to create new economic and political spaces (cf. Siniscalchi 2013a). Indeed, Presidia aim to give a social and economic meaning to productions threatened by the powerful agro-industry because they lack economic viability. The production of limited quantities by small peasants or artisans according to "traditional" techniques, and their inclusion in a limited list selected by Slow Food, constitutes an added value, transforming Presidia into "singular" products, defined by a "constellation" of qualities and limited production (cf. Karpik 2007). This ensures their presence on the market. The price contributes to singularizing these products: It shows that the quality has a cost. But it also has a political dimension: Producers must be able to gain their living from their production. At the same time the prices of some Presidia do not make them accessible to everyone, and this contrasts with some aspects of the philosophy of Slow Food evoked before.

Through Presidia, Slow Food also becomes an actor in the conflictual processes of regulation of food production. And Slow Food's political struggle is linked to the producers' battles, as in the case of Sardinian "Fiore Sardo" cheese. The producers are shepherds, and they are fighting against industrial producers who invade the local market with a cheaper cheese produced with pasteurized milk, often coming from other European countries. Their battle is also against institutions that have elaborated norms that do not protect the small producers, refuse them visibility, and prevent them from occupying a place in a real competitive market. "Fiore Sardo" cheese producers are not outside the market or market logics: They aim to modify these logics from inside and to improve the status of the Sardinian product. And the presidia project seems to them one way of achieving this.

At the same time, at the economic level, two visions confront each other: that of the producers, who would like a stronger and more concrete commitment to their place in the market, and that of Slow Food, which is above all political. Presidia are political projects, which, even if not always in step with what is really happening in local contexts, are part of a larger set of struggles. Presidia constitute examples to follow. They are prototypes that define a paradigm of production to be preserved. They allow Slow Food to be present around the world as well as in regions and countries where the movement is weaker. They help consolidate Slow Food's legitimacy. At the same time, Presidia integrate and synthesize the existing tension in the movement between an ideal dimension and concrete production activities, between the political message and the market, between morality and profit. This dual character of doing economy and being a model of political action gives them the role of an intermediary between these two aspects of the movement. The place they have occupied in the various editions within the Salone del Gusto and Terra Madre, and the conflicts that accompanied successive arrangements, reflect this concretely, as I will now show.

The Economy of Salons

Producers, and Presidia producers, sell on the market and also participate in performing the market that is held in the salons and fairs where they are invited: Cheese, Slow Fish, and Salone del Gusto. Real sales take place in these spaces of the market, but equally they model a direct relationship between the producer and the consumer, with Slow Food playing the role of both director and intermediary. The fairs and salons have been present right from the start in Slow Food's history. Its founders come from the circles of the left, but they are also lovers of wine and of good food, and their ranks include restaurant owners. Since its emergence, the association functions partly due to members' subscription fees but also thanks to participation in wine conventions, fairs, and salons. The Salone del Gusto—organized for the first time in 1996—has become one of the central events of the association, both a source of substantial income and a political platform.[10] The Salone del Gusto is a big food fair takes place in Turin every two years, in the pavilions of Lingotto Fiere, areas that shelter Fiat's old factories, at the same time as Terra Madre. The fair attracts around 200,000 visitors. During the five-day exhibition visitors buy and taste high-quality products from the different regions of Italy but also from other European countries and the rest of the world. The big stands of sponsors (Lavazza and Parmigiano Reggiano) dominate the entrance of the Salone del Gusto. At first glance, the contrast between these two events—the Salone del Gusto and Terra Madre—is striking. On the one hand are those who can buy; on the other, small producers coming largely from the southern and poor countries. These were two separate but closed spaces; visitors to the Salone could not accede to Terra Madre until 2012 when the two events were united.

Why does an association that aims to change the world, to defend peasants and local economies, continue to organize a commercial event such as the Salone del Gusto, which seems so far from Slow Food philosophy? First, for its commercial interest, because the Salone is a source of income to maintain the association. In the offices at Bra, everyone remembers the first edition of the Salone del Gusto in 1998 as a "mythical" edition, the one that brought Slow Food out from the restricted circles of lovers of wine and restaurants and made it famous by giving it a visibility in the national and international media. "This fair was a wreck"—the director of personnel told me—"from all points of view, physical and psychological: we weren't ready, we weren't prepared to deal with the dimensions of the fair and the masses of public.... This fair was a jump from all points of view, economic as well: an incredible number of visitors came and this was the only time when everyone received a bonus at the end of the year" (B. F., September 8, 2010). In its internal history, it is the 1998 edition of the Salone del Gusto that launched Slow Food. It formed a kind of bridge between an association that had little visibility and had really spread only in Italy and the movement that Slow Food subsequently became; at this moment the Bra offices "exploded," and recruitment shot up sky-high. But, above all, the Salone del Gusto became Slow Food's media and then political platform. Projects followed one after the other, and the Salone del Gusto became the showcase to display them to the association's members as well as to political authorities. If the Salone del Gusto seems to be simply a huge fair of food products—where produce is sold and bought in stalls—it allows the messages to be communicated to visitors who are not members of the movement but equally, and on a still larger scene, through the media. In this sense, it is one of the sites of visibility and dialogue with political powers as well as a space in which new forms of economy are staged, and economic messages, which are also political messages, are diffused. Through specific rituals that mark the rhythms and organize the exhibition, the sales and the purchases, the Salone is one of the places that allows the association to talk about itself and display the new themes at the heart of its philosophy. At each edition, the Salone del Gusto is a little different, a little bigger, with a different formula: the shift to the use of recyclable materials, the attention paid to "good, clean, and fair" producers—more than in the first editions—and consequently an increasingly selective choice of exhibitors; finally, the shift from an organization of stalls according to the category of products to "territorial" stalls, where producers from the same region or from the same country exhibit their produce side by side to recreate the impression of a local market that concentrates all the aspects of the region. This last change was adopted in the 2010 Salone and found its explanation in the (political) message that food is linked to a territory from the social, geographic, and climatic point of view but also from the economic point of view. Also, the "taste laboratories"—one of the key moments for the diffusion of Slow Food ideas and its activities around education in taste—have changed the focal point. Wines are not simply savored, but organizers try to place them in their context of production; products considered in danger are very present, but so, too, is the theme of "local production," which appears increasingly. The economy that is displayed and practiced here must also be considered as a ritual performance that talks to people of an ideal food, and of new ways of producing and consuming.

However, the economic level expressed through and in the Salone is precisely what exposes Slow Food to the strongest criticisms and reveals its weaknesses. The Salone del Gusto is the movement's Achilles heel. This is because it is directly linked to the dimension of classic consumerism that Slow Food attempts to rethink and that seems to contrast with the register of the moral economy. On the one hand lies the commercial dimension, the market and exchange of goods; on the other, commitment, debate, and exchange of ideas. On the one hand stand those who can afford to buy, taste, and savor; on the other stand the small producers, mostly from the Southern hemisphere, who are the heart of debates on food sovereignty, the environment, and local economies. Presidia are the intermediaries between these dimensions. In 2006 the exhibitors at the Salone were displayed in rows according to the category of the product (processed meat, cheese, oil, cereals, and so on). The Presidia found themselves all together in a central area of the Salone, right in the middle of the market, in a position that allowed them to display their difference in relation to the other products. In the following edition, the Presidia producers were shifted from the Salone del Gusto to Terra Madre; the aim was to valorize the political dimension of the Presidia project. The producers of Presidia scarcely appreciated this new organization that disassociated them from one of the reasons for their labeling: the market and the concrete economic dimension. During the 2010 edition, when the Salone's arrangement was completely transformed, rows of categories of products disappeared on the grounds that products are above all linked to a territory, and the exhibitors were placed according to the region of origin, in the case of Italy; or by country, for those coming from abroad; or by continent, for producers from the Southern Hemisphere, less numerous than those of the North. Thanks to this new logic, the Presidia reintegrated their places "of origin" symbolically and in the spatial organization of the exhibition. But, once again, the producers of Presidia do not appreciate this kind of organization. For many of them, this new organization, while restoring them to the heart of the marketplace, "removes" them and deprives them of the symbolic character acquired through the collective dimension when they were all together. They conceive that they are submerged among other products and producers, sometimes less good, less clean, and less fair, and, in any case, requiring less visibility in the market.[11]

These cases, which seem to reveal a deep contradiction, practically an oxymoron, also illustrate the poles of a continuum, which, even if they are partly contradictory, are not entirely in opposition but rather are complementary and compose Slow Food today: market, morality, and politics.

The Economy of Budgets

In the days preceding a national or international council or a meeting of the association's board or a congress, the administration's offices in Slow Food's old historical building, in the "via della mendicità istruita," Bra, are the last to turn off the lights. On these occasions preceding the political meetings, the personnel stay late, working to prepare the documents—above all the budgets—that will be discussed on the morrow. An association is also made by its budgets. They appear as Slow Food's real economy, made of costs and revenues, quite in opposition to the political idea of the moral economy. But this register is also political, like the others. The budgets reveal the political priorities, the projects that the association decides to invest in, such as the project of presidia or the publishing house, even if they are not directly profitable from the point of view of the relation between costs and economic benefits. Budgets are proposed in the movement's political bodies, then discussed, reworked, and presented in slightly different forms to put across its political ideas and strategic choices.

During a "restricted" meeting intended to rethink the budget of the Italian association, its place within the Slow Food structure, and ways of fund-raising and reducing and optimizing expenses, one of the leaders recalled Slow Food's diverse aims:

> We are a non-profit organization. The profits of our business—if and when there are any—are entirely reinvested in the institution. The allocation of any profits must be determined by the governing bodies and shared ever more fully with the membership. We are an economic entity, that is to say that this entity 'moves money', it generates and spends resources (it's essential to maintain this order), and it also produces economic activity. We are in some cases a business entity, such as in the sale of publications, or organizing major events: however, at every level the objective of implementing projects that contribute to the development of associative mission must prevail. (R. B., August 23, 2011)

At the same time this fact of being permeated with economic activity shifts attention to another topic: "Everything we do is economy in the authentic and noble meaning of 'stewardship of the home,' understood as 'stewardship of the common good,'" he said.

The association's existence and reproduction over time depend on its financial health. At the same time, its budgets reveal Slow Food's political choices in the international context. They are a door to understanding the relations between Slow

Food's various components and its internal structures: Slow Food Promozione, Slow Food Editore, the Slow Food Foundation for Biodiversity, the Italian association, and the international association. Moreover, budgets reveal "genealogical" links between the Italian national association and those of other countries, and the balance of power between them. The relationships between the international association and the national associations of different countries that are affiliated with it are governed not only by the statutes but also by budgetary ties: "Up until today, many of the resources generated by Slow Food have been invested to develop the global network of our association (including through the funding of projects of the Slow Food Foundation for Biodiversity). Obviously we cannot think that the commitment to Slow Food Italy will be less, since we are the ones who created these realities; nonetheless it is essential to redefine the terms and boundaries of the commitment to the Italian association" (R. B., August 23, 2011).

In the crisis that struck the French association and led to the closing of that national association by Slow Food International leaders in 2011, budgets became a central element in the negotiations between the French and Slow Food International leaders (who are Italian). To justify the contributions that France owed to the international structure, the general secretary of Slow Food International said, "The countries where Slow Food is stronger must support those in which Slow Food is less strong. So it was decided that where there was a national structure, there had to be a contribution. . . . In order to be sustainable as a national association, membership fees are not enough. The problem in France is that we did not find other funds" (P. D., June 4, 2011).

The logic governing transfers of money, in the form of contributions, from one structure to another is economic and political at the same time; it involves the costs of the headquarters of Slow Food but also the relative weight of each association, and involves a joint contribution, shown as an aid to the weakest. Transfers of money from one to the other define the political relations but equally the autonomy or dependence of one with respect to the others. They constitute a political language.

The budgets also reveal the political connections and relationships with the institutions. Slow Food has remained a militant association from different points of view but has also succeeded in obtaining money from sponsors as well as large subventions from institutions, thus remaining tied to more classic modes of financing. It has also shown itself capable of hobnobbing with current political powers. It acts in the political field through the economy including in and through the Salone del Gusto, which along with its sponsors is a source of income.

Conclusion

Slow Food elaborates new forms of economy that are visionary in some aspects and at the same time cause tensions between innovation and preservation of the economic models. One rhetoric of declared political action and another of economic utopia thus accompany a range of very diverse practices, including the management of budgets, or contradictory elements such as the indifferent economic treatment of certain categories of employees. The association is sometimes presbyopic about peasants' daily problems, conflicts among producers, or local political dynamics. Sometimes it has a very distant gaze but is myopic about the internal realities of groups and the countries concerned.

The various registers of economy mobilized by Slow Food allow us to analyze its members' visions of the future and ways in which they promote a "concrete" utopia. These registers are connected to each other, and they mutually reinforce and legitimate; but within each of them the tensions and the contradictions appear: between gourmets and producers, between political messages and the real economy, and between the budgets of the association and the movement dimension.

Partly, these aspects are tied to the association's complexity: The movement defends both "sober anarchy" and independent action by its local units as part of its philosophy. However, it needs to dialogue with political powers to exist as a legitimate actor in conflicting transnational and transversal arenas of production and food consumption (cf. Lein 2004).[12] For that, it needs to be governed, and also financed. External and internal constraints force Slow Food to adapt and compromise. In disregard of the differences or contradictions, it continues to convey "critical" messages about consumption and responsible production. Local projects in salons and international meetings generate concrete effects in economic and political supralocal scenarios equally.

As June Nash (2005a: 3) points out, social movements must be as flexible as the global institutions they challenge. Slow Food, like La Via Campesina and anti-GMO movements, displays this capacity for adaptation in its actions, alliances, political strategies, organizational structures, and rhetorics. Economic notions (exchange, morality, consumption, commons, and so forth) are often defined in dichotomous terms that obscure the complex realties of activism. As Richard Wilk suggested, "The real action takes place in between" (2006: 15). In Slow Food these notions are constantly reformulated in order to redefine the economic and political spaces and the possibilities of individual and group actions and control on some parts of the food system.

Notes

1. See Edelman 2001; Koensler and Rossi 2012; and Pratt 2001. Studies of social movements have shown the ties between globalization, transformations of capitalism, economic crises, and forms of mobilization (cf. Nash 2005b). Anthropologists are increasingly examining globalization (Abelès 2008; Appadurai 1998; Comaroff, Comaroff, and Weller 2000; Friedman 2005), including the

globalization of food and the resistance it generates (Grimes 2005; Inglis and Gimlin 2009; Lien and Nerlich 2004; Luetchford 2008; Wright and Middendorf 2008). See also Borras, Edelman, and Kay 2008.

2. My thanks go to friends of Slow Food who accepted me and put up with my presence over these last years with great patience and affection and to Carole Counihan for her suggestions and wise advice. The research was financed by the École des Hautes Études en Sciences Sociales (EHESS) Research Funds, by the visiting professor program of the University of Cagliari, by the international project "Patrimonialización y redefinición de la ruralidad. Nuevos usos del patrimonio local" (Universitat de Barcelona), and by DEVAMAP and EQUALIM-TERR, projects supported by the Provence-Alpes-Côte d'Azur (PACA) Region.

3. Roberta Sassatelli and Federica Davolio (2010) do a relevant analysis of texts and accounts of some of the movement's leaders. For others' analysis of the beginning of Slow Food, see Leitch 2003, 2009; Murdoch and Miele 2004; and Parkins and Craig 2006, even if they observe the movement from its periphery or from a point of view that is too internal. Even if I don't agree with Alison Leitch's whole analysis, and despite some imprecision, she presents a rich panorama of point of view on Slow Food.

4. On social movements see Nash 2005b. On alternative movements of consumers, see Dubuisson-Quellier 2009. On the fair trade movement see, among others, Grimes 2005, Luetchford 2008, and the Reichman chapter in this book. See also Carrier and Luetchford on ethical consumption (2012).

5. The same process has taken place in the opposite direction, and some elements of its philosophy—such as the notion of "slow," for example—have been understood and appropriated by other associations or movements with very different ideas (see Siniscalchi 2013b).

6. Extract from the Internet site of Terra Madre: http://www.terramadre.org (accessed November 2012).

7. See, among others, Hart, Laville, and Cattani 2010 and Hart 2013. On the notion of moral economy, see Thompson 1993 and, for a recent analysis, Fassin 2009. Cf. also Carrier and Luetchford 2012.

8. She refers to a racist massacre of Senegalese agricultural workers in the city of Rosarno, in the south of Italy, that took place in 2010.

9. The first Presidia projects emerged at the end of the 1990s. Today, there are more than 200 Presidia in Italy and around 160 international Presidia. On typical products and quality, among others, see Harvey, McMeekin, and Warde 2004; Meneley 2007; and Paxson 2010.

10. For some similarities, see Tonelli 2012.

11. I explore these topics more widely in Siniscalchi 2013b.

12. A consistent number of studies approach food not only as a social and cultural but also a political and economic object, which underlines the fact that food is involved in transnational processes and controversies. Marianne Elisabeth Lien

(2004) emphasizes that food policies cut across "classic" political spaces and that this demands taking into account controversies, balances of power, forms of resistance, and conflicting interests.

References

Abelès, M. (2008), *Anthropologie de la globalisation,* Paris: Fayard.

Anderson, B. (1983), *Imagined Communities: Reflections on the Origin and Spread of Nationalism,* Oxford: Verso.

Appadurai, A. (1998), *Modernity at Large: Cultural Dimensions of Globalisation,* Minneapolis: University of Minnesota Press.

Borras, S., Edelman, M., and Kay, C. (eds.) (2008), *Transnational Agrarian Movements Confronting Globalization,* Hoboken, NJ: Wiley-Blackwell.

Carrier, J. G., and Luetchford, P. (eds.) (2012), *Ethical Consumption: Social Value and Economic Practice,* Oxford: Berghahn.

Comaroff, J., Comaroff, J. L., and Weller, R. P. (eds.) (2000), *Millennial Capitalism and the Culture of Neoliberalism,* Durham, NC: Duke University Press.

Dubuisson-Quellier, S. (2009), *La consommation engagée,* Paris: Sciences Po, les Presses.

Edelman, M. (2001), "Social Movements: Changing Paradigms and Forms of Politics," *Annual Review of Anthropology,* 30: 285–317.

Fassin, D. (2009), "Les économies morales revisitées," *Annales. Histoire, Sciences Sociales,* 6: 1237–1266.

Friedman, J. (2005), *La quotidianità del sistema globale,* Milan: Bruno Mondadori.

Grimes, K. M. (2005), "Changing the Rules of Trade with Global Partnership: The Fair Trade Movement," in J. Nash (ed.), *Social Movements: An Anthropological Reader,* Oxford: Blackwell, 237–248.

Gudeman, S. (2008), *Economy's Tension: The Dialectics of Community and Market,* Oxford: Berghahn.

Gudeman, S. (2012), "Community and Economy: Economy's Base," in J. Carrier (ed.), *A Handbook of Economic Anthropology* (2nd edn.), Cheltenham, UK: Edward Elgar, 95–108.

Hart, K. (2013), "Manifesto for a Human Economy," *The Memory Bank,* January 20, http://thememorybank.co.uk/2013/01/20/object-methods-and-principles-of-human-economy/, accessed March 18, 2013.

Hart, K., Laville, J. L., and Cattani, A. D. (eds.) (2010), *The Human Economy,* Cambridge, UK: Polity.

Harvey, M., McMeekin, A., and Warde, A. (eds.) (2004), *Qualities of Food,* Manchester: Manchester University Press.

Inglis, D., and Gimlin, D. (eds.) (2009), *The Globalisation of Food,* Oxford: Berg.

Karpik, L. (2007), *L'économie des singularités,* Paris: Gallimard.

Koensler, A., and Rossi, A. (2012), "Introduzione: Comprendere il dissenso," in A. Koensler and A. Rossi (eds.), *Comprendere il dissenso: Etnografia e antropologia dei movimenti sociali,* Perugia, Italy: Morlacchi Editore, 13–32.

Leitch, A. (2003), "Slow Food and the Politics of Pork Fat: Italian Food and European Identity," *Ethnos,* 68/4: 437–462.

Leitch, A. (2009), "Slow Food and the Politics of 'Virtuous Globalization,'" in D. Inglis and D. Gimlin (eds.), *The Globalization of Food,* Oxford: Berg, 45–64.

Lien, M. E. (2004), "The Politics of Food: An Introduction," in M. E. Lien & B. Nerlich (eds.), *The Politics of Food.* Oxford: Berg, 1–17.

Lien, M. E., and Nerlich, B. (eds.) (2004), *The Politics of Food,* Oxford: Berg.

Luetchford, P. (2008), *Fair Trade and Global Commodity: Coffee in Costa Rica,* London: Pluto Press.

Meneley, A. (2007), "Like an Extra Virgin," *American Anthropologist,* 109/4: 678–687.

Murdoch, J., and Miele, M. (2004), "A New Aesthetic of Food? Relational Reflexivity in the 'Alternative' Food Movement," in M. Harvey, A. McMeekin, and A. Warde (eds.), *Qualities of Food,* Manchester: Manchester University Press, 156–175.

Nash, J. (2005a), "Introduction: Social Movements and Global Process," in J. Nash (ed.), *Social Movements: An Anthropological Reader,* Oxford: Blackwell, 1–26.

Nash, J. (ed.) (2005b), *Social Movements: An Anthropological Reader,* Oxford: Blackwell.

Parkins, W., and Craig, G. (2006), *Slow Living,* Oxford: Berg.

Paxson, H. (2010), "Locating Value in Artisan Cheese: Reverse Engineering Terroir for New-World Landscapes," *American Anthropologist,* 112/3: 444–457.

Petrini, C. (2005), *Buono, pulito, e giusto: Principi di nuova gastronomia,* Turin: Einaudi.

Petrini, C. (2010), "Se I pastori diventano un bene da tutelare. La sapienza va premiata in tavola," *La Repubblica,* August 18: 1, 33.

Portinari, F. (1987), "Manifesto dello Slow Food. Movimento per il diritto al piacere," *Il Manifesto;* reprinted in *Slowfood,* 19 (2006): 24–25.

Pratt, J. (2001), "Anthropology and Political Movements," *Journal of Mediterranean Studies,* 11/2: 297–318.

Sassatelli, R., and Davolio F. (2010), "Consumption, Pleasure and Politics: Slow Food and the Politico-aesthetic Problematization of Food," *Journal of Consumer Culture,* 10/2: 202–232.

Siniscalchi, V. (2013a), "Environment, Regulation and the Moral Economy of Food in the *Slow Food* Movement," *Journal of Political Ecology,* 20: 295–305.

Siniscalchi, V. (2013b), "Slow versus Fast: Économie et écologie dans le mouvement Slow Food," *Terrain,* 60: 132–147.

Thompson, E. P. (1993), *Customs in Common: Studies in Traditional Popular Culture,* New York: New Press.

Tonelli, A. (2012), *Falce e tortello: Storia politica e sociale delle feste dell'Unità (1945–2011)*, Bari, Italy: Laterza.

Wilk, R. (1996), *Economies and Cultures*, Boulder, CO: Westview.

Wilk, R. (2006), "From Wild Weeds to Artisanal Cheese," in R. Wilk (ed.), *Fast Food/Slow Food: The Cultural Economy of the Global Food System*, Lanham, MD: Altamira, 13–28.

Wolf, E. R. (2001), *Pathways of Power: Building an Anthropology of the Modern World*, Berkeley: University of California Press.

Wright, W., and Middendorf, G. (eds.) (2008), *The Fight over Food: Producers, Consumers and Activists Challenge the Food System*, State College: Pennsylvania State University Press.

Index

nuclear energy, 101

Obama, Barack, 42
Obama, Michelle, 42
obanzai cuisine, 90
Okely, Judith, 5
Olivier de Sardan, Jean-Pierre, 6
The Omnivore's Dilemma (2006), 169
organic coffee, 166
organic food
    activism over, 10
    consumption of, 104
    retailers of, 64, 70
    in Sicily, 113, 115, 118
Organic Food Emporium, 69
organic wine, 97, 99, 103–6
organization of labor with antimafia
        cooperatives, 123–4
Ortner, S. B., 9
Otero, Geraldo, 180

Parker, Robert, 104
Paulo Freire Stichting, 197
Peace Corps, 23
peasant-farmer identity, 100
Pechlaner, Gabriela, 180
Peña, Devon, 33
People's Climate Summit, 199
personal life worlds, 220–2
Petrini, Carlo, 225
Peyser, Rick, 171n6
Piras, Teresa, 67–8
Pitrè, Pippo, 117–18
place-making, 89–91
Polanyi, Karl, 78, 88
politics
    information politics, 186
    neoliberal anti-politics, 170
    over community gardens, 33
    over food activism, in Sri Lanka, 219–20
    Slow Food movement and, 226–8
    symbolic politics, 186
Pollan, Michael, 169–70
P-Patch Program, *see* Seattle's P-Patch
        Program
Pratt, Jeff, 91
Presidia, defined, 231–2
private farming, 123
private regulation issues, 159

PRODECOOP (fair trade cooperative), 163
producer's economy, 231–2
Puerto Rico, 5
Puget Sound Regional Food Policy Council, 37
purchasing power in Cuba, 55–7

Quist, David, 178–9
Quit India Monsanto, 200
Qur'an, 148, 150

race-based inequalities, 35
racial mixing *(mestizaje)*, 175
Reagan, Ronald (administration), 163
red meat production, 5, 214
refusal to consume in Cuba, 55–7
religious activism, *see* faith-based activism
Renaissance des Appellations association,
        106, 108
Ricardian theory of comparative advantages, 196
right-to-food perspective, 198, 203
Riina, Totò, 124n4
ritual actions, 213–15, 222
Ritz, Gerry, 132, 137
Robinson, Robert, 146, 150
Roosevelt, Eleanor, 42
Rosset, Peter, 202
Rossi, Amalia, 5
Russia, 22

S. Margherita di Pula Sapore di Sole tomato
        cooperative, 64–5
Sachs, Carolyn, 62
Salone del Gusto, 232–5
Sandinista revolution, 163
Santiago de Cuba food consumption
    background on, 48–9
    complaining and discursive resistance, 52–4
    domestic food-distribution system, 50–1
    everyday resistance in, 57
    food rumors and hidden transcripts, 54–5
    food system use, 50–1
    monthly rations, 58n1
    purchasing power and refusal to consume, 55–7
    resistance and household consumption in, 51–7
S'Atra Sardigna food cooperative, 70
Schiavoni, Christina, 36
school gardens, 37, 67
Schroeder, Kathleen, 71
Schurman, Rachel, 4